A Very Tall Story

A Very Tall Story

Martin Bayfield

With Gavin Mairs

**SIMON &
SCHUSTER**

London · New York · Sydney · Toronto · New Delhi

First published in Great Britain by Simon & Schuster UK Ltd, 2022

Copyright © Martin Bayfield, 2022

The right of Martin Bayfield to be identified as the author
of this work has been asserted in accordance with the
Copyright, Designs and Patents Act, 1988.

3 5 7 9 10 8 6 4 2

Simon & Schuster UK Ltd
1st Floor
222 Gray's Inn Road
London WC1X 8HB

www.simonandschuster.co.uk
www.simonandschuster.com.au
www.simonandschuster.co.in

Simon & Schuster Australia, Sydney
Simon & Schuster India, New Delhi

The author and publishers have made all reasonable efforts to contact copyright-
holders for permission, and apologise for any omissions or errors in the form
of credits given. Corrections may be made to future printings.

A CIP catalogue record for this book
is available from the British Library

Hardback ISBN: 978-1- 3985-1425-6
eBook ISBN: 978-1- 3985-1426-3

Typeset in Bembo by M Rules
Printed and bound by CPI Group (UK) Ltd, Croydon, CR0 4YY

To my wife, Jane, to Roseanna, Polly, Lucy, Ross, Alice and Clara, you mean the world to me. To my parents, John and Ursula, watching on from on high, thank you for letting me join the party.

'My pain may be a reason for somebody's laugh, but my laugh must not be the reason for somebody's pain'

Charlie Chaplin

CONTENTS

Prologue   1

1   'You're with the Big Boys Now'   9

2   Growing Pains   14

3   The Longest Arm of the Law   33

4   Face Down on the Beach   49

5   'Two Bits of Cotton Hanging Out of
    Your Shorts   61

6   The History Boys   79

7   'Are You Here for the Rugby?'   93

8   The Joy of Ceefax   105

9   'If You Don't Make It, Bayfs, Can I Have
    Your Sony Walkman?'   111

10 Revolting for Wade   123

11 It's Raining Beer (Cans)   135

12 Head on a Chopping Block   147

13 Deep Heat, Old Farts and Tackling
    Jonah   161

14 A Change of Perspective   181

15 Take That, Bayfs   191

16   Falling Down   199

17   Broon Frae Toon   207

18   A Pain in Robbie Coltrane's Arse   215

19   A Wheezing Darth Vader   229

20   Poacher Turned Broadcaster   243

21   The Ostrich, the Goat and the
     Golf Club   257

22   To Rugby, with Love   267

     Acknowledgements   279

     Index   283

PROLOGUE

'Bayfield, you fucking bastard, you should never have won that game.' The voice was vaguely familiar, but the words hit me like a thunderbolt. I have been called many things on a rugby pitch, and punched more times than I care to remember, but this barb nearly floored all 6ft 10ins of me in an instant. Everyone in the film studio stopped in their tracks. Then came the silence. *What am I doing here?*

My eyes darted across the room in desperation to locate the source of the abuse. It was one of my first days on the film set of an as yet unknown movie called *Harry Potter and the Philosopher's Stone* (you might have heard of it by now) and up to that point I had been an entirely anonymous presence, lurching around the Leavesden Film Studios near Watford like a lost soul.

No longer. I could feel the gazes of my fellow actors (listen to me!) and pre-production workers as I flushed with embarrassment. I could hear them all wondering: *Who the hell is the big guy in the fat suit?*

To the left, in one corner of the ramshackle studio, was an old horse carriage that had been used in the blockbuster film *Gladiator*, and across the other side were bits of *Star Wars* spaceships. For a massive *Stars Wars* fan like me – I

1

have to admit I still have a poster featuring Darth Vader on the wall of my office at home – this was the coolest place on Earth. But where, in my acute embarrassment, were Han Solo and his hyperspace-bound *Millennium Falcon* when I needed him?

Finally, our eyes met. There, standing in front of me, was the instantly recognisable figure of the Hollywood legend Richard Harris, decked out in his Dumbledore costume, sitting in a high directors' chair and grinning at me with a twinkle in his eye. 'Big man, you can fuck right off,' he bellowed.

What was I doing there? Years before I had been regarded as something of a celebrity myself. Well, at least I had played rugby with guys who were regarded as celebrities, at the heart of an England side that – by its deeds on the pitch and, at times, misdemeanours off it – had taken rugby union from a noble minority sport into the mainstream, with stories appearing on the front pages of the British tabloids as well as leading the sports pages of the broadsheets. At its best it had been a thrilling, white-knuckle rollercoaster ride which had rewarded me with life-changing experiences and memories to treasure. We were arguably the best side in the Northern Hemisphere and occasionally could lay claim to being the best in the world at our peak, beating Australia, New Zealand and South Africa, and winning three Grand Slam titles in five seasons. We had reached the semi-finals of the Rugby World Cup in South Africa in 1995.

At times I had felt like a film extra on the pitch, given the rugby royalty I had rubbed shoulders with – a stellar list that included Will Carling, Rob Andrew, Brian Moore, Jeremy Guscott, Rory Underwood, Wade Dooley, Mike Teague,

Peter Winterbottom, Dean Richards, Paul Ackford, Martin Johnson and Dewi Morris.

I was proud to call these guys my team-mates. Seeing them up close, with their heady combination of ferocious commitment, skill and warrior spirit (well, among the forwards at least), at times made my own sense of inadequacy more acute. Some of the players in the changing room beside me were my absolute heroes. I looked at them and thought, *You have absolutely nailed it*. If England wanted me to shift pianos, I would have been happy to do it all day to be part of this squad of galacticos.

I am quite comfortable to admit I was not one of England's greatest players. I would probably rate myself as one of England's 'good' players, who had his moments. And that's it. I remain one of the tallest forwards to have ever played the game, and despite my 18st frame, I had, as the football pundits might say, a good engine for a big man.

But my team-mates were in a different class. I was surrounded by some who I think are among the very best players ever to have played for England. They were not automatons. They were still fallible and did stupid things. But, more than anything, they were ruthless, single-minded and perfectly designed to be rugby-playing animals. And I just loved being in their company. It may not seem like a manly thing to say, but I not only admired their talent, I also looked upon them with great affection. I still do. They were my family.

I would go on to win 31 caps for England and play in two of the Grand Slam-winning sides – 1992 and 1995 – and was selected to play for the British and Irish Lions for the tour of New Zealand in 1993, winning three Test caps. I was also at the heart of the side that reached the World Cup semi-final in 1995 in Cape Town before we crumpled, in embarrassment and humiliation, at the feet of Jonah Lomu, rugby's game-changing sensation.

We might have failed to fulfil our potential at that tournament, and the defeat by the All Blacks left me with lifelong regrets, but it remains the greatest-ever World Cup, and certainly the one with the best stories.

But by the time I turned up at the film set of *Harry Potter* on that fateful afternoon to audition for the glamorous role of body double for Robbie Coltrane's much-loved character, the giant Rubeus Hagrid, I was in a dark place.

After being forced to retire with a serious neck injury two years earlier, I had walked away from the game with a sense of bitterness and despair. I had fallen out of love with rugby. *How had it come to this?*

Richard Harris loved a song, and he had been singing away in the director's chair with everyone fussing around him when he barked at me across the film set. The room was full of directors, publicists and personal assistants, many of whom (for the early days of the first film) were Americans who had no idea who I was. And the reason for his outburst?

The year was 2000 and Northampton Saints, my old club, had just beaten Munster in the final of the Heineken Cup at Twickenham. And Harris was a huge Munster fan. At first everyone rushed up to see if he was okay, but then calm descended as they realised he was just ribbing me and in fact wanted to talk rugby.

And by recognising me, it acted as an introduction to all these stars and gave me the confidence to feel comfortable in their world. He broke the ice and gave me a unique selling point. *If Richard Harris knows this guy who is trying out for the body double of Hagrid, he must be okay.* Instantly I was transformed from a nervous and anonymous bloke standing in a fat-suit to someone who was at least *relevant* again.

People said I was a fish out of water, but, actually, being on that film set was about as close to being in a rugby environment as you could get without actually being on the pitch. It ticked so many boxes for me and returned the smile to my face.

I started to feel tall again. *Very* tall. And in that moment I realised that the reason I was here was *because* of the game of rugby. It is just another crazy place that I have found myself in because of the game. *Without rugby I would not be here* I said to myself.

I developed a lovely relationship with Harris over the course of two films, talking to him and spending time with him. He had been a star of all these great Hollywood movies and yet he would never talk about his acting. I could tell you nothing about his films or about his plays. He just wanted to talk about rugby. He wanted to know everything. And it helped the rest of the crew work out who I was.

When he died a few months after completing the second film, *Harry Potter and the Chamber of Secrets*, I was contacted by his publicist to invite me to his funeral. Sadly I couldn't make it, but it was such a lovely, lovely touch to have received an invitation. I have no doubt that Harris would have loved the fact that it was my work on *Harry Potter* that put a smile back on my face and made me fall in love with rugby again, a game he loved to his core as well.

One day, the assistant director kindly asked me how I

had been able to excel in my role when I had no previous experience of acting. 'Because of rugby,' I replied. It was as simple as that.

It was many years later, at a charity function with several of my former England team-mates, including Lawrence Dallaglio and Jason Leonard, that the idea to write this book first struck me. I found myself sitting beside George Kruis, the England and Lions lock, who at the time was a member of Eddie Jones's squad.

George looked at me and said: 'I don't want to hear anything about the modern game. I just want to hear stories about your era. It just sounds insane!' So off I went.

What happened in that period from the late 1980s up until Sir Clive Woodward took charge in 1997 was as anarchic as it was remarkable. We pretty much made the rules up as we went along. I want to give a glimpse into that fascinating world when rugby transitioned from an amateur game to become fully professional, along with the fun and chaos that accompanied that journey.

I don't think the players of my era fully got the credit they deserved because it was they who laid the foundations for what was to come later: the red-letter moment when England won the World Cup in 2003. But they did it while still holding down day jobs and playing for clubs like Preston Grasshoppers. That's why I feel it's so important to maintain the link between rugby's past and present. This isn't a complaint at how professionalism has changed our game; as long as the link is maintained, the game can grow and change as it will always remember its roots.

My concern is that the link between the current generation of players and supporters and the past is in danger of being broken. There aren't so many of the old players around now. You don't have the old boys wandering into the team room after the games and having dinner and a beer with you and talking about the old days. When I played, the blokes on the wall in the black and white photos would still be walking around the place with their beer-stained blazers on and with a few extra pounds around their waists.

They were quite happy boring you with their stories and spitting all over your face when they did it. And you loved them for it. Those guys aren't there any more though. So now today's players are making their own memories – memories of the professional era which are shared among themselves but not with those who have gone before them in the bars of clubhouses across the country, breaking the connection through the generations.

Now I want to bridge that gap. I want to share with you my memories and insight into the characters I played with and against. My daughters have no recollection of me playing rugby because of the age they were when I retired, but at least the ghosts of my playing days can be found in video clips on the internet. This book will at least give some insight into the story behind those grainy images for future generations. Like any relationship, I've had my ups and downs with the game, but ultimately it has made me who I am. This is my love story with rugby. And what a *very tall* story it has been . . .

1

'You're with the Big Boys Now'

If you've seen the film *Sliding Doors*, then imagine me for a moment as Gwyneth Paltrow's character, running towards the train on the London Underground. The plot of that Hollywood blockbuster revolves around the premise of whether or not she managed to beat the closing doors as the train prepared to depart and the ensuing two different scenarios that would change her life completely. I may not be as alluring as Paltrow's character Helen Quilley, but I too have had such moments when I look back on my rugby career and wonder: *what if?*

Those lucky few of us who go on to represent our countries in the sport we love can look back at a moment in our playing careers that enabled us to set ourselves apart from the rest. For me, the closing doors of the London Underground train were in equal measure the vagaries of the British weather and the ribcage of former Wasps lock Sean O'Leary.

This story begins in November 1990, when I was picked to play for an England B team against the Emerging Wallabies.

'Emerging' requires some context. The pack included the great John Eales, the Wallaby legend who would go on to win the World Cup in 1991 and then captain them to victory in the 1999 tournament, as well as the powerhouse forward Willie Ofahengaue, while their star-studded backline included Jason Little and David Knox at fly-half. It was the third of three matches that weekend.

On the Friday night, another England B side had played Namibia; the following day, the senior England side faced Argentina, an afternoon made infamous by the right hook of an 18-year-old prop called Federico Mendez, who floored my former Met Police team-mate Ackers – aka Paul Ackford – and earned himself a red card. Finally, on Sunday, came our game. If the selectors were pleased with the 12-12 draw against such vaunted opponents, they were not overwhelmed with my display.

To be fair, in the build-up I had picked up a virus which had sparked an asthmatic reaction. I could hardly breathe during the game and boy, did it show. I was promptly dropped for the next game, against Italy.

But it was then that fate intervened. A heavy frost led to the Italy match being postponed until the following March. Sean O'Leary, who had first been selected for England B back in 1988 and who had originally been selected for the senior squad's 1990 tour to Argentina, only for a serious car accident to rule him out, was my replacement. His unlucky streak was about to continue. Before the match against Italy, O'Leary had played for Wasps against Northampton Saints. And once again the gods, *à la* Helen Quilley, would look kindly on me when Wayne 'Buck' Shelford, the great All Blacks No. 8, broke O'Leary's ribs.

Suddenly, I was back in the team for what was effectively the trial match for the tour of Fiji and Australia. I had an absolute blinder against Italy. Every bounce of the ball went my way. A few days later, I came home from work to see the blinking red light of my answer machine (these, remember, were very much pre-mobile phone days), alerting me to the fact that I had a message. It was Don Rutherford, the Rugby Football Union's technical director, who in a very formal manner informed me that he was inviting me to join the England tour of Fiji and Australia in June.

If Don Rutherford had been there in my front room, I might just have kissed him! I was going ON TOUR. With ENGLAND! How much *fun* was this going to be? Don, to be honest, you had me at: 'This is a message for Martin Christopher Bayfield . . .'

The only problem was that my season with Bedford, who I had joined from the Met Police, finished more than four weeks before the start of the tour. In those days, there were no tugs-of-war between clubs and unions due to seasons cluttered with fixtures and concerns about players' welfare. It was quite the opposite. My worry was not the effects of such a draining season, but that I was not going to be fit enough.

I might have been picked for England, but we were all amateurs then, holding down day jobs. So my lunchtimes were spent at the old-school gym in Greyfriars Police Station in Bedford trying to work how to use the rowing machine that had been given by the RFU to those players who had been picked for the tour. It was the first incarnation of the Concept rower. The gym had wall bars and a polished hard floor, like something from a *Carry On* film. The problem was that every time I did a session on the rower, it slid back slightly because of the polished floor and by the end of my lunch session I would be at the other end of the gym!

In my hour of need, I turned to Richard Greed, who was a friend and team-mate at Bedford and also a school rugby coach. He was also now my unofficial fitness guru. 'We can't get you much stronger in that time, but we are going to get you fit enough to cope with anything they will throw at you,' he said. 'So, I want you to go out running and training with me for the next four weeks.'

Cemetery Hill in Bedford became my unofficial running track. It was a hill beside the park that ran alongside the cemetery, appropriately, rising steeply before levelling off and then rising again. Richard would make me do shuttle runs, again and again and again, up the hill. I felt a little bit like Bedfordshire's oversized equivalent of Rocky, mimicking the fictional boxing star's famous training regimes, which always climaxed with a dramatic climb up steps – the Rocky Steps – to the Philadelphia Museum of Art.

But while 5ft 9ins Sylvester Stallone, who played Rocky, was treated to picture-perfect views of the Philadelphia sky-line when he reached the top, I was instead often greeted by a little old lady who lived in a small house at the top of the hill. I never knew her name, but she would see us doing these runs and one day she came out of her house just as I was being violently sick on the road. 'Would you like a cup of tea, dear?' she asked, standing over her gate. *No thanks, but an oxygen mask would be great if you have one.*

The hill runs were to build some strength into my legs but what came next was tougher. Richard took me to another location, outside a dramatic-looking old council building that would have been built in the 1850s. It had a long driveway, which was roughly one kilometre from one end to the other. Greedie said we were going to run it in three minutes, then rest and run it again. We did it again and again until I collapsed. 'Whatever you do in training, always be the first there and the last to leave,' was Richard's final piece of advice. 'Whenever you do a warm-up, make sure you are always at the front.'

When I departed for Fiji, feeling as fit as I had ever been, I became that annoying 'keeno' on the tour. Time and again Wade Dooley would shout 'Fucking hell! You are making us look bad' and would try to drag me back to slow me down. But it was all I could do to stand out. Some of the training sessions were tough too. The B side's midfield on that tour was Damian Hopley and Simon Halliday, with Ian Hunter at full-back. Hoppers was some player before he did his knee, while Hunts was a physical force. They were both big men in those days and poor old Will Carling and Jerry Guscott had to tackle them. I can remember Will saying, halfway through one session, 'Okay, I think that's enough, let's move on.' I didn't blame him.

My level of fitness got me through. In one match for the midweek side against the Fiji B team ahead of the first Test, the humidity was more than 85 per cent and the temperature above 95 degrees Fahrenheit. We went back to the hotel still in our kit and just fell into the swimming pool. Three hours later, we were still sweating.

I was not going to dazzle the England coaches with my skills, but I had to show them that, in the searing heat and humidity of Fiji, I could keep the pace, even without a cup of tea waiting for me at the top of Cemetery Hill.

*

I was standing in the blazing heat on a dusty training field in Nandi when Geoff Cooke, the England manager, named the team to face Fiji. The gathering had very little semblance to the elite international environment of today's game. There was no uniform training kit, and the players stood around Cooke looking more like a ragtag club team. All I heard was my name. The rest of the announcement was just background noise.

'Okay lads, let's split up – forwards down here and backs over there,' said Cooke. How many times had I heard that before? But this was anything but routine.

It was June 1991 and I had just been selected for my first Test match for England. *Bloody hell.* As I turned to assemble with the forwards, a familiar face stood in my way: Roger Uttley. *The* Roger Uttley, who had played 23 times for England at lock or in the back row, winning the Grand Slam in 1980 and playing in four Tests for the British and Irish Lions on their 'Invincibles' tour of South Africa in 1974. The same Roger Uttley who would be standing to greet us off our school coach when I was at Bedford School and we travelled to play his Harrow side, and who had helped me progress with England Schools back in the day.

Roger was now the England forwards coach and thus had been a reassuring presence for me on the tour. It felt like this would be a moment when the old coach welled up after seeing one of his young protégés finally come good. A knowing nod. A slap on the back and some brief words of encouragement. *You'll be all right. This is your time, son. It will be just like Bedford vs Harrow.* Well, it could have happened like that. The reality? It turned out Roger was a man of few words.

BANG! I am sure I saw stars as Roger's fist landed flush in my face.

'Concentrate, Bayfs, you're with the big boys now!' he growled. *Concentrate?* Nowadays I would have been sent for a head injury assessment! Talk about old school. Rather than attempt to motivate me verbally, he had opted for a dash of violence instead. Oh well.

I should have known better. I had already experienced some friendly fire earlier on the tour when Wade Dooley had punched me in the face during a line-out session. Geoff Cooke had made him apologise afterwards and it was hilarious to see the man known as 'the Blackpool Tower' come up to me like some naughty kid and say: 'Sorry mate.'

Now I was heading off to my first England training session as a player in the starting XV, rubbing my jaw and feeling mildly concussed. Well, as I said, this was the amateur era.

Later, when I got back to the hotel, I phoned my mum, more than 10,000 miles away in Bedford, to break the news of my selection. At least some things in this game never change. I was bursting with pride when she picked up.

'I'm going to play for England, Mum,' I said, grinning like a big kid. I wanted to tell Dad too, but she said he was asleep. He was 81 by then and quite fragile. He did not miss out on the celebrations, however. After I got home from the tour, Mum regaled me of the tale of what happened when Dad found out about my selection. On hearing the news, he got up out of his chair and walked down the road to his local pub and sat down in what was known as *his* chair.

'Boys, he has done it, Martin is going to play for England!' he beamed to his mates. Mum says he stayed for around four hours, toasting my selection before the lads carried him back from the pub, still in the pyjamas, dressing gown and slippers that he had been wearing when he left the house. Delivery for Mrs Bayfield.

He never got to see me play for England in the flesh as he was too ill and died a couple of years later, but the thought of him celebrating that night stays with me.

But back in my hotel in Fiji, deep in my stomach, was that feeling again. *What on earth am I doing there?*

2

Growing Pains

The first time I was aware of being tall, *very* tall, was when I was eight years old. You might think that having an extraordinarily big frame at that age has plenty of advantages. It's true. It did. But on my first day of prep school, as I wandered around the corridors of Beechwood Park School, near Markyate in Hertfordshire, not sure where to go, it felt anything but. A kindly teacher, sensing my distress, mistakenly directed me to a classroom full of 11-year-olds. It was not long until they quite rightly wondered who on earth the big lad was with the wobbling bottom lip.

By the time I *was* 11, I had sprouted from 5ft 4ins to 6ft. A year later, at the tender age of 12, I had reached the height of 6ft 4ins – taller than most England forwards even by today's professional standards.

From a rugby point of view, my height was – superficially, at least – like winning the lottery. I can't tell you how much *fun* it was. Even more hilariously, I started out on the wing. Almost every time I touched the ball, I scored. Not that it took a lot of skill on my part. All I had to do was run straight and hard and invariably it would end up with a try. And *another*. And *another*. No one could touch me.

In one of my first matches, a parent of one of the players in the opposition complained. 'No one is going to tell me that boy is twelve years old,' he boomed. My dad was beside him on the touchline. 'I will,' said Dad, 'because he's my son.'

From that day on, Dad brought my birth certificate to matches in his pocket, just in case anyone else queried my age. Thankfully, after a couple of seasons, I became well known on the circuit. The end-of-term report of my final year at Beechwood recorded that in our ten matches for the first XV, we had played ten and won ten, with a point-scored total of 543. And my contribution? A grand total of 45 tries.

In one match, against York House, we were leading 110-0 before the referee stopped the game 20 minutes before full time with some of the opposition already in tears. Many, many years later, I was speaking at a rugby dinner and had mentioned that match when afterwards I was approached by one of the guests, who was some big shot from the City. 'I was in that York House team,' he exclaimed. 'And it's true. You did make me cry!'

It made *me* smile. They were some of the happiest days of my rugby career. The fact that my dad had to bring proof of my age to matches when challenged by opposition coaches (or angry parents) was only a minor irritation. I was virtually unstoppable. I was fit, I could jump, I was taller than most adults and had a decent turn of speed. Yeah, this game of rugby seemed like a whole lot of fun. It's just that, sometimes, being that tall wasn't actually much fun *at all*.

*

I still have a photograph on my phone somewhere of a brawl during an England match. Brian Moore is looking to twat someone and I am standing there with a look that says: 'Calm down lads, let's just talk about this.'

It's true to say that, more often than not, my long arms were used to hold people apart, both on the beat as a policeman and on the rugby pitch, rather than land a punch. But I have always hated people thinking that I was soft. It has been an ever-present chip on my shoulder. I may not have been a fighter by instinct, but I was not a coward. The truth is that while I never looked to pick a fight, I would never run away from one.

I have a couple of commendations for bravery from the days when I was a constable with Bedfordshire Police to prove my actions have at times spoken louder than my words. Well, I say that, but to be honest I think my sergeant may have overstated the incidents slightly. The first was for disarming a guy in Luton who was brandishing a machete. It was almost a comedic moment if it hadn't been so dangerous. The guy was wearing a coat but we were pretty sure he was naked underneath. Our first thoughts were *Please don't take your coat off.*

He was swishing this machete around and threatening his parents. To make the scene even more surreal, he had put make-up on his dog, which was at his feet. We kept him talking and, as soon as he looked away, jumped on him. It was brave, I guess, but at the time also funny and weird. As we tried to put handcuffs on him, another colleague arrived and was holding the dog up in the air by the lead. It looked like he was trying to play conkers with it. But the dog was not going to attack anyone, so we told him to put it down as he was just embarrassing himself.

The other commendation was for a drugs arrest, but there were other incidents, such as when I ran into a house that was on fire. My colleague and I thought there might be someone trapped in a room. But as we opened the door, a ball of yellow and orange flames came towards us. In a slow-motion move, we shut the door and beat a hasty retreat. When I got outside, I noticed that my Gore-Tex jacket had gone a little bit tacky from the blast of searing heat. The next moment, a fireman arrived and gave me a right dressing down. 'Mate, you're the police, you catch the baddies,' he shouted. 'We'll put the fires out.' Fair enough. Yet none of these actions amounted to much for those who felt I lacked physical bravery on the rugby pitch.

In 2011, long after my international career was over, I was working as a rugby reporter for ITV in New Zealand. When the tournament reached the quarter-final stages, we were based in Auckland. All the ITV production staff had come out for the evening, including the main presenter, Steve Ryder. We were meeting for dinner and I walked into a restaurant with my colleague Craig Doyle. Already at a big table were a number of bigwigs from the world of rugby administration.

'Is that Martin Bayfield?' I heard one of the blazers mutter. The answer cut me in half. For the first time, my life-long mask as a peacemaker almost slipped. 'Yeah, you can tell by the yellow streak down his back,' came the reply, from perhaps the grandest of the grandees. I looked at him. It was the first time in my life when I really did feel like punching someone.

You don't know what I have done in my life, things that you would never do if you had a yellow streak on your back. You don't know some of the demons I have had to contend with in my life. Just because you don't throw punches doesn't mean you aren't tough.

I should have said something, but instead I hesitated and glared back at him with a look to let him know I had heard what he had said. From that moment on, it has been something between us. Even when we meet now, I always remember the remark.

It was Mooro who once said: 'If you're not going to bark when you're a puppy, you're not going to bark when you're a dog.' What no one else knew was that my experiences growing up as an oversized kid meant I was never going to bark.

Anyone who met my German mother, Ursula, would have been left in no doubt about where I got my giant frame from. At 6ft 3ins, with the physique of a second-row forward, she was a formidable force of nature. She was also an incredibly resourceful woman, a character trait forged from her remarkably challenging childhood experiences during the Second World War.

The youngest of four children, she was born in 1928 in Jädkemühl, Pomerania, in East Prussia. She shared the same birthdate as Adolf Hitler (20 April), which meant, after he came to power, she would get the day off school on her birthday as schools were closed for the Führer's official celebrations.

Her family moved to Halle, in the east of Germany, as the schools were better there and it also had a university. But when her father, Karl, died of cancer when she was eight years old, she was sent to live with her uncle in Hamburg for three months while her mother, Lotte, found a new home, a four-bedroom apartment in Kröllwitz, a suburb of Halle on the banks of the river Saale.

Hopes of a settled childhood, however, were short-lived. In 1938 she developed a heart condition and was sent to a children's home in Oberstdorff in Austria on the advice of a doctor, who suggested she would benefit from the mountain air. Austria was annexed by Germany while she was there and, when war came, she was sent to a state boarding school in Droyβig in the Saxony-Anhalt region.

At the end of each school term she stayed with her sister Thes, who had moved with her husband and four children to Czechoslovakia, to help with childcare. Her oldest brother, Klaus, meanwhile, was sent to the Eastern Front to fight the Russians, where he would lose an arm.

By January 1945, with the Russian advance through the east of Europe, she returned with her mother to Czechoslovakia to help her sister relocate back to Germany. It was a journey she would never forget. Her passage included travelling through the devastated cities of Leipzig and Dresden just after the Allied bombing. Years later she could still recall seeing ash falling from the sky as they crossed through the bombed streets of Dresden.

After meeting Thes and her family in Prague, they managed to catch the last train from Vienna to Berlin, via Dresden, and Mum managed to secure a wooden bench seat on the crowded train by climbing through the window from the platform. The journey to Halle involved passing again through Leipzig, during an air raid.

By now her school had closed and, with fears that Halle would become a target for the British and American bombers, she was sent with Thes and her children to stay with Klaus, who was living nearer Berlin, having returned from the Eastern Front in 1941. Once again the journey filled them with fear, not hope, as they passed many refugees heading the other way telling stories of the rape and killings being perpetrated by the advancing Russian army, and within a couple of months they had returned to Halle.

Soon there was nowhere left to hide. A trip back to her school with her mother to retrieve her belongings brought them face to face with a Russian soldier outside the building and they were saved only when her mother held up her shoe to indicate what they were looking for. The soldier lowered his rifle and let them pass.

It was the Americans who reached Halle first, but when they left in July 1945, the Russians quickly moved in and the family were ordered out of their apartment and rehoused in a much smaller flat with just two rooms and a bathroom.

The introduction of a border in Germany split their family.

Klaus somehow managed to escape to the newly formed West Germany – had he been caught in the East, he would have certainly been shot. But Mum's other brother, Ben, and Thes decided to remain in the East. She said he felt it was the right thing to do. So when Klaus got engaged in March 1946, the family had to cross the border illegally to attend the celebration party.

Those connections helped Mum get a job on a farm in the Western Zone but that too was a struggle to even get there. The border post separating the Russian and British zones was lit up at night, but the surrounding area was cloaked by darkness, a saviour to those like Mum, who was stopped at the border by officials and told she could not cross as her paperwork was not in order. As she turned away, Mum later recalled seeing a young boy run around the back of some buildings, so she followed him and crossed the border over farmland in the dark, away from the spotlight.

By the early 1950s her mother had also illegally crossed the border to relocate to a suburb of Hamburg. It was there that Mum saw an advertisement for manageresses at the NAAFI (Navy, Army and Air Force Institutes) and she was soon running a sub-canteen in Lüneberg, the first of a number of jobs across Europe in the hospitality sector that would include a stint in the billing office of the Savoy Hotel in London in 1958.

Five years later, she met my father, John, while on holiday on the Italian island of Ischia after being introduced by mutual friends.

My dad, who had been married before, was 19 years older than she was. Although the old dog looked younger, he was pretty straight with her. 'Look, I can probably give you 25 years,' he said. They got engaged within two days of meeting each other and married in September 1963, with the reception at the Dorchester Hotel in London.

Years later Mum self-published a book called *How Was It Then* to explain the remarkable story of how the girl from East Prussia ended up living in the English Midlands, how she escaped Germany as it was being split up and how she travelled before eventually reconnecting with her family again.

Many years later, we would visit her brother Ben when the Berlin Wall was still intact. We had to queue for hours to get through the checkpoint. I remember instantly being struck by the utter drabness of the east of the city. It was as if someone had turned the colour off. It was all greys and dark browns, and extreme contradictions.

The flat that had been given to Ben by the state would have cost millions of pounds in London. I remember it had wooden panels and high ceilings. But the sparse furnishings diluted any perception of grandeur. The state had given him and his family four chairs, a table and one bed. That was their lot. There were queues outside every shop and barely anything on the shelves, but at the same time the state provided jobs, healthcare, dental care – the core essentials of society. Ben and his family believed in the system.

When Germany was reunited, the family reconnected and we would visit Klaus too, who had worked as a forester before becoming a teacher. They were good people, but my abiding memories are of a stiff and formal reception. There was a language barrier too. My sister had picked up the German language easily from my mother but it was more of a struggle for me. And attempting to speak it only made me feel even more awkward than I already felt as a gawky young teenager. I was never made to feel very welcome but, looking back now, I realise I completely misread them. Their manner did not reflect a lack of affection. It was just the way they were.

Mum was strict too. In fact, she was absolutely terrifying, at times. But she would also have done anything for you. She was very proud of her German heritage, but she was also very proud to be a British citizen and very respectful of Britain. This was the country that never admonished her for being German, never ridiculed her background, gave her a family, gave her a job, gave her an income and gave her a new life, despite coming to England so soon after the war. That is why we never spoke German in our house. It was out of respect for her newly adopted country that had given her a second chance.

Her background made her the most pragmatic and

resourceful person I have met. She was also brutally honest in her assessment of everything I did. There was never any need to read the player ratings in the following day's newspaper when I was playing for England. Mum would always give it to me straight: 'England played well at the weekend. You? Not so much.'

Dad was 57 when I was born in 1966. 'Son, you were the last bullet out of the gun,' he would later tell me with a chuckle. My sister Karen had arrived two years earlier and I had a brother, Richard, who was born between the two of us, but sadly Mum had mumps early in the pregnancy and he only lived for two hours. Karen might not have had much time for me when I was a gangly youth, but when I started to excel at sports, she started to take notice and our relationship blossomed.

There had been no history of rugby in our family, and barely any interest in sport. My earliest memory of rugby was watching the Varsity match. My father, who was born in 1909 and grew up in Lowestoft, had been a grammar school boy who was smart enough to win a place at Trinity College in Cambridge. I've read some letters from his time there and initially he appeared to be quite homesick, trying to make his way in a world then dominated by public schoolboys. But he was very bright and a brilliant storyteller, and eventually he was accepted.

His first job was in the confectionary business. He worked for Cadbury Bourneville and was such a success that my god-father was Christopher Cadbury, of the second generation of the Cadbury family. So I was basically weaned on chocolate. Happy days.

By the time the Second World War came, he was not able to serve because he had bad eyesight and by then was 30 years old. Instead, he made his contribution to the war effort by playing a leading role in the rationing of food, for which he was awarded an OBE for services to the food industry during the war.

After the war, he ran a chocolate factory in Bedford, got married and then divorced, and there was quite a long gap before he met Mum. At his peak of his career, he had been a bon vivant, the kind of businessman who relished cutting deals over long lunches, cigars and with a handshake, not reams of paperwork and increasing computerisation.

By the time I arrived, the world as he saw it was changing and he barely recognised it. Driven on by that old-age fear of making sure that his family would be looked after before he was gone, he worked until he was 71. And to his credit, he did just that.

But the age gap meant that, despite my size as a teenage boy brimming with energy, I didn't grow up in an environment where I could let off steam with him in the garden of our house in Woburn Sands. There was never going to be any rough and tumble between father and son. He was an old man getting confused with the world, but with the responsibilities and challenges of a young family. Some days he would remain in his pyjamas. He was scared of getting old and at times he was frustrated by his age, and his behaviour reflected that. Looking back, he probably began to suffer from dementia in his later years, but it was never diagnosed.

He would slump into his chair after work, turning down my requests to go outside. 'I'm done, son,' he would say. If he had been my grandfather, it would have been fine. I had to wait until I started playing senior rugby to experience the fatherhood figure that I yearned for as a child.

The consequence was that I had a relatively lonely child-hood, even though I was not alone. The odd game of cricket with Dad was about it. I was happy but spent a lot of time by myself and missed the company of other boys my age to mess around with when I was at home. Some of that was down to my personality. Once I get to know someone, I'm all-in, but sometimes I find it difficult to make the initial connection with people and can appear a bit standoff-ish. There weren't many other children in my village, and those who were of similar ages were probably put off by my size. The kids that I was the same size as were four or five years older. I had an almost Edwardian upbringing because my parents were so formal. And if you were wearing clothes that look a bit weird because your mum has made them or they don't quite fit, other children looked at you slightly differently. I don't want to be disrespectful to my father because he did the best that he could, but I never felt I could charge around the house or garden in the way you would expect a father and son to do.

School was my saving grace. Mum knew that I needed to be with kids of my own age – not just through the normal school day, but also overnight and every weekend because I was not getting that at home – so decided I should attend a boarding school. I loved my time at Beechwood Park because, after a while there, no one cared about my size and I could charge around and be myself, even though teachers (perhaps subconsciously) tended to treat me as if I was much older than I was. But when I went home, it was very different.

My fondest memories of my dad are as the most fantastic storyteller. His friends who came to our house were older as well, but I was fascinated by the stories they would tell to each other. I would sit there, either in the room with them or sitting behind the closed door, taking in every word, mesmerised by their recitals. It is one of his legacies that I am blessed with the ability to tell a good story, and I equally love hearing other people's stories.

It was a loving family but a formal one. The message I constantly received because of my size was: *Don't be a bully, don't throw your weight around, don't do this, don't do that.*

There were times too when the atmosphere at home became tense. Dad could have a quick temper. He was tired and worn out by life; he just wanted to sit in his chair, drink a glass of whisky and read the paper. If the atmosphere did become tense and voices were raised and doors slammed, my response was to withdraw: it was time to disappear to the woods or to my bedroom to play with my Scalextric. My sister was always the brave one. She would confront the situation, but my approach was to try to be a peacemaker. 'It's okay, everything's all right, everything's fine,' I would say.

The emotional impact was that I would come to be repelled by aggression and aggressive behaviour. I didn't like what I saw when people lost their temper and so I shied away from that behaviour myself. I can remember telling my sister years later, when I was visiting her in New Zealand, that I had always envied her for being so courageous in the face of family tensions. Interestingly her response was that she had always envied me being able to defuse situations by calming everyone down.

While that wasn't always a useful character trait when things were kicking off in the white heat of a Test match, it didn't mean that I was a coward.

Part of the psyche that would dominate my rugby career

also stemmed from the reaction of others to my unusual height. From a very early age, I received a similar warning from my teachers not to use my size to bully people. Whether it was in the playground or on the rugby pitch, the message was constant: 'Don't throw your weight around, Martin.'

If another kid bumped into me on the playground, it was without any consequence, but even as an eight-year-old, at the back of my mind was the fear that if I did the same, it would be perceived that I *had* thrown my weight around, when inside I would scream back: *I didn't!*

My size also made me a target for the older boys. I guess it was bullying at the time, but I didn't perceive it as such. I just thought it was boys being silly. Some of the 12- and 13-year-olds wanted to have a go at the big kid who was several years below them at school.

I was tall, but I had no strength in me. So I would take a beating, or be put in a headlock and have mud shoved in my face. The strange thing at the time was that I could understand why it was happening. And rather than cry, I would laugh about it.

Instead of physical confrontation, I learned to use humour as my defence. I was equipped with a sharp wit thanks to listening to my father and his friends talk for hours when often the conversation would be full of quick-witted humour in the manner of *The Two Ronnies*. It meant I was able to come back to my adversaries with a quick retort or say something that would surprise them. And because I was happy to stand my ground and not run away or cry, eventually they lost interest in me. 'He's all right,' became the attitude.

If I never felt bullied, growing up in an environment where the assumption is that you have either done something wrong, or are on the verge of doing so, simply because of your size, had an impact. Home life only reinforced that sentiment. No, I was not going to start any fights but, equally, I would never run away from one, despite what others thought.

Of course, my England team-mates will also tell you that the real reason that I didn't throw many punches is that I was absolutely useless at fighting.

I found out from an early age that if I did try to fight anyone, I would just end up getting beaten up. I discovered that the easiest way was to try to talk my way out of trouble. I would rather have a laugh than a fight. I can remember in one England match trying to get involved in a scrap and my team-mate Wade Dooley shot a look at me. 'Bayfs, lad, just stick to what you're good at,' he barked. 'And you're not good at this.'

I even followed that advice when Wade punched me during an England training session. You would often hear stories about legendary punch-ups before games, but my reaction was: 'Oh, Wade has just punched me in the face.' It wasn't to punch him back. That was probably just as well. If I had, I'd have been in real trouble. But at least I knew I could take a proper punch now.

In fact, the only person I've ever punched properly in a rugby match was my fellow England and Lions second-row partner Martin Johnson. It was during the third Test on the Lions tour of New Zealand, as I attempted to throw a hay-maker at Ian Jones, the All Black lock forward. Jones ducked and I whacked Johnno instead. At the next line-out, Johnno came up to me. 'Bayfs, you better take this one. I don't know where I am.'

Dooley was right, I was no good at it. It was the last punch I would throw.

3

The Longest Arm of the Law

Was I ever ready to play rugby? Properly ready? Looking back, I think I spent most of my career worrying that I wasn't, apart from a few moments when I got everything just right. The honest answer is that I don't think I came into the senior game feeling physically comfortable.

I would compare myself to someone like Neil Back, the Leicester Tigers and England flanker, who was renowned for being remarkably physically fit, or Tim Rodber, my future Northampton Saints and England team-mate, for just being so strong. I never had anywhere near their physical attributes and it always played on my mind.

Sometimes I wonder what player I might have been if I had benefitted from more professional expertise and technical guidance early in my career.

If I were at school now, as a 6ft 4ins 13-year-old playing in Saracens' catchment area, I can guarantee I would have had a visit from the club. They would look at my parents, see that my mother was a 6ft 3ins, 18st German and practically offer me an academy contract on the spot.

Instead, insecurity about my physique was a thread that was always there, right the way through my playing days as I began to step up from schools rugby to age-grade national squads and when I started to play adult rugby with the Metropolitan Police, Bedford RFC and then Northampton Saints.

When I'm asked nowadays what advice I'd give to kids coming through, my answer is always: 'Ask questions. Ask lots and lots and lots of questions. And seek out experts from a multitude of sports.' In my time, any questions that I asked about my development were to those within rugby, and most of the time they didn't know the answers, because it was an amateur game back then. What I should have done was go to see a strength coach, or a strongman coach, to ask how I could make this big frame work to the best of my ability.

If you look at someone like John Eales, the great Wallabies lock forward, he wasn't that big. He was a little bit shorter than me, but had big strong legs compared to my Twiglet pins. Part of the reason for that might have been hereditary; I have also since found out that I have a condition called neuropathy which can cause muscle weakness. I may never have been able to get strength into my legs.

But Eales's strength stemmed from the fact he was an athlete who, as well as possessing a great understanding of the game, benefitted physically and skilfully from the fact he was also a great talent at basketball. At one stage, I thought I was a great talent at basketball too. But when I played, I was so tall that I could just shoot at will. If I missed, the ball would often rebound and I was able to catch it again and have another go. No one else could get near it. There was little need to develop strength in my legs or dribbling skills.

Still, it was suggested I should have a trial for the county and I went to Pilgrims School, across the road from where I lived. Suddenly I was up against kids who could actually *play* basketball.

When I was asked what position I played in, I stared back blankly. I didn't even know the names of the positions. All I knew was that I could just about bounce the ball, do a very simple lay-up and score a basket. I was a pretty good shot, but I was up against guys who could bounce the ball between their legs, spin and turn and I was made to look stupid. Five minutes into the game, everyone looked at me and thought: *The big guy's shit.*

While I loved barging through much smaller opponents during my school days, I look back now and can recognise that I also never had a proper grounding in the fundamentals of rugby. As everything came far too easily to me at school, it left me with gaps in my game that I struggled to plug later on. For example, I couldn't pass off my left hand because I had never needed to. I came from a world where the big guy always scored himself.

Going through the classic public school system, at prep school we would play ten games in the Christmas term and then not play again until the next September. As I was a boarder, I didn't play any junior club rugby. So in five years at Beechwood Park, I played 50 games, and in the first two or three seasons scored tries almost at will.

How do you actually prepare yourself for the big, grown-up game with 50 games? What do you think I learned playing

No. 8 during that time? A bit of line-out work, channel one and channel two ball, and that was about it.

When I came across Martin Johnson a few years later, I was stunned by his rugby knowledge and sporting brain. His family were sports mad, but it was never a topic of conversation in my house. Dad liked his cricket and that was that.

When I moved to Bedford School, even though I was already pretty much the tallest kid in the school, the physical difference between a 13-year-old and an 18-year-old was huge. I remember seeing the guys in the 1st XV walking around the school on a match day, wearing their blazers with this huge red badge with an eagle on it, and thinking, *Wow, these really are the main boys.* And even though I was bigger than them, I felt my age. I knew if I played against them, I would get absolutely battered. The days of rugby being easy were over.

The coaching was a bit scratchy to start with – a geography teacher taking the Under-14s and the chemistry teacher taking the Under-15s. But while they didn't know much about rugby, we were always aware that the two First XV coaches, Pat Briggs and Alan Thorp, were monitoring us from above.

Dad would still come and watch me, wearing a green sheepskin coat with huge horn buttons. He needed a walking stick by then and would plonk himself down in a seat close to the touchline. In one match, against Rugby School at Bedford, he was hit with a ball kicked into touch and toppled back on his chair, landing like an upside-down tortoise. Seconds later, he raised his walking stick into the air and twirled it around as if to say: 'I'm all right, carry on, carry on!' Bless him.

By the age of 16, I had started to play county and divisional rugby, as well as making my first connections with Bedford RFC. I went to watch a Bedford game one afternoon and was leaning against the barrier at the top of the ski slope that is Goldington Road when one of the coaches of the Colts team spotted me.

'Hey, you're the guy from Bedford School, aren't you?' he said. 'There's a Colts game in half an hour. Can you play?' Of course I could. I ran home, grabbed my boots, ran back and made it just in time for kick-off.

The next 70 minutes opened my eyes. Up to that point, I had no real point of reference for the game. I had seen the occasional Five Nations match on the television, while my first memory of the Lions was in the 1980 tour to South Africa and then in 1983 in New Zealand, when it pissed down with rain.

Now I was up against boys from state schools who were also playing club rugby. They were doing what most kids are doing now – playing for their school on Saturday and their club on Sunday. They might play 50 games a year, not over the course of five years. When I got the ball, I ran hard and straight, but rather than cut through the opposition defence like a knife through butter, suddenly I was smashed by a tackler from 90 degrees. At Beechwood Park and Bedford School, I would have run on. But for the first time I felt it.

Fuck, I've never been hit like that before. That was the thought that screamed in my head. It was mad but, bizarrely I quite liked it. After a couple of big hits, I thought to myself, *Okay, that's fine, I get this.* It was big-boy rules from now on.

Bedford School had a collection of great charismatic coaches: Ian Peck, who had been on the bench for England's Grand

Slam-winning team in 1980, Guy Fletcher, and Graham 'Granddad' Phillips, who also played for Bedford and was a real character. He was just one of a number who were playing at Goldington Road on the Saturday and would turn up at school on Monday morning with black eyes, cuts and bruises. I just loved it. They filled a bit of a void for me because they were about the same age as everyone else's parents and I related to that. They were like surrogate fathers (while my team-mates were like surrogate brothers who were so much more worldly-wise than I was).

It was a bond that was made even stronger when I began playing with some of them. It would never be allowed in today's game, but at the age of 16 I could play against senior sides. I was picked for the East Midlands to play against Buckinghamshire, and can still remember walking into the changing room and seeing Pecky and Granddad getting changed. Well, Pecky was actually sitting there with a fag in his hand. 'Bayfs,' he said. Suddenly I was being called Bayfs, not Martin, and I no longer had to call him 'sir'. 'When you get to my age, games like this are not really that important.'

I would get smacked and whacked on the pitch, and there was one of my teachers picking me up off the floor. There was no better feeling. I felt I belonged. And I just loved it on Monday mornings when I could look a teacher in the eye and give him a knowing look that said: *I saw you getting pissed on Saturday night!*

By the age of 17, I was 6ft 10ins, but still skin and bones, weighing in at little over 15st and nothing on my legs – and still little-to-no understanding of the game. But it was that experience of playing against adults that began to toughen me up. I started to do some weights and the sheer physicality of those contests turned me into a man.

I was picked for Bedford RFC to play against Pontypool on a Tuesday night. I should have known better that no one else fancied that fixture. I was up against John Perkins, a tough-nut lock forward who had played for Wales. At the first line-out, he screamed at me: 'Look at your man, there are fucking yards of him. Fucking yards of him.' Then he just looked me in the eye and winked. 'I am going to enjoy today,' he said, rather ominously. It was a long night as he proceeded to beat the shit out of me.

In my final year at Bedford, the kitchen staff, God bless them, would give me extra helpings of fish on a Friday to help me fill out. My body, finally, started to respond. I was up against guys who were just a bit stronger and a bit more streetwise, but I was starting to hold my own. If I drifted a bit at school academically, missing the structure that boarding at Beechwood provided me with, my steady progress in rugby eventually brought me into contention for England Schools. I had always looked on enviously at the senior boys, who strutted around the school in those famous purple tracksuits, having been selected for the England side. Now, for the first time, I was aware that divisional and national coaches were starting to take an interest in me.

Behind every England international there is always a backstory. And woven through that backstory are people who along the way have made a difference to that player, who have shaped them in some way, however small. It is why, when you run out at Twickenham, it's never just about the player.

It's about the people who have helped along the journey too. People like Guy Fletcher.

Guy was our head of PE and one of the things he said stayed with me throughout my career. I used to be in awe of the fantastic facilities at some of the schools we played against – Harrow, Oundle and Rugby – but Guy said, 'I can guarantee you, Bayfs, in years to come, when you bump into your old mates, no one will ever talk about the facilities. You will talk about the people. And the people here are the best.'

Alan Thorp, our deputy headmaster, was another who showed tremendous commitment to my development. He would drive me to all these representative training sessions, or trial matches, and then sit in the car for four or five hours, wait for me to finish and drive me back. I wish now I had been a bit more grateful.

I was overlooked by the selectors for a game against New Zealand after my first England Schools trial, which was held at what is now the Lensbury Club in Teddington, but back then it was the old Shell sports ground. The squad was read out and, for those of us who hadn't made the cut, that was it. We were told we had to leave. 'But how do we get home?' I asked. In classic RFU fashion, the answer was a simple one: 'Bye!'

Those were the days before mobile phones and so that night I was walking through the streets of Teddington to find the train station, thinking that if I could get the train into London, there must be a train up to Bedford. The trek home did nothing to diminish my frustration at missing out on selection.

Still, I did not have to wait long for my chance. England lost to New Zealand at Twickenham and there was then another selection and trials process. After the final trial at Rosslyn Park, I was selected for three internationals during the Easter period.

It was a huge moment for me. It opened my eyes to the fact that if I had a real crack at rugby, it could become serious. It was also the time when Roger Uttley had his first impact on my game. Uttley was head of rugby at Harrow School, but was also one of the England Schools coaches and we had always been aware of his presence when we played matches against them for Bedford.

It turns out he has been aware of me too, from the age of about 14. I can remember him coming up to me once and asking my name. 'You'll be all right,' he said, encouragingly. 'You might not make the team this year, but one day you'll be there.'

At my first England Schools training session, he really put me under pressure. He started jumping against me in the line-out and began pushing me as if to say: *Don't rely on your height. Start using your body.*

At the time, those three games for England Schools felt like the biggest games of my life. I had been lucky enough to pull on the white shirt with the red rose. Nothing else mattered. But as I progressed, I realised it mattered little. The side was very much selected out of the public school system. Very few players went on to even play senior club rugby, finding plenty of distractions at university. It wasn't exactly a great nursery for England players. The truth is the boys I played with at Bedford Colts would have breezed into that England side. They were harder, more streetwise and even hungrier. And thankfully, I was reaping the benefit of playing alongside them.

Between leaving school and joining the Met Police, I also

played a few games for Bedford RFC, which opened my eyes to the adult game. We played against Evesham in the first round of the old John Player Cup. A big box of free cigarettes was the perk of that game (if you didn't smoke you sold your box), but the highlight came in the post-match activities.

We had narrowly beaten Evesham but the main event was watching Northern Irish boxer Barry McGuigan making the first defence of his world title on a small portable TV in the middle of the pitch. Someone had rigged it up with about 20 extension cables and as it was early in the season, it was still quite light in the evenings. I had already overcome the embarrassment of singing my first song as a new player when both teams gathered together to watch it, and let's just say things progressed from there. It turned out to be a big old night; I was eventually returned to my parents' front door at 2 a.m. in a shopping trolley. Delivery for Mrs Bayfield. I was broken, but elated.

It was also a night with a remarkable legacy. Many years later, when I was working for ITV, I had to interview Chris Robshaw, who was the England captain at the time. It was a feature called 'Behind the Badge' and it involved beer-mat flipping. Robshaw was dumbfounded. He had no idea how to do it. But, from the dark recesses of my memory, I realised I knew how to flip a beer mat.

On that late summer's evening in 1985, at a pub near Evesham, someone had taught me how to do it as part of my initiation. I hadn't done it since, but 30 years later, sitting in the pub in Twickenham, it all suddenly came back to me.

And it turned out that while I might not have won a World Cup, I was fairly good at flipping beer mats. Which I guess pretty much sums up my career.

*

If club rugby was rapidly turning the boy into a man, it was winning those three England Schools caps that would still prove to be one of the decisive moments in my career, even if it wasn't a springboard for others. It was just as well, because before leaving school in July 1985, I had properly screwed up my A Levels.

My plans to go to Swansea University to study history were in the bin because of my laziness when it came to studying. It was probably just as well because going to Wales would have been a make-or-break moment for me.

At the time, I had ambitions of joining the Royal Marines but thankfully – for them – I didn't stand a chance.

I had a selection place to do the potential officers' course at Lympstone in Devon, but in my final England Schools game against Wales I was kicked in the head. I broke my nose and suffered concussion, injuries that forced me to delay my assessment. Then, out of nowhere, the asthma that I had experienced as a kid suddenly returned at the age of 18. That was the end of it. When I updated my medical records, I was told to cancel my assessment. The nation could rest easy.

It was just as well. I would never have had the strength to pass. And I would have been their biggest target.

Then, out of the blue, I received a call from Brian Baister, at the time the chief superintendent of the Met Police, who went on to become the chairman of the RFU. Baister, apparently, had gone through the list of players in the England Schools side and asked them if they fancied joining the Met.

I had never thought about joining the police before, but he came to our house and was almost uncomfortably flirty with my mum to convince her it was the right thing to do. But the more he talked about it, I started thinking: *This could be it.* So

I took the entrance exam, won a place and, by 1 November, was off to Hendon for a 20-week training programme. I also signed up to play for their rugby side.

It was there I first came across Paul Ackford, the England lock. Each week we were allowed four hours to train, initially at Hendon and then at Imber Court in Esher, when it opened up. Provided you kept buying your duty sergeant enough bottles of wine, you could usually wangle your shifts to make training sessions. Yet we were always up against it. Sometimes we would only have six or seven players because some of the guys would be in court or they had been asked to do a shift.

On match days, sometimes they would let you do an early shift, or a split shift – do four hours, go off and play rugby somewhere and then come back and do another four hours. So you might start off at 6 a.m., work half your shift and then meet the team bus, drive up to Crosby to play against Waterloo and then back again to finish off your shift that night.

When you got back, sometimes you would breathalyse yourself to see if you could drive, and if you couldn't and it was quiet, you could sleep it off in one of the cells. Sometimes the sergeant would just look at you with a sigh and say: 'Just go home. I'm going to get nothing out of you tonight.'

When we played the big teams, they would always beat us, but there was a great level of respect for the fact that we had got a team out. I was agog by the fact that our result would make it onto the Final Score portion of the BBC's *Grandstand* programme, when the rugby results followed the football scores. We had some great characters – including Vincent

Hill, the dad of Worcester and England back-row forward Ted Hill – and of course there was always a great night out afterwards, which occasionally involved the police being asked to police the police.

Once we were stopped on the M1 travelling back from Rugby. The look of the officers when they realised they had pulled over a crowd of Met Police was hilarious. Someone had taken the bar stools from their clubhouse and stored them in the luggage bays underneath so he could have them for his kitchen. Back you go, guys.

Another team-mate had this party trick of climbing out of one of the skylights at the front of the bus, crawling along the roof and then dropping down through the other one. That was until one journey when we decided to shut the second skylight and leave him hanging on the roof as we hurtled down the motorway for about 15 minutes.

Then there was the time we accidentally kidnapped a check-out assistant from a Granada service station. The bus drove off and we didn't realise she was still on it. We had to go all the way back to drop her off. After one game up north, we found ourselves in a nightclub in Chester. It was an old building with quite low ceilings, and I was standing with a pint, minding my own business, when the next thing I knew, I felt this smack on the back of my head which sent me crashing to the floor. The next thing I hear is: 'Someone's hit Bayfs!' A fight broke out, causing bedlam for a couple of minutes. Eventually order was restored when a guy from the corner came over, shouting: 'Stop, I saw everything.' It turned out that I had not been struck by a flying fist but had been standing too close to the spinning disco light which had knocked me to the ground when the

DJ had pushed his button to start the disco. 'Sorry everyone, it was just me . . .'

It was a great squad to be part of and I found it amazing how we managed to put a team out. It was not always easy for our opposition as they never knew which Met team would be turning up. We had sergeants, inspectors and CID officers, all of whom were doing significant work. It was not unusual for a player to turn up 20 minutes before kick-off, puffing and panting: 'Sorry lads, got caught up in paperwork.' Those guys who were coming off night shifts were allowed to sleep on the back seats. Some would try to catch an hour's sleep in their cars before meeting the coach at Hendon, or later the Hogarth Roundabout in Chiswick, where we would park at Fuller's Brewery. Occasionally on our return there would be a couple of packs of beer underneath your car because they all knew we were from the Met.

One of my first beats in the London borough of Hounslow gave me an insight into the charms of Twickenham on a big match day, as we would be asked to police the stadium. It was an eye-opening shift. The duty sergeant would drop you off at points around the stadium with the warning: don't get *too* drunk. *Interesting*, I thought, *that he didn't say don't get drunk.* I can remember walking around the old West Stand car park, where the more well-to-do supporters would be hosting picnics from the back of their Land Rovers or cooking food on the engines of their Range Rovers. 'Officer, come and have some foie gras and a glass of Bollinger,' they would often call out. *Don't mind if I do, thanks.* There was never any trouble we had to police, so we would end up watching the game from the back of the old green stands. The first game I worked at was the John Player Cup final between Bath and

Leicester Tigers in 1989, when Stuart Barnes kicked a ugly penalty to win it.

After the match, we would drive around the stadium in our van and pick up all the discarded foam cushions that the supporters had purchased for 20p to sit on to soften the hard wooden seats. We would then park up outside the gates at Twickenham and throw the cushions like frisbees back into the stadium. Was this the best use of police time? Probably not. But a few weeks later some cases of beer would be sent to the station with a thank-you note from the RFU.

As much as I loved the rollercoaster ride, I never dreamed it would take me any further, but playing for the Met would open the door of opportunity. I was asked to attend a training session for Middlesex at the Bank of England ground in Roehampton. Dick Best, who went on to become England and Lions coach, was in charge. Suddenly I was in big-boys' territory.

Besty was not one to mince his words. I was having a nightmare in a line-out session and he stopped the session, threatening to call me a taxi and send me home if I didn't sharpen up. We briefly moved on to another drill, but when we returned to do some more line-outs, I could not help but notice that parked up near the training pitch was a black cab. I made sure I caught the next ball. Besty just waved at the driver, dismissing him with a 'You can fuck off now.'

My big breakthrough came when I was selected for a training session for the Midlands Division in 1988 for a match against Australia, who were touring the UK and Ireland. Although I played for the Met, as I had been born in Bedford, I could represent the Midlands. The first session was at Welford Road, the home of Leicester Tigers. As I walked into the changing room, I was gripped by a similar sensation of apprehension as I would be years later on the film set of *Harry Potter*. *What am I doing here?*

As I gingerly sat down, I could feel the eyes on me again. Literally no one knew who I was.

Alan Davis, the coach, introduced me to my new team-mates. He went around the room and pointed to several England legends – Brian Moore, Dean Richards, Les Cusworth – who were putting forward ideas about how they thought we should play against Australia. 'Hi,' I said nervously. 'I play for the Met Police. I'll just be happy if I see the ball. If I can touch it just once in the game, I'll be delighted.'

Everyone started laughing. *What the hell are you doing here?* 'I have no idea,' I roared back. The ice, at least, was broken.

4

Face Down on the Beach

In the end, despite my hopes, I don't think I did get my hands on the ball during that Midlands tour match against Australia. But it was a game that would change everything for me. The journey to Nandi and my England debut began that fateful day at Welford Road.

Despite my peripheral contribution, the experience opened my eyes to rugby at an elite level. I just loved the noise and colour of Welford Road. It's one of my favourite grounds, even though I ended up playing for Leicester's fierce midlands rivals Northampton Saints. Before the game, we stayed in a hotel and during the training sessions beforehand everything felt different. It felt *special*.

There was a kit, there was the traditional shitty nylon tie. I felt a million dollars. Well, maybe a million lira. And the Australian team was box office. There were several players who had lit up Europe on their Grand Slam tour of 1984 – Michael Lynagh, Nick Farr-Jones, David Campese, Simon

Poidevin and Steve Cutler – in their side, and their famous green and gold kit was just so cool.

At times, I was running around simply staring at the opposition, in awe of the atmosphere of the occasion. I was up against Cutler, who was a giant of a man, and it was not long before the Wallabies landed their first blow. Farr-Jones came around the blindside of a ruck and scored their opening try. It was all too easy. We were huddled underneath the posts and Mooro bellowed: 'HOW THE FUCKING HELL DID THEY GET THE BALL?'

In my enthusiasm to get to the ball, I had accidentally kicked it straight into the hands of the Australia captain. 'Er, that will have been me,' I admitted, instantly realising that I should have kept my mouth shut as the glares from my teammates bore into me. We lost the game 25-18 against a side that would go on to come unstuck at Twickenham the following week on Will Carling's debut as England captain. Still, we had given them a run for their money.

Bob Dwyer, the Australia head coach, would be England's nemesis three years later as he coached the Wallabies to their World Cup triumph at Twickenham in 1991, defeating England in the final. But that night in the clubhouse at Welford Road, as I proudly wore my cheap nylon tie and rubbed shoulders with the Australians in their olde-worlde striped blazers, he would prove to be a catalyst for my international career.

He came up to me afterwards to share a beer. 'Mate, you are wasted playing for the police,' he said. 'You've got potential. I like what I've seen but you need to go to a higher level.' His words hit home. Later that night, I lay in bed thinking about my future. Having tasted the big time, I wanted more. Perhaps Dwyer was right. Perhaps I did need to get out of the Met and play for a bigger side and start pushing myself. Perhaps I really should start taking rugby more seriously. In the early days, my ambition was to play for the Met and progress through the ranks of the police. There was no way I was thinking about one day playing for England. But after playing for the Midlands, I began thinking: *This really could lead somewhere.*

As the beers flowed, some of the Leicester players said I should join them at Welford Road. Nottingham, who were one of the super clubs at the time, also expressed an interest.

But the definitive voice came from Mark Howe. Mark was a hugely talented hooker at Bedford. His misfortune was to be stuck behind three brilliant hookers during the 1980s – Steve Brain, Peter Wheeler and Mooro. But he was always the second-best hooker in England.

'Come back to your hometown – there is nothing like playing for your home club,' he said. Mark could have gone on and played for anyone, so his opinion carried significant weight. And so I did. Despite everything, it remains one of the best decisions I ever made. I still regard Bedford as 'my club' and my first England shirt still hangs proudly in their clubhouse.

I had initially asked my commander at the Met if it was possible to play for Rosslyn Park, who at that time were on a par with Harlequins. Paul Ackford had already moved on to play for them before joining Harlequins. He said I could, but they couldn't guarantee that I would have Saturdays off. The implication was that I was coming under pressure not to move. The message was: *Feel free to join Quins if you want, but you might be policing Chelsea v Millwall this Saturday. If you're playing for the Met, you can have every Saturday off.*

That made my mind up and I came up with some excuse as to why I needed a transfer to Bedfordshire Police, who had said I could play for whomever I liked. The only problem was that when I got to Bedford, they were truly dreadful. When you look at the teams struggling at the bottom of the Premiership nowadays, we were, in comparison, so much worse. Bedford Blues had just been promoted to the old First Division the year I joined, and the problem was that I don't think they had expected to go up to the top flight.

On the final day of the old Second Division in the previous season, Bedford had been fourth in the table but everyone above them lost. In the changing room afterwards, the players were celebrating a final-day victory, thinking it had been a decent season, when the word came through from the team manager. 'Er, guys, I've got bad news for you . . . we're promoted.'

There was no money, no recruiting had been done (apart from me!) and we got absolutely smashed in my first season. The First Division fixtures consisted of only 11 matches in those days, as you played a team once, home or away. And we lost all 11 quite comfortably. In our match against Harlequins, we were 4-0 up after 20 minutes but still managed to lose 71-8. And in those days, it was four points for a try. Yeah, I know. It was that bad. People used to ask: 'What time do Bedford kick-off?' The answer: 'Every four minutes.' Very funny, guys.

While Bedfordshire Police were great at giving me time off to play, I was based in Luton for the first two years after my move from the Met and it was full-on shift work: early turns, late turns and night duties. It meant that there would be times when I would turn up for a game with Bedford having just come off a shift, or go straight to work after a match.

Yet even though they were tough times, I still believe it was the right move for me. It allowed me to develop without any pressure or spotlight and I still take great pride from the fact that I won my first cap while I was technically still a Bedford player.

Our coach was Ian Snook, who had come from Taranaki in New Zealand and had obviously been sold this vision of coming to the northern hemisphere to coach an English First Division team. But when he rocked up, I am sure he thought we were an absolute shambles.

We used 70 players in our first season. Playing for the Blues was always considered a huge honour for players at junior clubs in our area. But it got to the point when the club would ask a player if he would be available and he would say 'Er, no thanks, am sure you'll be all right.' In the first season we had been obliterated in the First Division and in the Second Division we were hanging on, desperate not to get relegated again. But it was Snooky who first said to me that he thought I could play for England. 'I'm going to gear your training and your preparation around getting you into the England team,' he told me.

At the same time, Bedford signed two gnarled veterans from Gloucester – a second row called John Brain and the prop Richard Pascall. It was just what I needed. Suddenly, instead of playing in what was practically a pub team, I had a prop I could scrummage behind and who could help me with a bit of illegal lifting in the line-out, as well as an old head in the second row who could drag me around the pitch and make me more streetwise. I responded to what they were saying and it gave me a huge lift.

Training with the Midlands squad when we got together

underscored this development, thanks to the Leicester boys in particular – Richard Cockerill, Graham Rowntree, Neil Back and John Wells. Everything you had heard about Leicester was true. They just fought each other all the time. And, I mean, all the time. They wouldn't fight me, but when they ran past each other, an elbow or a fist would come flying. Why? Just for fun.

They were completely insane. Backy, with a massive chip on his shoulder, would fly around as the fittest man in the world. When he played in a 12-12 draw against the Emerging Wallabies in 1990, I remember their head coach asking afterwards: 'Why is this guy not playing for England? He is the best player we have come up against.' Backy didn't get capped until 1994. By then, he had a whole bag of chips on his shoulder. But he would have the last laugh, playing in three World Cups, including the 2003 triumph, and touring three times with the Lions.

It was this combination of working with Snooky, having the space and time to find my way with Bedford, and getting a glimpse at the competitive nature of the Midlands players, that allowed me to develop into a player knocking on the door of the international stage. But there were moments when could I not help myself thinking: *Why me?* I can remember John Reason, the former rugby correspondent of the *Daily Telegraph,* writing about a Divisional Championship match between the Midlands and the South West. It was at the time when the South West never won a game. If you put Bath in the Divisional Championship, they would have won it. But put them in the green of South West and they lost every game.

Reason wrote that: 'Martin Bayfield was taken to the

cleaners by Nigel Redmond but he had the last laugh by finally winning a line-out from which the Midlands scored a try. It does reflect credit on the Midlands that they are trying out this nobody.' It was one of those reports which, when you read it, made you think *What a bastard*. But it was true. England were giving this *nobody* a chance. Someone, somewhere was thinking that I had something that was worth indulging. Not for the last time in my career, I would also benefit from a massive dollop of luck.

The England tour had started in Australia, beginning with New South Wales, but I was not required as Nigel Redmond and I were the second-choice locks behind Wade and Ackers. The tour didn't start well. We lost first the game. I played in a low-key win against the Victorian President's XV in Melbourne, but the second big provincial encounter, against Queensland, hardly went to plan either. But it did open the door of opportunity for me.

The build-up to the match included one of the funniest moments of my career, which I recently recalled with Simon Halliday, who years later went on to become chairman of the European Professional Club Rugby organisation, the body that runs the Champions' and Challenge Cups. Neither of us were in the Saturday team and Besty had taken us off for a training session. What we didn't notice was that the pitch had these water sprinklers that came out of the ground. Hallers, unknowingly, was lying on top of one while he was stretching. The next moment, in a scene like a cartoon, the sprinkler starts gushing out water, drenching Hallers as if he was lying over the blowhole of a whale.

We reminisced about the number of times we would do

training sessions in random bits of parkland where people would be eating picnics or flying kites. They would look across and ask who we were. 'Oh, that's the England team.' It was just so wonderfully amateur.

My big break? It was literally Wade's hand. Wade, being Wade, broke it after punching Queensland's Sam Scott-Young and was ruled out of the Tests against Fiji and Australia. We flew on to Fiji for the B match before the moment arrived when Geoff Cooke read out my name for the Test team.

My elation at my debut was tempered by seeing for the first time just how tough international rugby could be and observing players trying to cope with the disappointment of being dropped, a sensation I would come to know well.

My room-mate, who shall remain nameless, had missed out on selection from the Tests. We had a few beers after one of the games and later that night back in our hotel room, I was awoken by a noise and saw my team-mate, clearly sleep-walking, bump into the chair that had his clothes hanging on it. He started pissing all over them. 'Take that, Cooke, you bastard,' he murmured in sleep talk. When he woke up in the morning, he went over to the chair to get dressed. 'What has happened here?' he asked me, as I creased up laughing. 'Yeah, you pissed on your clothes during the night.' 'Oh, sorry about that.'

Of course, there were plenty of fun times, but it could be tough too. One evening we had a big night out and Dick Best, who was seen as a visionary back then for the work he had done with the London Division, told us he was going to sweat that evil out of us. And we ran and ran and ran all afternoon.

I'm not sure whose decision it was, but John Hall, who had

messed up in training, was told to run back to the hotel in the 90-degree heat. He didn't have any trainers with him so had to run on the concrete with his boots on. It was brutal. He had a dodgy knee at the time and not long after he had to be sent home. He would only play for England one more time, winning the last of his 21 caps three years later against Scotland at Murrayfield.

After the Fiji B game, and with the tour back on track, Cookey addressed us in the changing room. 'Look, no messing around tonight. We've got a Test match coming up,' he told us. Yeah, *sure*, Geoff. Of course, we all got pissed and at the hotel resort we stumbled upon some instruments that a band had left behind in a room. Damian Hopley, the Wasps centre, could play the piano and others had a go at the rest. As we entered the early hours, someone must have made a complaint because suddenly Geoff appeared, steaming towards us.

Nigel Redmond, who is quite a quiet bloke, piped up. 'Fair play, Geoff is still up as well. Top man.' 'No, Nige,' came the response. 'Look at his face. He is not happy.'

'Back to your rooms, lads, NOW!' barked Geoff.

I'm not sure what I thought would happen in the build-up to my first cap, but few people said anything to me. If I expected Will Carling, our captain, to come over in a quiet moment and talk me through what to expect on the Test stage, I was mistaken. In fact, I got the feeling that most of the lads were probably thinking: *I wish Wade hadn't whacked that Queensland bloke.* The attitude was: you're in the team, what else do you want us to say? Just get on with it. And I suppose that was fair enough.

We didn't have a dedicated media manager for the England team then, a stark contrast to the phalanx of staff that accompanies the national side these days. Even the age-group sides have press officers. Colin Herridge travelled with us, but his main job seemed to be turning up with a cheque book if there had been any damage caused and asking: 'How much?' Colin was a fabulous man, full of kindness and energy. Most importantly, as I would discover, he was a man who turned several blind eyes to any nonsense. I was so sorry to hear that he recently passed away.

I remember one day walking through the reception of the team hotel and David Hands, who then was rugby correspondent of *The Times*, asked if I wanted to have a chat. So I sat down with David and had a natter, but I didn't know what to expect until the next day, when there was an article published in the paper. There was nothing exceptional to report. It was a bit of a weird time. In fact, it was rare that any media took interest in me throughout my career and I got that. Everyone largely wanted to speak to Will, Mooro, Jerry Guscott, Rob Andrew or Dean Richards.

One team-mate who was brilliant to me was Mooro. He told me what was coming my way and prepared me for it. I don't remember much about the game. We won 28-12 and afterwards Geoff Cooke said some nice things in a newspaper article. 'Whatever happens now, we will go back to England having discovered an exciting player,' he said.

To be fair, I remember even less about the after-match celebrations. The England management had clearly not expected anyone to make their debut on tour as they had nothing to present to me to mark the occasion. No cap, no tie. Uttley – perhaps feeling guilty for that punch – pulled off his tie and handed it to me after the game. 'Congratulations on winning your first cap, mate,' he said. That was it. I was given Roger Uttley's tie.

'By the way, I need that back.' Oh, okay, of course. Eventually one was posted from the UK and I would finish the tour with an England tie of my own.

Rooming with Mickey Skinner, the Harlequins flanker, was an experience in itself and he took it upon himself to make sure I enjoyed the night. We were drinking Fiji's national drink, kava, and after a while on it, you realise your legs don't work any more. Then it was off to the official function, where we ate curried turtle. From then on, everything became a bit of a blur until I woke up the following morning, face down on the beach outside our hotel, still wearing my blazer. Welcome to international rugby.

In the next Test, against Australia, we were taken to the cleaners. It was a match that registered little in the national sporting narrative back home, but it would have huge ramifications just a few months later, when England faced the Wallabies in the World Cup final at Twickenham. England, in Carling's first game as captain, had comfortably beaten the Wallabies in 1988, and the Lions had triumphed against them the following year. Even though Wales had lost to the Aussies, in the back of our collective minds, that was *Wales*. It was a sense of complacency that would come to bite us then, and again in the World Cup in 1995 against New Zealand. That afternoon in Sydney, they caught us totally by surprise.

They did so with a few subtle changes that made them an infinitely better side, taking us on at our perceived strength up front. Willie Ofahengaue and John Eales trampled all over us, while Jason Little and Tim Horan were awesome in the midfield. We were thumped 40-15.

A few months later, Bob Dwyer's side would be crowned world champions at Twickenham. It was the legacy of that performance in Sydney, rather than pre-match taunts from David Campese, that led England to change their tactics for the final, moving away from the forward-orientated game that played into the hands of the Wallabies. Australia had already landed their psychological blow on the tour. As for my own World Cup hopes, well, they wouldn't even survive the trip home to London.

5

Two Bits of Cotton Hanging Out of Your Shorts

I sometimes wonder how I would have responded to Eddie Jones's abrasive style as England head coach. I am fairly sure I would have loved it.

In 1992, we had our own version of Eddie Jones in the form of Dick Best, who had been appointed as coach under manager Geoff Cooke in the wake of England's defeat in the World Cup final the previous autumn. I loved Besty. He had been seen as the coming man for several seasons based on the brand of rugby that his London Division had been playing, stretching back to their victory over Australia in 1988. Will Carling, who knew him well from Harlequins, was among those who had been keen to get him involved with England.

Yet if he was seen as 'new school' in terms of tactics, there was plenty of old school about his dealings with players. He was always brutally honest with you, and would often rip you to shreds. Some players he would bury and they would just disappear, but given my personality I found his manner and methods hilarious. I just clicked with him and he became one of the guys who had the most influence on my career.

Compared with his peers, he was a relatively young coach, who had come in with innovations and new ideas. Like Jones, he was not a former international himself, so he had to impress you with his coaching abilities rather than saying: 'This is what I did with England and the Lions.' Besty was a different animal. He would needle away to see how you would react and where your weaknesses were and then how to improve them. I just loved his approach. It was perfectly suited to get the most out of me.

It is fair to say this wasn't a view shared by some of my team-mates, however. Some players didn't like it because he could be vicious. But I was a bit like an overstretched, milky-white Incredible Hulk. If you got me angry, I really went for it. And Besty could make me angry, without me being *angry* angry, if that makes sense. Having got me worked up during a session, I would look across and he would be looking back, with a little smile on his face. He knew exactly what he was doing. He would just push those buttons at the right time and in the right way.

He was able to find that aggressive streak deep inside me that I couldn't find myself, which I had subconsciously kept hidden because of my childhood experiences. I guess I had always sup-pressed it because there were times when I got angry and had to quickly calm myself down; I knew, at 6ft 10ins, I could do a lot of damage in that state. I didn't want to get angry as, when I lost my temper, people could get scared. That's where Besty was so good with me, helping me bring out a more aggressive streak in my game when it was the right environment.

He also had an acerbic wit. After one of our matches, we stopped for some drinks in the Roebuck pub in Richmond on our way to the Petersham Hotel. One of the wives of a RFU committee member was with us and she appeared to be just a little bit too happy to be with the England players. She was having a few drinks and getting a bit flirty. Besty just turned around to her and said: 'My dear, you need to stop acting this way. Otherwise we will just think you are cheap, white trash.' Ouch. No one else would have got away with saying something like that.

He was also a trained pastry chef, of all things, and loved his food and wine. It was always the very best wines for Besty. He and Mooro used to sit and discuss wines and we would wind them up when a new bottle of wine arrived at the table and we added it to the glass we were drinking a different bottle from.

Despite his abrasive tongue on the pitch every now and then, he would give you a word of encouragement that would mean the world to me. He was the kind of coach who only needed to say 'That was good today, that was better' and you felt even taller than 6ft 10ins. It was all that was needed. I would be ready to run through a brick wall for him.

The problem I had when we reconvened for a fitness test at Twickenham after the Fiji tour, as part of the preparations for the 1991 World Cup, was that I could barely run the length of myself. It was in the old Rose Room in the stadium, and the test involved running up and down on the carpet.

I immediately knew something wasn't right. I felt inexplicably lethargic and sluggish. A few days later, I started coming out in boils, but when I saw a doctor, he could not establish what was wrong with me. I did a bit of self-surgery on the boils (first with a needle, before squeezing out a disgusting plug of pus with a pair of tweezers) before seeing another doctor who took a swab from my nose. 'You've got bugs living up your nose and you've picked up a virus,' he told me. I had picked them up from the soil while playing in Fiji, apparently.

The treatment was to shove some paste up my nose for a few days to get rid of the bugs, but by then any hopes I had of making the World Cup squad were gone. With Wade fit again, the selectors went for Nigel Redmond as the back-up second row and I can understand why. He was a far more experienced player than I was. I think the only person more disappointed than I was at my omission from the 24-man squad was John Eales, who no doubt would have been licking his lips at the prospect of facing me after the rout in Sydney.

Missing out on the World Cup at least allowed me to settle into my new club, Northampton Saints. There had been something of a revolution at Franklin's Gardens at the end of the previous season and it was the vision of the new architects that prompted me to leave Bedford, who had failed to return to the top flight after another difficult season in the Second Division.

Northampton had recently been in dire straits themselves. In the 1987-88 season, despite having players of the calibre of Gary Pearce, Vince Cannon and Frank Packman, they had finished bottom of Division Two, only to be saved from the embarrassment of falling into the third tier of English club rugby by the absence of relegation that season. It prompted a takeover by a group of former players and supporters known as 'The Gang of Seven', following stern warnings that the club would face extinction unless it underwent radical changes.

The proposals were put to the club's annual general meeting and passed by an overwhelming majority. One of the first steps was for the Saints to become the first club in England to appoint a full-time director of rugby. Barrie Corless was appointed to the position, on the condition that he was not allowed to coach but could act as an administrator. A recruitment drive followed, with the likes of John Steele, Ian Hunter and Tim Rodber joining the club. Then I got a call. I was told that Buck Shelford, the great All Blacks No. 8, was on his way too. With Bedford at the time falling apart, it was a no-brainer for me to move on.

I spoke with Bedfordshire Police to check if they were happy if I switched clubs to Northampton and they were fine with it. The only catch, I told Saints, was that I would miss out on the opportunity to earn overtime with the police if I had to train with the club on Tuesday and Thursday nights. But there was an old-school solution. In the car park of the Green Man pub in Lavendon near Milton Keynes, I was handed a brown envelope with £1,500 of cash in it. 'That should cover your expenses for the year.' Excellent. What they didn't know was that I would have joined them anyway.

It was an exciting time. A new generation of young English talent soon arrived at the club – Matt Dawson, Paul Grayson and Nick Beale – who created a potent mix with the likes of older hands such as John Olver. It was a great team to be with and I absolutely loved my time with the club. During my first season we came within a whisker of winning Division One. And, away from the spotlight of the World Cup, I started playing some really good rugby.

Not being involved with England allowed me to reboot after the tour. It was not that I had come back feeling cocky. It would have been nice to be picked for the World Cup squad, but I hadn't expected it. Instead I focused on improving my game, keeping my head down and settling into Northampton.

I was helped by the fact that by this stage Bedfordshire Police had transferred from Luton to Bedford and I was working in the town-centre unit, which was pretty much a 9 a.m.–5 p.m. shift, meaning I was free to train in the evenings with my club. I perhaps wasn't as focused as I should have been on my day job. A shout would go out at the end of my shift that we had a shoplifter at Marks & Spencer. I would turn up, speak to the store detective and to the bloke who was alleged to have stolen fifty quid's worth of salmon. 'Do you really want to prosecute?' I would ask, thinking inside that I did not want to take this case on as I had training in a couple of hours. Of course he wanted to prosecute. First thing was a quick phone call to my coach: 'I'm going to be late.'

But the fact is that I couldn't have done what I did without the support of the police. It was more than support. They were genuinely enthusiastic about what I did. There were some officers who resented it, and I got that. But the rest of the guys were chuffed to bits for me. They were great characters too.

Training with Northampton on Tuesday nights was the tough session. At the start we would ask: what are we doing tonight?

'Oh just scrums, line-outs, kick-off receipts, penalty moves, backs moves, forward moves.'

'What, so everything then?'

'Yeah, everything.'

It would last around two hours. We had players like Phil Pask, who was training to become a physiotherapist – and who became one of the most respected physios in rugby, working with the England and Lions teams for many years – putting our strapping on.

Thursday was a much lighter session and we would normally finish by having a big pot of curry and a few beers for pre-match bonding purposes. I also trained by myself at least three times a week. On Monday morning, I would get up early and go to the gym in the town centre to do a weights session before work. Then, after work on Mondays, I would head to Bedford Athletics' track to do some running, speed and plyometric training.

It was there that I first came across a young Paula Radcliffe, who went on to become one of world's best long-distance runners. She must have been around 16 at the time and was training with a group of around 20 girls, many from the nearby Sharnbrook Upper School (now Sharnbrook Academy). I think I was referred to by them as 'the dirty old man'. My routine involved doing a set of ten 300-metre 'repeats'. My goal was to complete one in 55 seconds, then have a two-minute rest and then go again. I would start my session at one bend of the track on my own, while Paula and her gang would start at the far end. But their session normally involved running 400-metre repeats in under one minute and only one minute's rest. I would normally let them go past me by 70 metres or so before I'd set off to try to catch them. All they could hear was my heavy breathing behind them (hence the nickname) before I would collapse to the ground as they set off again. They were seriously good athletes, but Paula stood out as the fastest.

My own fitness and speed improved, but the plyometrics would later lead to pelvic injuries because of the pressure

I had put on it by landing on one leg. I tried resistance work too, to improve my physique. One night I found an old tyre and filled it with shots used by shot putters before attaching the tyre to a weights belt and putting it around my waist. I started to run down the field in the middle of the track, but the groundsman must have cut the grass that day because it was covered with loose cuttings. As I charged forward I slipped and went face down only to emerge totally covered in grass. I quickly stood up, brushed myself down and mumbled, while trying to look cool, 'Yes, international athlete here.'

I probably should have had a more balanced training pro-gramme but I concentrated on what I liked, and what it did do was improve my mobility.

My dedication to training was matched by my com-mitment to enjoying myself off the pitch. Memories came flooding back a few months ago when I was walking through my village and I saw this woman walking towards me who looked a similar age. It was one of those moments when you think you recognise someone, and I think she recognised me because of my height. 'If you are wondering,' she said. 'It was Aunty Ruth's.'

That was all that needed to be said. *Aunty Ruth's*. It turned out she was a former barmaid from from the famous club in the centre of Northampton. What a place. It was owned by the Richardson brothers, Colin and John, who were big characters in Northamptonshire and owned property, hair salons and clubs. They had this band called Ginger Pig, a very well-respected New Orleans jazz band. One of them played the piano and the other one the guitar, and they had really good people who would come and sing.

One of the cocktails in Aunty Ruth's was also called The Ginger Pig, a name that I will never forget. In the early days of European rugby, we went out to play Bordeaux and Nice and, on the way back at the airport, the boys clocked Geri Halliwell from the Spice Girls, aka Ginger Spice. She was looking at lingerie in a shop and Matt Dawson, Northampton's England and future Lions scrum-half, bold as brass, walked past and said: 'Hey, you'd look amazing in that.'

We got chatting and she was telling us how the Spice Girls were about to head for India and for some reason thought they were going to die out there. 'You're looking at the worst-case scenario,' I replied. 'You're going to go out there, you'll have a curry, get food poisoning and you'll suffer for a few months, and *then* you'll probably die.' Oh yes, my banter was gold back then.

But the joke would soon be on me. Andy Blyth, one of our centres, came in and saw me talking to Ginger Spice.

'Oi, Bayfs! We're trying to get the guy in the bar upstairs to do the cocktail they serve at Aunty Ruth's. What's its name again?' he shouted over.

'Ginger Pig,' I shouted back. Ginger Spice, standing beside me, looked up at me and smiled painfully. And then just walked off. Cheers, Andy.

Naturally, we celebrated winning the final of the Divisional Championship at Aunty Ruth's, after defeating London at Franklin's Gardens on the day that England played France in the quarter-finals of the World Cup in Paris. I can still remember hearing the cheers during our match, emanating from the old clubhouse. 'I'm not sure anyone is watching our game,' someone quipped. 'Those cheers are certainly not for us!'

When the big news came through that Ackers had decided

to retire from international rugby after the World Cup, I was in the perfect position to push for a recall in time for the start of the Five Nations Championship. If Ackers had decided to play on, I am pretty sure it would have been a different story. But, thankfully, the call came.

Given that Besty had been on the tour of Fiji and Australia, it made my return to the England squad less terrifying. I also had Wade Dooley to take me under his wing. It had been a bit of a slow burner, our relationship. But with Ackers out of the picture, he was brilliant at preparing me for what was to come in the Five Nations.

It quickly became clear that it was going to be a completely different level of intensity to the tour. The senior players in the squad were looking to make immediate amends for losing the World Cup final; there was also the matter of attempting to become the first England side to win its second successive Grand Slam in 68 years.

And who did we have first up? Scotland, in Murrayfield, our first return to Edinburgh since the infamous afternoon in 1990 when David Sole's side snatched the Grand Slam from England's grasp despite being overwhelming favourites. The same Scotland players who had turned up at Twickenham for the World Cup final the previous November wearing Australia jerseys, after England had beaten them in the semi-final when Gavin Hastings missed that penalty in front of the posts. You can just imagine how that went down with the likes of Mooro, Deano and Jeff Probyn.

Yet, surprisingly, Mooro was once again a calming presence for me. We had met up on the Wednesday before the game, trained that night and again on Thursday before travelling to Edinburgh on the Friday. Tim Rodber, my new Northampton team-mate, was making his England debut against Scotland, and there was more pressure on him as he had been brought in ahead of Deano, who was on the bench. Some were questioning why this young lad had got the nod. What people didn't realise at the time was that Tim was going through his Sandhurst training (he would become a major in the Green Howards infantry regiment of the British Army), but the exertions of the training had seen him lose over a stone and a half, leaving him absolutely knackered, so he wasn't at his best for his debut.

In contrast, I was lucky in the sense that Ackers was gone, so I never felt the pressure of the old guard over my shoulder like Tim did. It was reassuring therefore when Mooro, in a surprisingly measured mood, called us to his room in the Balmoral Hotel in Edinburgh to talk through the game.

'This is Murrayfield. The crowd will try to get on top of you and there will be pressure and nerves like you have never felt before,' Mooro told us. 'But just remember, you have got the rest of the team around you, which is hugely experienced, and you will be fine.'

Later we went to a park near the Balmoral Hotel and did what we called a few 'spotters' – a bit of line-out practice. People who were walking their dogs were saying: 'Is that the England team?' It all helped to calm the nerves. A bit.

When I played in the Tests against Fiji and Australia, it had felt almost surreal – new venues, new players, new kits – and it really did not mean as much to me. But I had seen Scotland vs England matches at Murrayfield many times. It did not matter what you did on tour, the Five Nations was your bread and butter. We were expected to beat Scotland and my nerves were more shredded than anything I had experienced in Fiji. When we got to Murrayfield, all I could think about was that this was the venue I had seen on the telly. I knew the colour of the shirts, the noises and the songs, and sensed, from the intimidating atmosphere, that a repeat of 1990 was on the cards.

Yet first things first. My initial major task had been to get prepared for the after-match dinner and that required hiring a dinner suit. So off I went with Martin Hynes, my Northampton team-mate, to go shopping in Richmond before we headed north. The suits barely fitted, but who cared?

Now Martin was also quite keen to buy what he described as some 'naughty knickers' for his wife, so we went into a lingerie shop. There was Martin trying to explain to the assistant just how big his wife's breasts were. I remember thinking that this was hardly great preparation for my Five Nations debut, but you know what, looking back it was moments like these that defused the tension that might have been building up.

What helped too was that the preparation was otherwise strangely familiar. It was almost exactly what I would have done with my club, except with a nicer hotel, nicer bus and famous faces. Oh, and the match programme was a bit fancier. And there was also a marching band on the pitch.

Perhaps the ultimate tension-breaker would later come from Wade as we stood for the anthems. It was my first Test match with him and I was feeling it. Remember, this was the guy that I had idolised as a schoolboy. On my debut against Fiji, I had played with Nigel Redmond and in the second, against Australia, I had played with Paul Ackford.

I was standing beside Wade as we lined up just before the anthems started, when he turned to me. 'Mate, there are two bits of cotton hanging out of your shorts,' he said. 'Oh, hang on, they're your *legs*.'

So there I am, chuckling away at this stupid gag before the biggest moment of my career.

Scotland 7 England 25, Murrayfield, 18 January 1992

I hear so many players describing their international debut as a blur. Well, my Five Nations debut was anything but. It went on *for ever*.

My first hurdle was the line-out. The coaches had wanted me to jump at No. 2, largely because Wade had said: 'I'm jumping in the middle, lad.' Of course you are. The problem was that I had never jumped at the front of the line-out before and, for the first half an hour, I was like a rabbit frozen in headlights.

When I look back at the game, it's quite embarrassing to see my efforts. I was all over the place. I was up against a guy called Neil Edwards, who was quite a chunky bloke and didn't really look like a modern second row at all, but he had great handling skills. He had played for the Saints and, ahead of one training camp with Scotland, was asked by Ian McGeechan, the coach, what training he had been doing.

'Ach, Geech, I've been doing altitude training,' he said. 'Really?' said McGeechan. 'Bloody hell, that's impressive.'

'Yeah, I get on the running machine, put it on an incline and run until I'm at 10,000 feet!'

Jumping at the front of the line-out, certainly in my day, was a completely different skill to jumping at four because lifting was not allowed back then. So traditionally the front jumper was smaller and more powerfully built because the ball was in the air for less time as it was a shorter distance, so a more explosive moment was required.

Martin Johnson was brilliant at it. The technique was to almost open yourself up in front of your opponent so they had no way of getting to the ball. The classic line-out throw was for the ball to go right into the shoulder. 'Just give it to me here.' *Bang.*

In contrast, in the middle of the line-out, where I preferred to jump, there's a bit more movement, a little bit more time and you can get your body into position for a more dynamic, higher jump. There is also a little bit more kidology – feinting and running around. So, effectively, I was learning a new skill in the white heat of a Calcutta Cup match.

But even if it took me a while to get into the game, Mooro had been right. The big names in the side stood up that day and in the end we ran up a convincing victory, with tries by Rory Underwood and Dewi Morris, four penalties and a conversion by Jonathan Webb, and a nonchalant drop-goal by Jerry Guscott. We were up and running.

There had been moments in the game when, just for a fraction of a second, I stood back and almost became a spectator watching the England shirts piling into the navy Scotland shirts. It just seemed so familiar. It felt like I was now placing myself into the rugby narrative. It hadn't felt that way seeing England shirts against Fijian or Australian shirts. When I played against Australia, there hadn't been a particular point of reference. But against Scotland? Plenty.

That's my white shirt up against that blue shirt. This is the oldest game in international rugby and I am now in the narrative. There were moments when I found that quite suffocating during the game. I remember thinking: *If this never happens again, I have played in a Calcutta Cup match*. How epic is that?

And maybe it's a fault of mine to allow those thoughts to go into my head at various times during the game when I probably should have been concentrating on winning the next line-out. I guess that's just the way my brain works.

That feeling intensified when we came back into the changing room afterwards, having won the Calcutta Cup. Of course I wanted more. But if I never played for England again, well, this was still a moment to cherish.

It was as if my team-mates sensed my mood. While Skinner had made sure I had celebrated my debut in Fiji, there was a more focused collective effort in Edinburgh to make sure I didn't get away lightly with my first Five Nations appearance. They went after me. And they got me. That was the night when I also realised that whisky is not really my drink. By the time I got back to the hotel, I don't think Helena, my girlfriend at the time, who would become my first wife, was too impressed by the state I was in. I expect the menswear shop in Richmond was even less impressed when I handed back the dress suit.

England 39 Ireland 9, Twickenham, 1 February 1992

I was still hugely wet behind the ears for my first game for England at Twickenham. It was my first experience of staying in the team hotel right up to the game, of training at The Stoop, and of the drive to the stadium. Our next opponents were Ireland, so there was plenty of history there too. On the Friday night before the game, we all went to Richmond to watch the B match. It was great to be able to wander around the pitch with the team and watch another game. It also served as a reminder that if you don't perform the next day, there was another group of players ready and eager to take your place.

But remarkably, when you consider the detail that goes into preparing for Test matches nowadays, including analysis of opponents' strengths and weaknesses – and even of the referee's – I had no idea who I was playing against. These were the days when there were no cross-border club competitions, so international matches were the only time you came up against players from other countries. In today's game, if an England player is making his first appearance at Twickenham against Ireland, he might have already come up against players from Ulster, Leinster, Munster or Connacht six or seven times in the European Champions' Cup. But I had no exposure to the Ireland team. At all. I was playing against guys about whom I knew nothing.

However, it was my biggest advantage that season too. Not only was I making my Five Nations debut, but in the previous season I had played in the Second Division with Bedford, so I am certain that none of my opponents knew who on earth this big gangly kid was. Nowadays, new faces might be targeted but I don't remember any kind of sledging because no one knew anything about me. It was quite nice that that element of pressure was not there. I was very lucky that I was in this strong and dominant team which I could ease my way into. And against Ireland, I felt a bit more comfortable. The scrums and line-out went well and it ended up being a fairly straightforward win. Jerry, Hallers, Dewi and Rory scored tries while Webby, who also scored twice, kicked two penalties and four conversions.

There was a great moment during the game which crops up now and again when classic rugby matches are repeated. It shows Jerry making a fantastic break and his flying into the 22. I am running a support line just beside and as he is tackled, he turns to pass the ball on to me. Then he stops and throws this big loopy pass past me to Jonathan Webb on the outside. And as he falls to the ground, he has this big grin on his face as if to say: 'I am not going to let *you* score.'

Thanks a lot, Jerry. I think even I could have finished that one off.

Afterwards, in the Hilton Hotel, we were in the foyer, drinking at the bar because no one wanted to go to the dinner. We were more interested in drinking with the Irish lads. A representative from the RFU came over to us and told us we had to go back into the room.

But just at that moment, 50 stunning women, all wearing ball gowns, walked into the foyer. Suddenly all the boys are fixing their shirts and thinking *Oh, hello.* Then this woman, who seemed like the mother hen of the group, looked across and made a beeline for Colin Herridge, as he looked like the most sensible chap to have a conversation with.

Moments later, her eyes opened with shock and her face turned pale. She suddenly hurried back to her group and began ushering the women out of the hotel. Herridge came back to us, chuckling as he walked.

'It turns out they're candidates for Miss World and she didn't think it was wise for them to be in the same hotel as two rugby teams,' he said, almost crying with laughter.

'Herridge, what have you done?!' we replied. Mind you, it was probably just as well. Can you imagine the headlines the next day? Still it was a great night and one that did not go unrecorded by the national press. I was later sent a clipping of a diary story in one of the newspapers. It read: 'England players will be given a formal reminder this week of their social obligations after nine of them left the dining table to drink before the speeches at the men-only banquet following the victory over Ireland. England captain Will Carling congratulated Peter Winterbottom on his 50th cap and Martin Bayfield and Tim Rodber on their Twickenham debuts, only to discover all three were absent.'

Oops. Oh well, it could have been much, much worse. Of course, we would face a completely different experience in Dublin the following year but, for now, we were already halfway to the Grand Slam.

6

The History Boys

Let me begin the story behind our bloody victory against France in Paris by making an admission. My name is Martin Bayfield and Wade Dooley is my hero. There, I've said it. Such declarations of admiration were not common in any changing room that I was lucky enough to be in. I'm pretty sure nothing has changed. But who cares? This is my book and I think it is important to declare my interests. I simply love that man.

At 6ft 8ins tall, the 'Blackpool Tower' was the tallest lock forward in world rugby at the time – until I came along. Like me, he was also a policeman when he played for England. Like me, he also jumped at four in the line-out. But that, I'm afraid, is where the similarities stopped.

I might have been one of the tallest players in world rugby, but while I wanted to be like guys like Wade, I was never big enough. As much as I idolised him and wanted to play rugby like him, I knew I was never going to. The guy was simply a man mountain. In comparison, I was a mere beanpole. And that sense of physical inadequacy was always there, right the way through my playing days, from school, junior rugby, age-grade national squad and when I started to play adult rugby.

No one could ever accuse Wade of being soft. He was one of the hardest forwards to have ever played the game and was simply terrifying as an opponent. Between 1985 and 1993, he won 55 caps for England and played in two Tests for the British and Irish Lions on the tour of Australia in 1989. He was also selected for the 1993 tour of New Zealand, only to have to return to the UK following the death of his father. But more of that later.

All this he achieved while he was playing for both Preston Grasshoppers and Fylde in the fourth tier of English club rugby – a phenomenal achievement at the time and one that will never be replicated in the professional era. Playing down the leagues mattered little to tough-as-teak Wade.

Even when the England training schedule clashed with his club fixtures – it was designed to dovetail with the rest of us who played for clubs in the old First Division – it never broke his stride. Once, when we had a week off club duty, England organised a fitness test at Bisham Abbey. As Wade had just played a game for the Grasshoppers, he assumed he wouldn't be tested when he arrived and promptly got stuck into five or six pints – only for Geoff Cooke to tell him he had to do the test as well.

'Right, let's get on with it,' he said, before going out and recording his highest-ever score on the bleep test, a lung-busting fitness test that involved running 20-metre shuttles, trying to beat the bleep. Running under the influence appeared to have brought the best out of him, until at the end he collapsed to his knees and vomited violently. That was one of the reasons why they stopped doing the bleep tests in the Rose Room at

Twickenham: the complaints from the facility manager that the players were vomiting on the carpets too often.

That was Wade all over. Hard as nails but also a brilliant athlete. Yes, the Blackpool Tower was a guy you wanted with you in the trenches. They say never meet your heroes but, in my case, it was anything but a disappointment. Even when I played alongside Wade for England, I remained in awe of him. I would go on to play with and against some of the greatest locks ever to have played the game, including England's World Cup-winning captain Martin Johnson. But to me the greatest England pairing remains Ackford and Dooley.

My affection for Wade is such that I often mention him in a story in my after-dinner speeches to reflect how influential he was as a physical force at the heart of the England pack and my admiration for him.

The story goes something like this:

'We were momentarily stunned when a haymaker from the France lock Olivier Roumat floored Wade,' I say. 'You know it's a good punch when the referee goes up to the man and shakes his hand. With Wade poleaxed on the floor, it looked like a massive psychological blow had been landed by the home side.

'Of course, we needn't have worried. After a few seconds he got back to this feet and then looked Stephen Hilditch, the Irish referee, and then Roumat in the eye. "Ref," boomed Wade, jabbing his finger towards Roumat. "Do not send that fucker off."

'You have never seen blood drain from a man's face quite so quickly. Welcome to the Battle of Parc des Princes.'

What started out as an apocryphal yarn has grown legs over the years. If it may have been somewhat embellished, what is undeniable is just how tough a competitor he was, making him the perfect team-mate to have beside you during that particularly violent afternoon in Paris.

France 13 England 31, Parc des Princes, 15 February 1992

History has determined that the fractious World Cup quarter-final between the two sides four months earlier is now remembered as the low-point in Anglo-French relations in 'Le Crunch', but this game came close to matching it in terms of brutality, violence and infamy. And I just loved it.

It was the moment when I finally felt at home on the international stage. Everything clicked. It was the game when I thought to myself: *I can do this*.

And what a venue.

To those of you old enough to remember watching Five Nations matches at the Parc des Princes on television, do you remember the sort of tinny, ringing noise in the background? I don't know about you, but I used to think it was just because it was an overseas broadcast. But when you're in the stadium, that's actually how it sounds. It remains one of the best atmospheres I have experienced. Similar to Cardiff, the stadium was in the heart of the city, so to get there we had to be driven through Paris, passing the most beautiful architecture with police outriders just booting cars out of the way, and then we drove down, underneath the stadium. The drive to Twickenham is great, but you're driving through suburbia. In contrast, driving through Paris was special. Even the police officers looked like they had stepped out of *Vogue*.

The French players even had metal embroidery on the

badges on their shirts. Imagine having metal embroidery on your shirts. 'How did you get injured?' 'Oh, I hit his badge.' They even used a different match ball, the Adidas one with the black tips, and the language all added to the sense of occasion. Everything was just so achingly cool with Les Bleus.

That's everything apart from the temperament of the French players. I have never seen a side implode so spectacularly as Pierre Berbizier's side did that afternoon. For the first 30 minutes, they were completely in control, running us ragged. Sébastien Viars scored a try to put them in front, but by half-time we led 15-4, thanks to a penalty try after we had demolished their pack at a scrum, before David Pears, on for the injured Rob Andrew, fired a long cut-out pass to Jerry, who scythed through the defensive line to put Jonathan Webb over for our second try.

During that time, I had played my way into the game. The advice I had been given was to get myself into the contest early and, when they put a kick through, chase back, recover the ball and take a couple of steps into contact to clear up the mess. It was simple stuff but I was in the game.

Little did I realise that perhaps my biggest contribution to England's victory was to come, when I lay prostrate and was stamped on by Grégoire Lascubé, the French prop. I think frustration had been building because we had been able to extend our lead. You could sense their growing irritation. They tried things but nothing was working for them, despite their early pressure, and they started bickering at each other.

It was then that we cut loose. Rory Underwood raced over for his 35th international try after Viars and Webb exchanged penalties. When Alan Penaud scored after charging down a kick by Will Carling, the game was already beyond them.

France had not lost to England on four consecutive occasions since the 1920s and, on the back of the World Cup quarter-final defeat, were now facing making unwanted history. Like pressure building under a dormant volcano, the searing pain of Lascubé's studs on my head signalled their eruption. I had little idea of what had happened until I saw Mooro's snarling face above me.

'Stay down. We will have this fucker off,' he barked.

Thanks for the words of concern for my wellbeing, Brian, I thought. But I did what I was told. In the end, Hilditch had no option but to send Lascubé off. I had received a right old kick to the head. I afterwards described it as 'doing a Fred Astaire on my head' and the touch judge Owen Doyle had seen every brutal step.

Cue all mayhem breaking out. The French crowd howled with derision. Mooro was now in his element, winding up the French pack. At the next scrum, Vincent Moscato moved from hooker to loosehead prop, while Jean-François Tordo switched from the back row to the middle of the front row. For the first engagement, Tordo and Moscato head-butted Mooro and Jeff Probyn, who was at tighthead. It all kicked off.

Hilditch did his best to calm things down, but as they went down again, Jeff blew Moscato a kiss. Afterwards the Frenchman was described as having 'tears of rage' as he butted Jeff again. All I knew as I stood up from the scrum was that Hilditch had already pointed to the touchline to send him off as well. *Bloody hell*. Never before had two players from the same team been sent off in a Five Nations match. So this is what 'Le Crunch' is all about . . .

*

In the end, France were lucky not to have finished the game with just 11 players, so violent were the closing minutes. A disciplinary committee was swiftly assembled 90 minutes after the final whistle and both Lascubé and Moscato would receive bans of six months. Neither played for France again.

And yet by the time we had reassembled for the post-match dinner, all the aggravation had evaporated. We might have smashed them, but when the French team turned up (naturally they were fashionably late), they looked immaculate in their blazers, jeans and white trainers.

The mood was broken by Mickey Skinner picking up this flan that was on his plate and lobbing it across the room at his opposite number, Tordo. He didn't hit him, but the ice was broken and there was a bit of chuckling. The next thing the waiters brought each of us was a little lemon meringue pie. Skinner turned to me and said: 'Do what I do.'

He proceeded to tuck the tablecloth into his shirt so that he was completely covered. 'It is all going to kick off,' he warned. Within seconds, these meringues were bombing around the room. It was the sort of behaviour that nowadays someone would catch on camera and we would have been branded as a disgrace. But back then it helped to ease the tension and we were able to have conversations with the guys who just a couple of hours earlier had been piling into us.

Eventually the French players went off into the night to do their own thing and we ended up in some club in Paris. I remember stumbling out to get a taxi back to our hotel. 'The Hilton Hotel please, driver,' I asked politely. 'Which one, monsieur? There are 15 in Paris.'

'Take me to the one you think I should be at,' I said, not that helpfully, to be fair. I could see him smile in the mirror and he drove me to five or six Hiltons, with the fare rising with each stop. Eventually he began to head towards the bright lights of the Eiffel Tower and pulled up outside another Hilton.

'Is this the one?' he asked, before presenting me with an outrageous bill.

'Yeah, this looks right. That's it,' I mumbled.

When I opened the taxi door and stepped towards the hotel, all I could do was chuckle. Across the road was the nightclub we had been in before he had taken me on a magical mystery tour of Paris. I could have walked home but instead was hit with a bill of more than £100. All I can say is thank goodness for RFU expenses.

Many years later, I bumped into Wade at an event. 'I hear you're still making money out of that Roumat story,' he boomed, in reference to my after-dinner speeches. 'You could have at least made it about someone a bit harder. That Roumat was a soft fucker.'

It's just a moment in time, but one of the most treasured photographs of my career captures our last training session at The Stoop in Twickenham ahead of our final match against Wales. In some ways it's remarkable because of its ordinariness. But that's the thing that I love about it. It's just a mishmash of training kit.

Nowadays, when you see the England squad training they are pristine, all wearing exactly the same gear. In the photo, most of us are in club shirts, with sponsors such as Scrumpy Jack or Courage, or the odd Australian shirt in there. Some have got tracksuit bottoms on with their shorts over the top of them so there was something to lift on. People of a certain vintage will remember that look. We look an absolute and glorious mess.

Just as the photographer clicked his button, Deano had elbowed me in the face and I was falling over. Not my best look but it's the one the newspapers wanted because we were going for back-to-back Grand Slams. This rag-tag group were about to become the history boys of English rugby.

England 24 Wales 0, Twickenham, 7 March 1992

There are moments in elite sports when, amid all the uncertainty, there is certainty.

And if I could describe the mood in that England camp in those final days, it was of absolute belief that we were going to win the game.

From the outside it might have looked like arrogance. It wasn't. But we were utterly ruthless in our attitude. There was complete confidence that we were going to win. Training had gone smoothly, a potent mix of edge and expectancy, and there was a lot of press interest, although obviously no one wanted to talk to me, which allowed me to carry out my preparations in a pressure-free environment.

For once everything went to plan. It was a procession. There were no stress points in the game. It was a comfortable victory given the circumstances and context. It was also Wade's 50th cap and fittingly he scored one of our three tries. Will and Mickey also scored, while Webby kicked two penalties and three conversions. We thought it was going to be Wade's last game, but we should have known better.

At the final whistle, we were carried off the pitch by our supporters. In those days, they were allowed on the pitch and it was completely flooded by fans. We went up onto the balcony afterwards, even though there was no trophy in those days, to wave to the crowd. The supporters started singing 'Swing Low' to us and we responded by doing the actions to the anthem.

Mickey Skinner had taken his shirt off but, in typical RFU fashion, if you look at any of the official photographs of the moment, they had painted a shirt on him. They didn't need to paint one on me.

Perhaps it was the sense of history that had been imbued in me by my father, but it means the world to me now that it was the last time that the England team wore the pure-white shirt. My dad had not been able to travel to the game because of illness, but my mum and sister were there. I know Dad would have loved the photograph of me with the backdrop of the old East and West Stands, the green sheds in front of which so many England players before me had stood. At that moment I look like every other England player who had worn the shirt before me, going right the way back in time to when those sheds were built, in the 1920s.

After our historic victory, first the East stand and then the West stand would be redeveloped, while the pure-white shirt was gone for ever, replaced with tweaks, like stripes on the shoulders – anything they could do to sell shirts every year. But back then my shirt had a red rose and a number on the back. That was it. You could run another 20 metres after someone grabbed you because of it stretching. But I loved it.

There are some photographs of me being chaired off the field along with Dewi, Will and Mooro. To be carried off like this was just awesome. Looking back, it seems even more remarkable that, in my first proper season with England, we won the Grand Slam. *This is easy*, I thought. *Why don't we do this more often?*

I would win another Grand Slam, but it would take three years to achieve it. And no England side has yet been able to replicate our feat of securing back-to-back Grand Slams. The closest England came to doing so was in 2017, the second season under Eddie Jones, when, having already won the championship in the penultimate round, England travelled to Dublin to face Ireland and attempt a second successive clean sweep. Ireland won 13-9.

In the build-up to the game, replays of our triumph had been shown on television and there was plenty of press coverage about us, the last team to have achieved the feat. Dylan Hartley, England captain at the time, came up to me. 'I didn't realise you played in that team,' he said. 'Yeah, I did play a bit of rugby, you know,' I replied.

Of course, at the time you don't realise how special it was. Only France, in 1997 and 1998, have managed to win back-to-back Grand Slams since ours. It's a point I make when I hear people in the southern hemisphere crow about how good New Zealand, Australia and South Africa are and say that England should have won loads of Grand Slams. Yes, we should have done.

But the Five Nations, and now Six Nations, is actually far more difficult than people think. It only takes one team to beat you and Grand Slam hopes are over for another year. And everyone wants to beat England.

How many Rugby Championship titles have New Zealand won without losing a game? Because that's a Grand Slam. It's tough and it brings a level of pressure that I don't think people really understand.

To be able to call yourself a Grand Slam winner is special. I realised I was surrounded by far better players than me. You could have put any second row in there in my place and England would have won a Grand Slam. But I played my part.

Players nowadays are likely to receive a six-figure bonus for winning one, but it doesn't bother me in the slightest that all we received were some commemorative cufflinks and another cheap nylon tie as mementos, as well as one shirt. I like to think I'm forward-thinking, but I really do cherish the history of our sport too. I can remember after our Grand Slam win seeing all these old alickadoos dotted around the room at our dinner in the Hilton, wearing their blazers, and I remember thinking *They are what I am going to be in 40 years' time.* Yes, they can be a pain in the arse. They corner you and spit down the front of your blazer and have stains on their trousers which shouldn't be there. But they had earned the right to do that. And they are actually quite good fun.

As Grand Slam champions, we had a lot of fun on that Saturday night. Before the official dinner we were up in Will Carling's suite and Jason Leonard looked a bit out of sorts. 'Are you all right, mate?' I asked him.

'No, I can't move my right arm.'

'What are you going to do?'

'Drink left-handed.'

It turned out he had a disc problem in his neck but, Jase being Jase, he had a discectomy and was back playing again by the autumn. The next morning was spent reading the coverage of our triumph in the Sunday newspapers. There was another wedge again in the papers on Monday. But in those days there were no rolling 24-hour news channels. That was it. It was done and everything disappeared. As a group, our journey for now was over.

Rugby World would come out a few weeks later with a big picture of Will Carling on the front, but by then we had all returned to our clubs and our day jobs. I remember turning up at Northampton for training and David Elkington, our scrum-half, smacked me in the face. 'Well done, you won a Grand Slam, but now it is back to your bread and butter. We don't want any of this England big-head about you.'

By Monday morning, I was back on the beat in Bedford. Don't worry, Dave. By the time I had dealt with the drunk in the Debenhams car park, my feet were well and truly back on the ground . . .

7

'Are You Here for the Rugby?'

If the England team in 1992 was the unstoppable force, then Norm Hadley was the immovable object. 'Stormin' Norman' was 6ft 7ins with a fighting weight that tipped 21 stones. An enormous man. He was like a cross between Wade Dooley and Dean Richards, with the height of Wade and the man-strength of Deano. A simply terrifying man.

The previous year he had been at the heart of the Canada side that had almost shocked New Zealand in the quarter-finals of the World Cup and was later named in the world team of the year. The Canadian captain struck fear into the hearts of all his opponents, including, it would later transpire, two drunken thugs who were abusing passengers on the London Underground a couple of years later, earning him national recognition as a vigilante hero and a mention in the House of Commons by the prime minister of the time, John Major.

At Wembley in October 1992, however, his two victims were myself and Wade Dooley. Canada back then were a formidable side. It makes me so sad to have seen their decline on the world stage in the decades since, especially when you look at all the investment that has gone into the US in a bid to make them competitive and tap into their broadcasting market.

Well, in 1992, Canada were a genuine top-eight contender and should have received greater financial backing to cement their place there. They had players of such quality as Gareth Rees and Al Charron, with Hadley the rock upon which the team was founded. Although we would go on to win the game comfortably, 'Super Norm' came through the contest unbroken and unbowed.

It was the only time in my career when I heard Dooley ask for help. Norm made Wade look small. And that was some achievement. 'Bayfs, I'm getting nothing out of this fucker. You better have a go.'

So we switched positions in the line-out, only for Norm, who had played for Wasps and Bedford, to bounce me off like a twig in a storm. But Jason Leonard had a plan. 'Don't worry, lads,' he said during a break in play. 'I've got this.'

Jase was famed for flying into rucks and invariably someone would fly out the other side. So at the next ruck big Norm could be seen exiting 'stage right' at a rate of knots.

The big man stood up, dusted himself down and then shot a withering look at Jase. Hadley said: 'Is that the best you got, princess?' Oh shit, we're in trouble now. Or rather, Jase, *you're* in trouble now. *All yours, big man!*

The occasion was also noteworthy for my Saints team-mate Ian Hunter scoring twice on his debut, and for the shambolic state of Wembley. Don't get me wrong, it was fantastic to play there, but by 1992 the old national stadium was in a dilapidated state.

Back in the more comfortable surroundings of Twickenham, the first visit of South Africa since the sporting boycott was lifted, following the end of apartheid, felt like a truly historic fixture. When I talk about the special jerseys I played against, there was something mysterious about the Springbok one that afternoon as it was so long since we had seen one. The last time South Africa had toured England was 1969. The colour of the jersey and the emblem were unfamiliar and there was such history about them. And boy were they big. They really are the biggest humans you will play against. Samoa, Tonga and Fiji also produce big sides. But, across the board, the South Africans are bloody massive. They are solid.

I was up against a guy called Drikus Hattingh, a former shot putter who had given up athletics when he tested positive for drugs. And he looked like a guy who had been banned for drug abuse. The other second row? He was a strong ball-winner from Northern Transvaal called Adolf Malan. I mean, *seriously*?

You can imagine the jokes in our dressing room and in the team talks about playing against a guy called Adolf. Some of the line-out calls Mooro came up with were just horrific. Just as well there weren't pitch-side microphones then.

In the event, we won the game easily, despite the presence of some of the great veterans such as Naas Botha. It was tough for South Africa because they were still trying to get up to speed, having been in the international wilderness for so long. And it was the last Test match Adolf would play for the Springboks. I hope that wasn't our fault.

There had been a danger during the run-up to the game that I might have missed it because – in between this and playing for the Midlands against the Springboks at Welford

Road ten days earlier – my daughter, Roseanna, was born. There had only been a small window for her to arrive that would mean I did not have to miss either game and, with impeccable timing, she obliged.

I would hear of other players who came home from a tour or missed a key match to be at the birth of their child and wondered what decision I would have made. I'm still not sure yet what I would have done, even now. But thanks to Rosie, that was one call that I never had to make.

After the match, I travelled home to see my mum and dad with Helena to show off baby Rosie and celebrate what had been a clean sweep of victories for England in my first full calendar year wearing the red rose. In true fashion, however, my mother delivered the kind of post-match review that may even have made Dick Best wince a little. Er, thanks Mum.

No team in the entire history of the Five or Six Nations Championship has won three successive Grand Slams. I did say it was tough. We were about to find this out.

Following our comfortable wins at Twickenham in the previous year, both Wales and Ireland would have their revenge during the 1993 championship. Perhaps the strangest thing about playing for England in those days was the lack of continuity in training and preparation. After the South Africa victory, within a couple of days we were back to our day jobs and then there was nothing. It was back to Northampton for me and no contact whatsoever with England until we met up again two days before the start of the Five Nations Championship two months later.

Our attempt to go for a triple Grand Slam had stirred up

some media interest and there was also the added spice of it being a Lions year. But the reality? We had just two-and-a-half days to prepare for an international. We would meet up on Wednesday night at The Stoop after work. Everyone was still in their work clothes. Then a quick training session before heading down to the pub – the Sun Inn or the Roebuck in Richmond.

Thursday would be the hard training session, followed by a few more drinks around Richmond. Friday was the captain's run, with a bit of media. Game on Saturday, dinner in the evening at the Hilton. Back home Sunday and then work on Monday. I would be walking the beat in Bedford and people would drive past in their cars and either shout 'Well done mate!' or 'You were shit!'

That was just the way it was. And on the Monday morning after our game against France, I'm pretty sure I received the latter reaction. I didn't have any thoughts about making the Lions tour to New Zealand in any shape or form and, after our first two games in the Five Nations, that probably was a good state of mind to be in.

We only stumbled past France in our opening game at Twickenham. Ian Hunter got us off the hook by scoring from a Jon Webb penalty that rebounded off a post and securing a 16-15 victory. France were much improved from their Paris shambles, but we had failed to replicate our form of the previous year in a match that was seismic only for the fact that an unknown 21-year-old lock called Martin Osborne Johnson made his debut alongside me in the second row.

Wade had been forced to pull out of the game at the 11th hour with flu, and when they were looking for a replacement, Dean Richards turned to Will Carling: 'We've got this guy at the Tigers. Get him in. He won't let you down.' The rest is history.

I knew very little about Martin Johnson, other than he'd been due to go on the England B tour with me to New Zealand in 1992 but dislocated his shoulder and a guy called Dave Baldwin went instead.

Johnson had been due to play for England B against France at Leicester, but was dispatched down the M1 to Twickenham to join us on the Friday before the match. He only had about 20 minutes to get up to speed with our line-outs but then proceeded to produce a near man-of-the match performance in his first game. Against the French. Typical Johnno. You could tell then he was in a different class. A clash of heads with French prop Laurent Seigne might have seen him go off but he just grew into the game with aplomb.

His career would soar as mine began to fall but, at least for a period of time, we met in the middle. Lawrence Dallaglio would enjoy a similarly phenomenal rise and, like Johnno, was one of a rare breed. I can remember being at a spon-sored coaching session for schoolkids which Dick Best was running and one of the kids asked Besty who was the player to look out for.

'There is this young guy who has started playing for Wasps called Lawrence Dallaglio,' said Besty. 'He is going to be huge.' No one had heard of him either, but he did turn out to be huge. And I know Besty backed up his words with deeds by trying to sign him for Quins on many occasions.

If we thought the performance against France was under-whelming, the wake-up call would come with our trip to Cardiff. It began with concerns we had a serial killer in our camp and concluded with me being trailed by a police car along the M4 as I tried to escape from Wales.

A serial killer, I hear you say? Well, of course, I am joking. I think.

Peter Winterbottom, like Dooley, was a hugely respected member of the squad. But after watching a documentary on serial killers back at the Petersham Hotel before we departed for Cardiff, we started to have our doubts. The documentary highlighted these warning signs to spot a serial killer and all of them seemed to match Winterbottom.

He was a loner ... not many friends ... kept himself to himself ... 'Wints, this is you!' we cried. As if to underscore our point, you could see Wints' eyes begin to twitch. There was trouble brewing.

But things were only about to go from bad to worse for him. We drove separately in our own cars to Cardiff, but on the way back on the bus from a training session, one of the lads starting singing the song 'Under the Boardwalk'. After a couple of verses, Wade stood up, completely out of the blue. and changed the lyrics to 'Under the floorboards!' Wints had a complete sense-of-humour failure.

When we got back to the hotel, some mannequins had been set up in the foyer displaying traditional Welsh dress and a few hours later, when we were having a team meeting, John Olver came into the room with one of these things on his shoulder.

'Wints, mate. Security wants a word because they found this in the boot of your car!' he said, with a straight face. Wints jumped straight out of this chair, ran over to the buffet that had been laid out in the corner of the room, grabbed a knife and chased Olver right through the hotel as we howled with laughter.

If this was not exactly the best preparation for what was my first appearance at the old national stadium (I had played at the Arms Park for England Schools), it showed in our lacklustre display. We should have won the game, but ended up losing 10-9 and I played a rather embarrassing part in our defeat by squandering a golden opportunity to score what would have been my first try for England.

Dewi Morris popped the ball to me as I was just a yard from the goal line. My first try beckoned. The problem was that I had failed to gather the ball properly. It was down on my hip, I was a bit too upright and as I went over the line I was held up. What made it worse was realising that the guy who had prevented me from scoring was the smallest guy on the pitch, Neil Jenkins, who had stripped the ball out of my hands. It was the closest I would ever come to scoring a try for England.

Wales went on to win the match when Ieuan Evans kicked the ball past Rory Underwood, who did not see him coming up behind him as he was in his blindspot. It was my first defeat with England and hopes of a third Grand Slam were quashed.

Some wise guys in the Welsh police ensured I wouldn't forget, either.

I was crawling along the M4 in the queue to get over the Severn Bridge and I passed a raised layby where a police car was sitting. The officers obviously recognised me because as soon as I passed, they pulled in behind me and turned on the tannoy speaker on top of the car. The next thing I heard was: '10-9, Mr Bayfield, 10-9 . . .' *You bastards.*

I have to admit it was very funny. I don't know what the ordinary members of the public must have thought because I turned around in my seat and gave them two fingers back.

When we got to the point where they had to turn off as we approached the bridge, they flicked on their lights to say 'cheerio' as I sped back to the welcoming arms of England.

Rob Andrew was the biggest casualty from the defeat in Cardiff. I had feared for my place too, but in the end it was Rob who paid the price, with Stuart Barnes coming into the side to face Scotland at Twickenham. It was a massive call by the selectors because Rob had been one of our star players, but Barnes was brilliant against Scotland and we romped to a 26-12 victory with both Underwoods, Rory and Tony, scoring, as well as Jerry Guscott, to set up the championship decider on the final weekend. All we had to do was beat Ireland in Dublin . . .

It was an ambush from start to finish. From the moment we arrived in Dublin, we were lulled into a false sense of security, starting with the moment when I attempted to check into our team hotel.

It's one of the delightful, and at times frustrating, challenges of being an England team playing away from Twickenham, and certainly characterises the uniqueness of the Five Nations, which has only been accentuated with the inclusion of Italy since 2000. In Cardiff and Edinburgh, you expect to face hostility. But in Dublin, it's much more subtle yet can be no less effective.

'Are you here for the rugby?' enquired the guy behind the reception desk, with a mischievous smile. *Of course I'm here for the rugby. I'm Martin Bayfield. I'm not some punter over to get smashed with my mates and watch the England game. Can you not see the blazer I'm wearing, with the red rose? And the England squad standing behind me?*

Of course he had seen the blazer. And the entire England squad standing behind him. *Okay, very good, you got me.*

It set the tone for the weekend. Everywhere we trained, the people couldn't do enough for you. 'Just go easy on our boys,' was the constant refrain. It was a rugby ambush waiting to happen.

Given the backdrop of the Troubles, trips to Ireland in those days meant precautions had to be taken against an ambush of a different sort for those players in the forces and the police – me, Wade, Deano, Rodders and Rory. We were all assigned an armed guard as an extra layer of protection. Someone later told me the IRA had a list of the top 200 targets of the British Establishment, including members of the royal family, politicians . . . and all those England rugby players. If the Queen was number one, I think I must have been 200.

But I was never aware of any threat. There were no messages or random phone calls, so we just got on with things in blissful ignorance. If there was something going on, we weren't aware of it. All we knew was that there was someone in the background watching us, someone who was there at the game too. That was, at least, until the post-match function, when we would see our armed guards absolutely shit-faced. All I can say is that seeing your security detail drunk in charge of a firearm was not a reassuring sight.

Nor was the sight of Paddy Johns, that gritty Ulster lock, smashing into Dooley as he tried to claim the deliberately high, hanging kick-off that had been delivered perfectly by Eric Elwood, the Ireland fly-half.

Lansdowne Road was magical that afternoon. We might have taken a hammering but the atmosphere was incredible.

It reminded me of Parc des Princes the previous year. It was everything I had seen on the TV – the little cottage in the corner of the ground, the tram running around it and hordes of people everywhere. It's a shambolic joy and I loved it – apart from the result.

The writing was on the wall when Johns mullered Wade. He absolutely smashed him and it took the big man a while to get back onto his feet. Mick Galwey also had an inspired game. It was a classic ambush by the Irish at Lansdowne Road. They had a fantastic game and while I don't think we were complacent, we just didn't turn up. And they rattled us.

This was an Irish team the majority of whom we had beaten comfortably the year before. I think they probably felt it was payback time. Also, we weren't very clever. I won a lot of line-out ball, but was basically just tapping it down to Dewi Morris, our scrum-half. I was giving him shit ball and one of us needed to say 'For God's sake, just catch the ball and set up a maul!' But we had got it into our heads that we could run our way around these guys, and tapped ball from the line-out was the key to that.

And so our hopes of a third Grand Slam campaign back in January had deteriorated to a second defeat away from home and a third-place finish in the table. It's fair to say that things had not gone to plan and the repercussions of our defeat would have major implications for the selection of the British and Irish Lions squad for the tour of New Zealand. Dick Best, who had been appointed as assistant to Lions head coach Ian McGeechan, was hastily summoned, while still in his dinner suit, to an emergency selection meeting at Heathrow the following morning. It seemed the initial plan for England to provide up to 23 members of the 30 squad now lay in tatters.

8

The Joy of Ceefax

Any rugby aficionado will tell you the two most memorable speeches in the history of the British and Irish Lions came on the 1997 tour of South Africa.

The first was the 'This is your Everest, boys' rallying call by Jim Telfer, the Lions forwards coach, to his pack ahead of the first Test victory. The second was delivered by Geech in the build-up to the series-clinching 18-15 second Test victory in Durban. Watch a clip of the speech on the Lions website and I bet it will make the hairs stand up on the back of your neck.

'There are days like this that many rugby players never have, they never experience it,' Geech tells a rather anxious-looking squad. 'It is special. Jim and I have been involved in rugby a long time. I can tell you that these are the days that you never think will come again. They have.

'And I can tell you that I've given a lot of things up. I love my rugby. I love my family. And when you come to a day like this, you know why you do it all. You know why you've been involved. It's been a privilege, it is a privilege, because we're something special. Because you'll meet each other in the street in 30 years' time and there'll just be a look. And you'll know just how special some days in your life are.'

Well, I hate to break it to you Geech, but as Lawrence Dallaglio later pointed out, this is actually a load of old cobblers. Do you know what happens when, 30 years later, I meet up with a former team-mate from the 1993 Lions tour of New Zealand? We look at each other and snigger like naughty schoolboys: 'Do you remember '93?' we snort. 'Christ, how on earth did we get away with it?' *How did we get away with it?*

It saddens me that the 1993 tour has, to some extent, become the forgotten Lions tour. Supporters remember the 1989 tour for the dramatic Test series victory over Australia and for getting the Lions back to winning ways after all the series defeats since 1974. And they remember the 1997 tour as the most famous tour since that of Willie John McBride's Invincibles in South Africa.

Not only did Martin Johnson's 1997 side probably save the Lions brand going into the professional era, but the compelling *Living with the Lions* fly-on-the-wall documentary captured that Corinthian spirit for ever. Our tour, in contrast, has tended to be defined by a split between the Test team and the midweek side, a corrosiveness that would slowly eat away at our spirit and resistance, and eventually bring about our downfall just when we had the All Blacks there for the taking.

That might have all been true. But for all the problems that we had to overcome, the tour was wonderfully chaotic. It was the last amateur tour and while there were issues that stemmed from the fact that the Test team became identifiable quite early on, and some of the players selected should not have been there at all, it still created some brilliant moments and lasting memories.

My sister, Karen, who came out on the tour as a supporter and ended up emigrating to New Zealand, says people there still talk about the 1993 Lions. I remember Sean Fitzpatrick, the All Blacks captain, saying afterwards that the rugby might not have been that great, and the New Zealand team might not have been at their best, but as an advert for fun and cama-raderie, it was a fantastic tour.

It also laid the foundation stone for Lions supporters to tour with the team. About 3,000 made the trip in 1993, small in comparison to the 30,000 that toured New Zealand in 2017, but it was a significant step forward.

In truth, I still have no idea how we got to the end of the tour, given the amount of drinking and partying that went on. It was crazy. We partied too hard and there was always something going on wherever we went. There were times when we probably lost focus about why we were actually there. Yes, there was too much drinking, too much horsing around. But it was so much fun. And, despite everything, we nearly won.

It all started with a page on Ceefax. Those of you old enough to remember the now-defunct teletext information service will remember the frustration when you were just seconds too late to read the page that you were interested in and then had to patiently wait as the pages flicked through local news, then traffic, weather and TV pages until it got back to the sports pages.

Well, that's how I found out about the greatest honour of my rugby career. The announcement of the British and Irish Lions squad has become something of a glittering event in recent years. The razzmatazz includes the unveiling of each selection live on host broadcasters Sky Sports in front of a packed audience at a swanky London hotel, with huge media interest and sponsors' commitments to fulfil.

Even when the global pandemic struck, forcing the announcement of the squad for the 2021 tour of South Africa to be done behind closed doors, technological innovations ensured that head coach Warren Gatland was able to do it virtually, appearing on stage like he had just been beamed up like Mr Spock in Star Trek. But there was no one to beam me up as I peered through the window of Tavistock Sound & Vision shop on The Broadway in Bedford, straining my eyes to read the Ceefax pages on one of the television sets on sale.

To make the image even more preposterous, I was on the beat at the time, in full uniform; passers-by must have wondered if there'd been a break-in at the shop. I don't know why I didn't just go inside, as I must have looked very odd standing outside in uniform peering through the window. And just to strip the announcement of any remaining semblance of glitz and glamour, I narrowly missed the page with news of the Lions squad.

Perhaps it was the suspense. I thought I might be in the mix, but the fact that England had won two and lost two in the Five Nations was hardly convincing. I knew they were definitely going to take Wade. Of course they were going to take Wade. But I thought they might go with Paddy Johns and Gareth Llewellyn, the Wales lock.

It's said that a watched kettle never boils. Well, you should try watching pages turn on Ceefax. It took an age before the squad was finally displayed and I feverishly scanned the names . . . M. Bayfield. Yes! I was going to be a Lion.

Further investigation revealed, however, that several of

my England team-mates had not made the cut, including, remarkably, the best tighthead around, Jeff Probyn. Rather than the expected 23, we ended up with an English contingent of 17. Don't get me wrong, the thought of touring with Jeff for ten weeks would have filled anyone with fear, but if you needed a prop to lock your scrum in the muddy depths of a New Zealand winter, it was Probs.

It appears the Lions selection meeting had descended into unedifying horse-trading between the home unions, but they hadn't even managed to get that right. Ireland had been magnificent in their victory over us, but only two of their side made the squad: Nick Popplewell and Mick Galwey. But where was Paddy Johns or Peter Clohessy? I thought Johns would have suited New Zealand perfectly; he was super-fit and hard as nails. But more of that later.

My first job was to return immediately to the station and see my superintendent, a guy called Alan Marlow, who had been brilliantly supportive of my rugby career. 'I've just been selected for the Lions tour of New Zealand and would like to apply for special leave,' I told him. I needed a total of 50 days off.

'Well,' said Alan. 'The regulations state that I can give you two days of special leave, so I can give you two.' He held it just long enough for a feeling of panic to surge through me. Was he serious? 'It would be my honour to grant you your special-leave request,' he added with a smile.

Of course, issues such as obtaining leave from your day job have long stopped being a concern for the players since the game turned professional in 1995. Despite Alan's generosity and support, the matter would later come back to bite me on the white heat of the tour. Fast-forward to the early hours of the morning before the first Test at Lancaster Park in Christchurch. I was already struggling to get any sleep, such were my nerves ahead of my Lions Test debut, when the phone in my hotel room rang. It was around 3 a.m. You can imagine my mood when I lifted the receiver.

It was a journalist, a guy who I had been at school with but was now working for *Bedfordshire on Sunday*, the local newspaper. He said he was writing an article about how there was resentment in Bedfordshire Police that I was getting all this time off to play for the Lions and asked if I wanted to give a quote.

So at 3 a.m., just hours before I was due to face the mighty All Blacks, you can imagine what my quote was. Yes, the second word was 'off'. I was livid.

After the game, I phoned my superintendent to let him know what was going on. 'Tell me if there is a problem and I will address it when I get back,' I told him.

'Don't worry about it,' he said. 'We'll sort it.' And they piled into the newspaper the next day, telling them the story was unacceptable and threatening to remove co-operation with them.

I subsequently found out that the journalist had spoken to a mate of mine who had jokingly said 'I don't know why he gets 50 days off to play for the Lions. I want to go shopping with my wife – why don't I get special leave off for that?' He was taking the piss and how anyone could take that as a serious complaint, I have no idea. Can you imagine Maro Itoje having to deal with this rubbish?

9

'If You Don't Make It, Bayfs, Can I Have Your Sony Walkman?'

It was the waiting that was the problem. Between getting picked for the Lions and the start of the tour, there was a huge gap in the schedule. There were no Premiership vs Lions squabbles back then. It was the reverse. Our season with Northampton had finished four weeks before we met up as a squad in the Woodlands Park Hotel in Surrey.

The first guy I saw was an old mate of mine called Roly Williams, who had played for the Met Police and Middlesex. He was a brilliant guy who always seemed to land plum jobs. As I entered the hotel, there was a big sign up for a meeting of the local Masonic Lodge and there was my mate walking into the room. *Ah, so that's why he always got those jobs . . .* When I first started with the Met, Roly would always ensure we got on the beat together. 'What are we doing?' I would ask. 'We are going training, that's what we are doing,' Roly would tell me. And we would disappear into the local gym.

Geech was the head coach, Geoff Cooke was the manager and Dick Best was the assistant, a tiny management compared to this generation of Lions tours. Receiving our Lions kit was just as haphazard as those early days on the beat with Roly. It did not compare well with today's kit, either in quality or quantity, but none of us cared.

This was the moment when we would finally get to properly break the ice with our Celtic cousins. We introduced ourselves to each other and I was rooming with Ieuan Evans. I was in awe of the guy. I just remember thinking: 'What on earth am I going to say to this guy?' And he clearly had no idea who I was.

An experience with Ieuan would also give an early indication of just how difficult it is to bring a Lions squad together. In one of the early training sessions in New Zealand, I was working with him on a contact session and he wasn't quite getting it right. Bestie was watching us. 'Ieuan, I realise that this isn't your forte,' drawled Besty, 'but do try harder.' I'm not sure what Ieuan made of it. The England boys would have known Besty's dry humour, but Ieuan was probably trying to make some sense of it. You must remember that our entire coaching team consisted of Geech and Besty, as Geoff Cooke had a managerial role.

The Scotland boys would have known Geech, but they also would have known nothing about Besty. And as I have explained, he is a bit of an acquired taste. It made me realise it's a miracle these tours work at all. In a matter of weeks, you have to get used to different coaches and different styles. What works with your own national side might not work with the Lions. This is why I have sympathy with someone like Damian Cronin, the Scotland lock. He was a good player and a great bloke, but I think he must have felt he was not going to get near the Test team, and it's hard to stay motivated for that long away from home if that's the case.

But everyone's hopes were high on that first afternoon at London Irish's old ground at Sunbury. It involved a bit of a training session and then it was off to the pub for a massive piss-up, which is where I first met the infamous Richard Webster, who established a phenomenal friendship with Besty. They made an unlikely couple: a rough, hard-nosed flanker from Swansea, and Besty, the wine connoisseur and pastry chef.

One of the first things we did on the pitch was a really simple fitness session. I don't know why they bothered because there is no way you are going to get fit in a day. You had to lie on your stomach, then get to your feet and sprint 30 yards within a certain time. And if you didn't do it, you had to do 20 press-ups. Well, Webster was missing the mark every time. There was Besty at the finish line, ready to deliver a laconic drawl. 'Webster, by the end of this tour, you are either going to be fucking fast or fucking strong,' he said. Somehow, from that point on, a lifelong friendship had been founded.

I had two seasons of Five Nations rugby under my belt, I was playing pretty well for Saints and was fit and getting stronger, and just like my first England tour two years earlier, was determined to make the most of this remarkable opportunity. And yet I had only been in New Zealand several hours before I had to overcome an alarming setback: in our very first training session, I pulled my hamstring.

I know, I probably don't look the type of player that ever pulled his hamstring. To make it more embarrassing, I managed to do it while I was stretching. We had gone for a run on the beach in Paihia in the Bay of Islands to get the flight out of our legs and I was stretching before our training session when my foot slipped on a bit of mud. My hamstring felt tight but, like an idiot, I carried on training. I was running when I felt something go quite high up the back of my leg and I stopped mid-step, with my leg up in the air, scared to take another step. Kevin Murphy, the physio, looked across at me. 'Don't move, Bayfs,' he said, and ran over to me. He helped me off the pitch and took me straight up to my room for ice and rest.

It was the only time in my career that I had any problem with my hamstrings. I don't know whether I was tight from the flight, but at that moment I was terrified that my tour was over. I'd been scheduled to play in the first game against North Auckland alongside Andy Reed, but for the next three or four days, Kevin worked on me non-stop.

'If you had taken another step, it would have been the end of your tour before you had even played a game,' Kev said afterwards. 'It's a minor-grade tear so you'll be back after a week.' That was enough to reassure Geech and Cookie that there was no need to send me home.

But perhaps Kev wished I had been, after all. During a training session with the midweek side, I started doing some jogging around the field as part of my rehabilitation. After a while, Kev said we needed to check if I had any spring in my leg. So he ran ahead in front of me, dropped down onto his hands and knees and told me to try to jump over him. But instead of clearing him, I only managed to kick him in the ribs. 'Yeah, I don't think I'm quite ready for jumping yet,' I said. 'Oh, sorry, Kev. Have I broken your ribs?'

*

I think I had also pissed off Damian Cronin, a guy I get on well with now, because I think he felt I had feigned the injury so that I could miss the first match and play in the next game alongside Wade in the second game, against North Harbour. Wade was expected to start the Test matches, and playing alongside my England team-mate could have been seen as a way of fast-tracking my own ambitions.

His suspicions were no doubt heightened when they were doing their Captain's Run before the North Auckland match. It was then that I was doing my runaround with Kev, and I probably looked like I was doing pretty well until I tripped over him. But the injury was genuine. I also had to contend with the nagging feeling that no doubt every Lion has felt before and after me: you don't feel part of the tour until you've played your first game. That made watching our narrow victory over North Auckland an even more uncomfortable experience.

And a painful one. Although fears that my tour might have been over before it had started had eased, my good mate Ian Hunter was dealt the cruellest of blows when he suffered a dislocated shoulder during the match. His tour lasted just 39 minutes before he picked up the injury while attempting to tackle David Manako, the All Black trialist wing. Hunts had endured a tough run of injuries (including, remarkably, having his tear duct ripped out of his eye), but this was the most bizarre. While attempting the tackle, he got his thumb caught in the pocket of Manako's shorts (again, for those of you not old enough to remember, rugby shorts used to have pockets on them) and as he fell his arm twisted and twisted until it popped out as he hit the ground. His tour was over.

I know Gavin Hastings, as captain, was always going to

start at full-back in the Test side, but I believe Hunts would have pushed him really hard for one of the places on the wing, without a doubt. When he was fit, he was a remarkable player. The trouble was getting him fit . . . and keeping him so.

To make matters worse, they had to cut his Lions shirt open to treat him. Before he was sent home, he asked if he could have a replacement as a memento but was turned down on the grounds that he had already been given one. It was the same with England. We were only ever given one shirt. It was not until Sir Clive Woodward became England coach in 1997 that he introduced the policy of giving players two shirts per game.

It summed up the attitude of the administrators to players at the time. It was just a shirt, and a shirt that stretched and stretched, but it had that Lions badge on it. And that is all that mattered. Yet there seemed to be an attitude of: 'Thanks for your efforts, now off you go.'

The footnote to this story is that I was recently contacted by Lennie Newman, a former player and team manager with the Saints, who got in touch to ask if I could get hold of one because it was really eating away at Hunts that he didn't have a shirt from the tour. I had managed to come home with two shirts, one of which my wife had framed, while the other was in a kit bag somewhere in my attic. I bumped into Hunts recently and I thought, *Why am I even thinking about this? I have a shirt stuffed in the attic somewhere. Why don't I give it to him?* It's the least I could do for an old mate and fellow Lion.

It must have been tough for Gav, given his responsibilities as captain. He was an inspirational leader but he had the task of captaining a tour which at times could have blown apart.

And he also he was up against a bunch of English players who just took the piss all the time. I don't know how on earth he controlled us.

Mike Teague would later tell me the story of Gav's speech before the game against the New Zealand Maori in Wellington. It had been billed as the fourth Test and was the first time the team would face the Haka on tour. I was not in the team that day, but in the changing room beforehand, Gav was fired up. 'Right, we're going to face the Haka today. Now let's run out there and shove that Haka right up their arse,' he boomed.

When the NZ Maori raced into a 20-0 lead, Teaguey turned to his captain as the team gathered under the posts. ''Ere Gav, when exactly can we start shoving that Haka up their arse?' Thankfully we managed to do just that in a remarkable second half, racking up 24 points, with Ieuan, Rory and Gav scoring fantastic tries.

It was a moment when the tour could have wobbled, but we got through it and, after our comfortable win over Canterbury in Christchurch, we headed to Otago with significant momentum generated by four successive victories.

But as we landed in Dunedin to play Otago at the Carisbrook, a stadium known locally as the 'House of Pain', everything was about to change.

The mid-tour blues is one of the challenges of a Lions tour. Being thousands of miles away from home for so long – constantly on the move, hotel after hotel, training session after training session – can hit you hard. The 1993 tour involved 13 matches, whereas the tour of South Africa in 2021 was reduced to eight.

The players in each of the sides that we played against all had the luxury of going home to their own beds after the match, eating their own food and seeing family and friends. So, sometimes it's necessary to blow off steam. Well, that was what the group of players who would become known as the 'Otago Five' decided was the best way forward. To counter the blues, the boys decided to go out for a bite of lunch. However, a few quiet glasses turned into several bottles of red and when the players turned up for the team meeting that evening, they could barely speak – a situation pointed out by Teaguey, who could hardly speak himself he was laughing so hard.

During line-out practice in the warm-up for the game against Otago the next day, the hooker, Kenny Milne, was getting increasingly frustrated with Dooley, who clearly couldn't see straight. Even Dewi, who was himself one of the miscreants from the previous day, was getting fed up with Wade's erratic ball delivery – on the rare occasion he actually got a hand to a ball. Clearly hurt by this criticism, Wade rose impressively for the next throw and, courtesy of a lower trajectory than normal, managed to head it into Dewi's hands. 'Any better, Monkey?' he quipped.

It was not a surprise that we lost the game. It was a glimpse of what was to come from New Zealand over the next few years, which should have acted as a warning sign for 1995 World Cup plans. A young Josh Kronfeld, the future All Blacks flanker, tore us apart that day.

The Otago defeat didn't just leave a mental scar. We paid a heavy price in injuries too. Scott Hastings, or 'Klunk' as I like to call him, suffered a fractured cheekbone. One of my penchants was giving team-mates nicknames. Klunk was the

What a shambles!

Mum and Dad off to the
Palace. Classy!

Holiday + cigar + champagne
= one happy Dad!

A first taste of silverware – Beechwood
Park winning the Hymers School 7s 1978.

Yup, very tall! Overall look not helped by the home-knitted jumper (by Mum, not me).
Love the fact we're wearing spikes on the wooden gymnasium floor!

April 1986 – PC 794 graduating from
Met Police College, Hendon.

Early days in new club colours – the black,
green and gold of Northampton Saints.

Not quite the distraction of an Eva Herzigova 'Wonderbra' advert, but still a shock to the commuters of Bedford.

Nearly got it – my second Test, versus Australia in 1991 – it didn't go well.

Recording England's 1991 Rugby World Cup song at Abbey Road studios. Destined for the Woolworths bargain bucket.

An early introduction to the pain of an Ergo. Not sure what Mooro is up to behind me. Notice the lack of any standard sponsored training kit.

First Cap v. Fiji.

Astonishing to think that was the sort of team you could assemble for a charity match.

Avon Rugby Football Club

Jeremy Guscott Invitational XV

A.SPREADBURY, G.DAWE, D.CRONIN, M.BAYFIELD, M.TEAGUE, J.PROBYN, M.CRANE, R.HILL,
(Referee) (England) (Scotland) (England (Bath) (England)
P.BLACKETT, R.UNDERWOOD, J.HALL, S.BARNES, J.GUSCOTT, I.EVANS, J.BAKER, A.ROBINSON,
(Bath) England (Wales) (Avon) (England)

Played Avon All Stars on Sunday 23rd August, 1992, for The Bath Spa Cup, Sponsored by The Bath Spa Hotel.

Nothing to see here! Bedfordshire and Lancashire Constabularies unite to keep the peace in a fractious Le Crunch at the Parc des Princes in 1992 – Mooro was in his element.

Grand Slam achieved v. Wales in 1992, alongside my hero, Wade Dooley.

Being chaired off (no, I'm not walking) following our Grand Slam triumph over Wales.

Second Test victory for the Lions over New Zealand – great feeling! Awful gum shield.

Not a happy bunch – leaving the pitch at Eden Park
having lost the final Test and the series.

Happy chaps after victory over Australia in the Rugby World Cup quarterfinal of 1995 – Will looks slightly nauseous. Well, it was a hot day.

Two awkward second rows.

Chats with the stars of stage and screen are not unusual... Unscheduled but joyous interview with Tom Jones ahead of England's ill-fated pool match with Wales at the 2015 Rugby World Cup.

Filming the final fight scene of *Harry Potter and the Deathly Hallows*. When it all came to a close and the cameras stopped rolling it was an emotional wrench walking away from such amazing people.

Joe Scott, skilled animatronic designer, great companion and utter joker, sporting my undersuit, which he and the equally fab Gemma De Vecchi decided would look better in a shade of bright pink.

Any time spent in the company of Robbie Coltrane was a hoot. Happy to be his 'arse' for ten years; an experience I will never forget and which put a smile back on my face.

mechanic in the 1960s cartoon *Wacky Races*, whose language was largely made up of silly noises. Well, that was Scott all right. He didn't stop making funny noises. So Klunk he was. He was a fantastic player, but his tour ended when his face was smashed in that afternoon. Will Carling was also forced off with a thigh injury early on, while I suffered another injury scare which threatened my place in the side just a week before the first Test.

I landed heavily on my neck when I was tipped over in a line-out. Some people later thought that I had been targeted ahead of the Test series, but looking back at it, it was just an accident. I had leapt at least four inches off the ground, one of their props went through to bind and just flipped me over. Bang, down I went. I was carried off on a stretcher. It was incredibly painful and I lost feeling in one of my arms. This sparked major concern in the medical team and my neck was put in a brace for a few days. With three of us off, there was carnage in the physio room after the match.

But I could rely on Will to take my mind off the pain. As I waited for an ambulance to take me to hospital, he came up to me, being the caring England captain that he was. He had been with me the day before, when I had gone into town to buy myself a Sony Walkman cassette-tape player (young things, google it, but be reassured they were pretty cool pieces of kit back in the day).

'Are you all right, mate?' he asked.

'Yeah, I think so, but it's bloody sore.'

'Well, you know that Walkman you bought yesterday?'

'Yes, Will.'

'Well, if you don't make it, can I have it?' *Cheers, skip!*

Thankfully the X-rays showed nothing untoward and,

although I missed the game against Southland, it had eased within a few days. I would be fit for the first Test, earning me the nickname 'Lazarus'.

The injury would come back to haunt me a few months later as it grew progressively worse through the summer, forcing me to miss the first half of the next domestic season, including the Test against the All Blacks at Twickenham in the autumn. But in New Zealand I was just glad it was not deemed to be serious.

Will would also recover from his injury. It had been a difficult tour for him.

He was an intriguing character. Awarded the England captaincy at the age of 22, he became the pin-up boy for the team and attracted all the media attention. I didn't envy him having to captain a side with some dominant personalities. And I always got the sense there was a little bit of friction among them. Certainly I had the impression that Rob Andrew and Mooro looked at Will and thought he had the captaincy that they should have had.

To be fair to Will, he was always keen to make sure that the players were not taken advantage of. It was one of his best attributes. Rob and Mooro were similarly minded. It was an indication of the game edging towards professionalism. But he was struggling in New Zealand. Given his profile, it must have been a tough blow to lose out on the Lions captaincy to Gavin Hastings and his attitude was poor in the first weeks of the tour. I don't think he was in the best frame of mind.

The one guy who he really looked up to was Peter Winterbottom, and at one stage Wints told him he was acting like an idiot and to sort himself out. But while I know Will had his faults and attracted bad press, and at times he may have handled himself poorly, I've got a lot of time for him. He's tough. He's tougher than people realise and, by the end of the Lions tour, despite everything, he would go on to prove just why. Even without my Walkman.

10

Revolting for Wade

I can remember having a laugh-out-loud moment when hearing about Scott Gibbs' assessment of the England players on the 1993 Lions tour in his autobiography, *Getting Physical*. 'When I came back from the tour, everyone was asking me: "How were the English? Were they bastards?",' wrote Gibbs. 'To be honest, the English were the best and most professional on tour.'

Really, Scott? *Really*? No wonder Wales didn't win anything back then! God help us all if we were the beacons of professionalism on that tour. I think it might have been more accurate if he had written something like: 'I thought they would be much better than that.'

This piss-taking bunch of Englishmen continued to make life tough for Gav. In his speech before the first Test in Christchurch, he was trying to get us pumped up. 'Lads, we're going to run out and hit them hard,' he shouted, before instructing us to take a deep breath. He carried on talking and we all noisily drew air up through our noses. But about a minute or so later, Gav realised we were all still holding our breath, starting to turn purple.

'You didn't say breathe out,' someone blurted. 'Ah, that's how you do it,' said Mooro, gasping as we chuckled like schoolboys.

Warm-ups on that tour involved a lap of the pitch, a bit of jumping up and down, and touching your toes. I would never have survived the routines that the players go through these days before a match. It was moments like that which make you realise just how threadbare the coaching structure was compared to the modern Lions tours. Geoff Cooke didn't really get involved in the coaching side as he was our manager, so it was just down to Geech, Besty and Gav as captain to prepare us.

And thankfully we had players like Gibbsy with us, because, in my eyes, he was a remarkable player. And I can remember being struck by *his* professionalism and by the fact that he was such a deep thinker about the game. Most people remember his achievements on the 1997 tour to South Africa, when he bulldozed over the top of Os du Randt, the 21-stone Springbok prop. But he was also a brilliant talent in 1993. He was a relatively new player in the Wales team at the time and was up against two hugely experienced centres in Jerry Guscott and Will Carling for a place in the Test team.

He would strike up a firm relationship with Jerry on that tour and they are still best of mates. Of course, Gibbsy would become the new best mate of all the English players when he took Will's place in the side for the second Test . . . (Only joking, Will. Honest.)

I also found it spellbinding to see how players like Gav and Ieuan went about their work, both in training and during matches when the heat was on. There were others too, such as Tony Clement and Robert Jones, who may not have made the Test team but to me were stand-out players. You won't meet many more talented players than Tony. He could do everything; he could have played anywhere in our Test back line.

I guess Gibbsy's thoughts about the professional attitude of the England players was coming from what he was experiencing with the Welsh national team, which at the time was in all sorts of turmoil, coaching-wise. They weren't getting the best out of their group. Scottish rugby was a little bit threadbare, and Ireland were only slowly starting to wake up because it was before the dawn of European club rugby.

Irish rugby was always waiting for European rugby because, with four provinces already in place, it suited their format perfectly. They didn't have to invent anything, or come up with any daft names or silly super-districts. They had a manageable number of sides controlled by their Union, as opposed to the English clubs all controlled by separate owners. It ensures that they get the very best out of their system nowadays and that they punch significantly above their weight. But that didn't exist back then.

Looking back from the perspective of players from the other countries in our squad, they may have thought the English were more professional. I suppose we were, but we had strength in numbers and maybe, because the competition for places was tighter in the England squad, we were more switched on. We liked a drink and the banter was relentless. But we could get the job done when we needed to.

But as I say, Tony Clement would have fitted brilliantly into the England set-up. Ieuan would have absolutely walked it, as would have Gav too. These guys were brilliant. I could go on ... Robert Jones, Scott Hastings too – at least until he had his face rearranged in the match against Otago.

Despite our childish japes, Big Gav's team talks were very focused and to-the-point. He liked a beer and wasn't aloof at all. And his experience as Lions captain made me realise how difficult it must have been for Will at times with England. Every time he wanted to have a drink as the England captain, there was a camera shoved up his nose or someone waiting to write a story.

As that tour went on, I think Will relaxed a bit, realised he could go on the lash and have a laugh. And as he wasn't tour captain, he knew there wouldn't be a camera hidden or, just as importantly, he didn't *feel* as though there would be a camera hiding in every bush. By the end of the tour, he was an inspiring figure. The petulant behaviour from the start became just a memory.

It's true that there was this feeling of a split within the squad. There was, for whatever reason, a clear demarcation between the Test pack and the midweek pack.

Yet there was one issue that united us all, including the coaches and management: the shambolic treatment of Wade Dooley after he learned the devastating news that his father, Geoff, had suffered a heart attack and died.

We had just arrived in Invercargill, still smarting from the Otago defeat. Understandably, Wade decided to return to the UK to be with his family and attend his father's funeral. The least we could do was send him on his way with a few drinks in a rough old pub in the centre of the Southland town. It was a bit of an England clique – Wade, Teague, Dewi, Mooro and myself. And 'Iron' Mike seemed intent on providing some light entertainment to help cheer him up. A ferocious-looking local woman approached us.

Teaguey, mischievously, enquires: "'Ere love, how much?'

Not surprisingly, she stormed off in disgust but, to our astonishment, half an hour later returned to our table.

'Me and my mates have been talking. You can have all three of us for two hundred dollars,' she said, matter-of-factly. *Uh oh.*

Teaguey's face collapsed. I had never seen the granite-tough flanker from Gloucester, the man of the series from the Lions tour of Australia in 1989, ever look scared before. But there was terror in his eyes when he said: 'It's time to leave, lads. Sorry love, I wasn't serious.' And we were gone.

We said our farewells to Wade the following day. He'd been certain to start the Test team and I knew that, with his departure, I was going to have to step up and accept greater responsibility at the heart of the pack. To lose such an experienced figure was a major blow for a touring party that was already starting to become blighted by strained relations in the camp. It almost led to a mini-revolt by the squad against the Lions administrators.

Dooley's replacement, Martin Johnson, who was flown in from Canada, where he was on tour with England, proved to be an outstanding substitute and ended up starting in the second and third Tests, which no doubt further exacerbated the divide between the Test team and the midweek dirt-trackers. But the issue would escalate further. The problem was that we all expected that Wade, who at 35 had been due to retire at the end of the tour, would be allowed to return to New Zealand after the funeral.

The New Zealand Rugby Union confirmed they were happy for him to do so, but the Lions blazers insisted the squad could not exceed the original party size of 30. Wade was told that if he returned to New Zealand, he would not be able to play again under the terms of the tour agreement. It was a decision that lacked any sense of empathy, particularly as New Zealand, as hosts, were happy for the rules to be relaxed.

The whole squad signed a letter of complaint to the committee of the four home unions, while Cookie spoke out publicly once it became clear that Wade had been told he would not be permitted to play if he travelled back to New Zealand. When the home unions secretary Bob Weighill arrived in New Zealand, all the players ignored him in protest.

'The whole squad is incensed,' said Cooke. 'It's an appalling way to treat a person who has given so much to the game. For our people to raise objections is staggering. It shows a lack of sensitivity and understanding.

'We talk about the amateur ethos of our game and if ever there was a case for displaying the amateur ethos, this was it – by saying, "All right, the regulations don't allow for it but we understand the situation and on grounds of sheer compassion he should be allowed to rejoin the party without any conditions."'

Sadly, the great man never played rugby again. He deserved so much better.

By the time we had reached the first Test, I was pretty confident that I would be in the team. With Wade out of the equation, the question was who would be my partner. They went with Andy Reed, the Scotland lock, as the first Test had come too soon for Johnno.

There were some strange selections for the first Test. Kenny Milne and Paul Burnell started in the front along with Nick Popplewell, who was another fantastic player who would have fitted into our England set-up. Will, despite his poor form as a tourist on and off the field, was given the nod in the midfield, along with Jerry. Otherwise, the team more or less picked itself.

Ben Clarke had come through in phenomenal form. He was unbelievable on that tour, while Deano and Wints made up a formidable back row. England team-mates Dewi Morris and Rob Andrew gave us cohesion at half-back, and there was no doubting our back three, with Ieuan and Rory Underwood on the wings and big Gav at full-back.

In terms of selection, the only player who I thought could feel aggrieved was Richard Webster. He had been playing really well and, as I said, Bestie had taken a real shine to him. But he injured his ankle in the first game against North Harbour and he was struggling to regain his fitness from then on. If he had been fit, he would have pushed Wints hard for a spot in the back row.

But that was about it. It felt like Mick Galwey went on a booze cruise the whole tour and, hilariously, he went AWOL several times. Jeff Probyn was an infinitely better tighthead than Peter Wright, but Wright was one of the Scots who had benefited from the selection horse-trading following our defeat by Ireland in the final game of the Five Nations.

And, despite the angst over the handling of Wade's situation, at least our victory over Southland ensured we headed to Christchurch for the first Test in good spirits. No one knew how we would hold together as a team in the white heat of a Test match, but we were up for it. Bring on the All Blacks . . .

*

Christchurch is the most English of all the cities in New Zealand. I love it, but it was horrific to go back there for the 2011 World Cup, when I was covering the tournament for ITV, and see the devastation that had been caused by the major earthquake in February that year.

There was an exclusion zone around the centre, the cathedral had collapsed and the lovely hotel where we had stayed, the Marriott, was shut down. It looked like a pyramid. It had a great big crack right the way through the wall. Looking at the devastation, memories came flooding back of a city full of life 18 years earlier as we prepared to face the mighty All Blacks in the first Test at Lancaster Park, which itself now lay in ruins because of the quake.

The beautiful park nearby was still there, with the River Avon running through it, where we had run to from our hotel to hold a training session. It was during the run that someone ripped the shirt off Ieuan's back for a laugh. It was so childish, and everyone was howling with laughter. The problem was that Ieuan didn't have a spare with him, so he just did the whole training session for an hour and a half topless, despite the freezing conditions. Talk about elite preparation.

I remember Ieuan was nervous going into the first Test because he was up against Inga Tuigamala, who was the Jonah Lomu of his time, a giant and powerful wing. All the pre-match talk had been about whether Ieuan would be able to stop him. I had my own issues to deal with in the anxious countdown, thanks to my 3 a.m. wake-up call from the journalist in Bedford, but receiving our Test shirts from Geech was a special moment.

Otherwise, it felt like we were just preparing for another international. I think the fact that a lot of the guys had played against New Zealand Maoris had helped acclimatise us for facing the Haka and playing against the black shirt. I had wondered how I was going to feel standing in front of the Haka. When it happened, I wouldn't say I was under-whelmed, but it didn't provoke any emotional response. All I was thinking was that we had to get through this before the whistle was blown.

I've been lucky enough to face it four times and at no point did I think, *Oh shit*. I just watched it and thought, *Okay, that's the Haka, great*. Let's get on with it. I suppose it is whatever you allow it to be, whatever emotion it stirs in you. There were, though, moments as I stood there and, like during my debut for England, my mind wandered briefly. *I can't believe I am actually here. This is the All Blacks and this is Christchurch.* Another deep breath needed.

My mind flashed back to 1985 when I played for Midlands Schools against New Zealand Schools and faced the likes of Robin Brooke. Here he was again standing opposite me. Then my mind skipped back further, to 1983, when I remem-ber watching the Lions tour of New Zealand in 1983, Terry Holmes against Dave Loveridge, and it pissing down with rain. This is just like it was in '83.

New Zealand 20 British Lions 18, Lancaster Park, 12 June 1993

Ieuan need not have worried about Tuigamala. The giant All Black wing got past him a few times, but never prop-erly because Ieuan was all over him, grabbing hold of him however he could. Ieuan was knackered by the end of it, but he had prevented his opposite number from scoring a try or making himself look stupid. I mean, you don't make someone like Ieuan look stupid, but he was up against a winger with the kind of physique that he wouldn't have experienced before. It quickly became apparent to all of us that the All Blacks were not supermen. They're bloody good hard rugby players, really hard rugby players, but the pre-match fears melted away. And we could have won if a couple of key decisions had gone our way.

As with my early games with England, I'd been asked to jump at two in the line-out, but halfway through the game, I said to Reedy to switch to two and I dropped back to four. We got a lot more change out of that.

Frank Bunce was awarded a try in the second minute, even though Ieuan had caught the ball in goal from a high ball by Grant Fox. The remainder of the contest was a kicking duel between Gav and Fox, and we had edged into an 18-16 lead before Deano was penalised for wrapping up Bunce in one of his trademark bear tackles to give Fox the chance to win the game at the death.

Despite the defeat, we had a big old night out. The next day we had to assemble for another squad photograph because there had been a few additions, including Johnno. And if you look at us, we are absolutely *hanging*.

The following day, I received a phone call from a woman who said she had seen the first Test and that I was an absolute double for her husband. The reason for her curiosity was that her husband's family name further up the line was also Bayfield. She wondered if there was a family connection.

I wasn't going to meet up with some random person to have a cup of coffee, yet now I really wish I had. Back in my parents' house, there was a family heirloom, a miniature portrait of Horatio Nelson. On the back it says 'Presented to D. S. Bayfield, architect from the Roebuck Kensington Cross on his departure to Canterbury, New Zealand on HMS *Himalaya*.' My sister later told me that on a flagstone at Canterbury Cathedral chronicling the original settlers, his name is there. Sadly, I was too focused on the demands of the tour to make the connection.

11

It's Raining Beer (Cans)

We might have lost the first Test, but in doing so, we had managed to shatter the perception of the All Blacks' invincibility. Despite the defeat in Christchurch, we fancied our chances of winning the series. It was a sentiment boosted by Johnno's remarkable impact. He came in for his first game against Taranaki and he simply ripped up trees. It was clear to everyone that he was a player that would dominate the game for the next decade. Everyone stood watching him thinking: *This guy is amazing.*

Not even the piss-taking from Mooro about the Taranaki tradition of throwing bread into the crowd at half-time (I mean, who does that?) could distract us from Johnno's brilliance. He played again with me in the game against Auckland at Eden Park. Yet before we arrived in Wellington, the gap between the Test side and midweek team was brutally underscored.

We narrowly lost the game against an Auckland side that was stacked with 13 All Blacks, which was far from a disgrace, but the following game against Hawke's Bay was an absolute shambles. One of the few players who stood up to be counted was Will. He had been dropped for the second Test, with Gibbsy coming into the midfield, and yet he played his heart out at the very moment that he could be forgiven for going off tour himself. He earned a lot of respect from the entire squad, despite the defeat.

It was in Napier, ahead of that 29–17 defeat, that I also came to fully appreciate the legendary status of Peter Winterbottom. Brian Moore, Dewi Morris, Winters and myself decided to go for a couple of drinks in what looked like your classic New Zealand Hicksville pub. As we were walking up the stairs, this guy was climbing down them. He took one look at Wints, turned on his heels and ran back inside.

Back in the 1980s, Wints had played for Hawke's Bay and starred for their side in two classic matches: narrow defeats to the touring Australia side and Ranfurly Shield-holders Wellington. It might have been over a decade earlier, but the rugby bonds remained very much intact. As we walked into the room, everyone stood and cheered and clapped their returning hero. Of course, knowing Wints, he would have absolutely hated the attention and we just ripped the shit out of him, calling him the 'son of god'. Yet for all our ribbing, it made me think of what an accolade it was to be revered in this small town more than 10,000 miles from England. To see that reception was something pretty special. And it was an honour to play alongside him.

He was a big presence on the tour, delivering some strong words to Will when he needed them and then to the mid-week team, some of whom had clearly gone off tour by the end, when the Test team needed them the most. The true impact of that split would not be felt until the third Test, however.

As the squad landed in Wellington, we were in a buoyant mood and absolutely full of confidence. We knew we would beat them – we almost felt they'd shown their hand . . . and we should have won the first Test.

The Auckland game hadn't been that bad. It was disappointing to lose but I felt we had played okay, given the circumstances. What drove us on was the fear of being in New Zealand for another week if we lost the series, because if there's one thing we didn't want, it was a load of All Blacks crowing and being patronising until the end of the tour.

Everyone in New Zealand has an opinion on rugby. Just after our first game against North Harbour, which had been a comfortable 30-17 victory, we were in a shop and the woman behind the counter, who must have been around 75 years old, started to tell us where we could improve. We had just had our team meeting and she basically came out with the same feedback we'd had with our coaching staff, telling us how our body positions were too high, we weren't deep enough and so on. Okay, okay, we *get* it.

That would only get worse if the series was lost. At least the forwards were already well-briefed. During a two-hour team meeting, Geoff Cooke had explained to the forwards that if you lost two matches in a three-match series, that was a bad thing. 'OK then, we'd better win,' we thought. Big Gav led the way. 'We're taking this to the death,' he announced, 'otherwise we've got a week of absolute hell.' While motivation to keep the series alive was huge, we also knew that we could beat them up front. Mooro had come into the front row along with Jason and we knew we could get the edge on them in the set piece. We also knew we had the backs to inflict damage out wide. In Ieuan and Rory, we had two wingers who could absolutely shred them, while Gavin was a rock at the back. He was struggling fitness-wise with a slight hamstring problem and it was a bit touch and go. Yet with Geech urging him on, he knew all he had to do was cover the back field and kick goals.

New Zealand 7 British Lions 20, Athletic Park, Wellington, 26 June 1993

In 2017, an aerial photograph was posted on social media that had been taken above the Lions test against New Zealand in Wellington. The All Blacks are in full flight doing the Haka and it looks fantastic – marching bands, lights, flags, advertising banners everywhere. Someone else then posted an aerial shot of our team standing for the Haka 24 years earlier, before our second Test in Wellington. There are us, there are the All Blacks, there are a couple of cameramen and that's it. Nothing else. Just a shambolic stadium with a garden shed on top of one of the stands for the television commentators. But it was still a Test match against the Lions. If you had gone back 12 years earlier, to 1971, there would be even less of a spectacle. But the connection between the three tours remains unbroken – three brilliant victories for the Lions in Wellington.

And what we achieved that afternoon against Sean Fitzpatrick's side was the most emphatic victory the Lions have achieved to date against the All Blacks. It began seconds after the Haka had finished. Ieuan just winked at Tuigamala and then tapped his arse on the way past as they changed ends. The message was unequivocal: *No problem, mate, I know what I'm dealing with now.*

It was one of those days when everything goes your way. It was also one of those moments when I had briefly caught myself thinking that I had the best seat in the house, with time standing still as I watched the likes of Deano, Ieuan, Jerry and Rory go about their work. Christ they were good. *Shit, come on, Bayfs. You better get involved, you big lump.*

And I did. It was a red-letter day and I totally dominated the line-out, taking the ball towards the back, having sent my opposite number forward, and then took a good old lob, tapping it to Dewi, who was already running round, feeding it to Ben Clarke on a brilliant line and smashing it up the middle. Clarkey was phenomenal, absolutely phenomenal. He's what, 6ft 6ins and around 17st? But he's also rangy and fast.

The All Blacks had no answer and one of the proudest moments, on a personal note, was forcing them into what was the first ever 'tactical' substitution. Replacements were only allowed in those days for injured players unable to continue. But Fitzy later told me that because of the job I had done on Mark Cooksley at the line-out, he was effectively told to go off at half-time. Cooksley at the time was the tallest-ever All Black, at 6ft 9ins. He had done reasonably well against Wade in the Maori game and had come into the side for Ian Jones, who had started the first Test.

At half-time both sides remained on the pitch in those days. Someone ran from the New Zealand bench and handed Fitzy a bit of paper. Fitzy nodded, returned the scrap of paper and told Cooksley that he had to feign an injury. I spoke to Fitzy about it afterwards and he admitted he'd had to tell the big man he was off. It was brutal. But it also could not save the All Blacks that day.

Deano was a formidable presence in the loose, while Jason locked our scrum admirably, having switched to tighthead prop. Our scrum didn't go anywhere, and now we had Gibbsy playing in the midfield, where he started causing them all sorts of trouble with his strong and direct running, the sort of stuff he would deliver so emphatically four years later in South Africa.

The stand-out moment was when Rory scored his famous try. Fitzy knocked the ball on, Dewi pounced on it before Jerry put Rory into space just beyond the halfway line and he scorched past John Kirwan. Up in the commentary box (er, garden shed), his brother Tony was commentating on ITV with John Taylor and described it as 'like watching a Porsche going past a Lada'. Which, to be fair, may have been a touch harsh on JK, however good a try it was. Our 20-7 victory was a remarkable performance, not least because the series was on the line.

The match also produced one of the funniest moments of the tour, when someone in the crowd threw a six-pack of beer onto the field just after Gav had landed his fourth penalty to take the game beyond the All Blacks. Unfortunately, it just missed Mooro, who picked it up, pulled a can off, opened it, toasted the crowd and downed it in one before jogging back for the restart. Can you imagine that happening in today's game? A six-pack landed on the pitch and no one batted an eyelid. There was no security, no outrage, no disciplinary hearing . . . Just a player ended up downing a can of beer that had fallen from the sky.

Of course, at the next scrum, we go down and it smells like a brewery. All you can hear from the middle of the All

Blacks scrum is one of their players shouting: 'No wonder they're winning. They're all pissed!' Five minutes later, the final whistle went and we went and did just that.

First, though, Mooro and I had our numbers called to do a drug test after the game. We went into this room to give our samples. I was so dehydrated that I couldn't go and my tester had to come with me to the post-match dinner because, once your number is called, you're not allowed out of their sight. So we had to set a place for him at the dinner table.

Mooro, however, had no such problem. Fitzy was in the room with us too because he was the same number as Mooro. He was sitting there, head in his hands, devastated by the defeat. Mooro, without even bothering to go into the cubicle, pissed in his container in front of Fitzy. 'See, we can even piss better than you,' he said. All I could think was: *Oh you really are a horrible individual, Mooro.*

We had a big court session that night. I have a picture that my sister took of me standing on a table singing into a wine bottle. I do like a sing-song. It was great, great fun. There were a few fans with us too, but everyone could let their hair down without worrying about someone recording the night. We had kept the series alive into the final week.

The Lions in 1993 were a lot better than people think we were, but as we headed to Auckland for the series decider, we just fell into a trap, the same one that England would fall into two years later at the World Cup in South Africa.

What we should have done was analyse the first two Tests and pose ourselves the question: how are we going to win the game and what do we need to do differently? Instead, we ploughed on in the belief that what had worked so far would continue to work. The problem was that as a squad we were physically and mentally drained at that point. It was the biggest challenge for the Lions, because at this stage we had been away from home for weeks, and the options to innovate, even if there was the desire to do so, were extremely limited.

Throughout my career I was hardly a big gym monkey anyway, but I don't think I went to the gym once during the eight-week tour. How on earth were we meant to keep up our strength? When you follow the Lions in the professional era, they're at the gym all the time. But, back in 1993, I know I was fitter at the start of that tour than I was at the end of the tour, and I would argue that all the players felt the same. Our fitness tailed off just at the point when we should have been peaking for the defining game of the entire tour. In contrast, the All Blacks could go back home to their families after each Test, eat what they want, train where they want to train, and freshen up their squad by bringing in a few new players.

Of course, we didn't help ourselves. There were probably times when we should have told each other not to party so hard after this game or that game. But in the final week of the tour, when we really needed to have the midweek team on song, many of them had already checked out. I have a degree of sympathy with them because it was a long time away from home, and if you knew you were nowhere near the Test team, it would be hard to sustain that commitment. What I do know is that the 38-10 defeat by Waikato in Hamilton three days later sucked all the feelgood factor from the squad after the heroics of our second Test victory.

Waikato had been lying in wait for us. Warren Gatland, the future Wales and Lions head coach, was in their side, as was John Mitchell, a future All Blacks head coach who became

England's defence coach under Eddie Jones. It was their big shot at the Lions, whereas we, in contrast, were knackered.

It was the game where Peter Wright got the nickname 'Teapot'. The Lions scrum was under pressure and, as it broke up, he was already standing at the side of it. Wints, sitting in the stands, asked who it was. 'It's Peter Wright,' someone said. 'Shouldn't he be in the scrum?' There was Wright, gasping for air, standing there with his hand on his hips. 'He's like a bloody teapot!' He, like several others, had already checked out long ago by then.

New Zealand 30 British Lions 13, Eden Park, Auckland, 3 July 1993

And yet the third Test started really well. Gibbsy scored quite early on and we had the lead we wanted to put pressure on them. There was nothing overly intimidating about the stadium, nothing intimidating about the opposition. But our strong start only papered over the cracks. It quickly became obvious to me that the spark I had in the second Test wasn't there. It wasn't mental, it was just the effects of feeling tired. Really tired. The All Blacks had also brought innovations to their game. They moved the line-out around a lot, and this is when, if I had been any good at it, I should have just twatted someone as they were laying into me and putting pressure on Johnno. I did try to thump Ian Jones, but he ducked and that was when I connected instead with Johnno. When we got to the next line-out, Johnno said I should take it as he was all over the place. It must have at least been a decent punch, even if it was friendly fire.

Whenever they got the ball they just ran hard at us. Lee Stensness, who had come into the midfield for his debut, stole the show. He only went on to win eight caps, but that day he made the difference, with his chip setting up a try for Frank Bunce.

A bit like England in the 2019 World Cup when they defeated New Zealand in the semi-final, the second Test had been our 'moment'. And like Eddie Jones's side in the final against South Africa, we had run out of steam by the third Test. We played the same game plan, but just were not able to do it as well and were out of it by the end. On reflection, to win the series, we had to win the first two Tests. It was a remarkable achievement that the Lions in 1989 had managed to beat Australia by winning the third Test.

It was devastating walking around the pitch to acknowledge the Lions supporters who had brought life and colour to the tour. But then very quickly we had a beer in our hands and were socialising with the All Blacks, talking, laughing, joking and drinking with them. And there was time for more antics.

On Sunday, we were all battered and bruised and sporting old hangovers, but we had a whole day off in Auckland. Some of the guys went out on a boat in the harbour, while a local businessman who had a magnificent house overlooking Auckland Bay laid on a party for us. He told us that he had hosted world-famous rock stars Sting and Eric Clapton a month before, but we replied: 'Mate, forget that. You've got the Lions here now.'

The property had indoor and outdoor swimming pools, and the owner told us we could eat and drink whatever we liked and go wherever we liked – apart from upstairs, which was out of bounds. 'Don't even try, guys,' he warned. 'The doors are all electronically locked.'

Of course, it was the worst thing he could have done. Someone worked out if you poured beer into the lock, it short-circuited it. 'Lads, the doors are open!' Shortly afterwards, we were booted out and headed back into town. Deano and Richard Webster ended up staging a sumo wrestling contest in an Auckland bar. The image of the two of them wearing only towels is still hard to get out of my mind.

We flew home the following day and there was no official reception when we landed back in London. By Wednesday morning, I was back at work, wondering to myself: *Did the last two months really happen? Did I really go on a Lions tour?*

12

Head on a Chopping Block

I made the front cover of *Rugby World* in October 1993, pictured with my new England and Lions second-row team-mate Martin Johnson. The magazine predicted a bold future for the pair of us on the back of our fledgling partnership that had flourished on the tour of New Zealand.

Not only were we compared favourably to my favourite England second-row pairing of all time, Paul Ackford and Wade Dooley, but the expert opinion suggested that we might become the finest locks England had produced in more than 40 years. It's fair to say they certainly weren't looking to flog any copies based on our looks. Still, I have to admit it was pretty cool to see my face staring back at me from the middle shelf of newsagents. It was not often in my career that I attracted much media attention. And who was I to argue with their expert analysis?

But to give you an insight into how fickle this game can be, just five months later I found my ugly mug on the back of *The Sun*, this time pictured with a few unfortunate

England team-mates with our heads on a chopping block and a guillotine hanging above us. It was a knee-jerk reaction to England's Five Nations defeat by Ireland at Twickenham. Ouch. It turned out *The Sun's* expert analysis was much closer to the mark than the high-brow punditry at *Rugby World*. For the first time in my career, the upward curve I had enjoyed since my school days suffered its first major dip. It turned out the finest second-row pairing in English rugby in 40 years would not even last the season.

It had all started with my neck, but the problem wasn't the guillotine. That would come later. While I had been relieved that the basic scan had not picked up anything serious after the Otago match on the Lions tour, when I got back to England, my neck had started to deteriorate. I was sidelined for four months and my rehabilitation required driving from Bedford to Aylesbury five days a week for three months to see Don Gatherer, the RFU's physio.

My problem was that the RFU would not pay my travel expenses because I had injured my neck while playing for the Lions, not England. It was always nice to know they cared. Within two years, the sport would be flung headlong into professionalism, but a strong defence of amateurism could still be found at Twickenham. Tight bastards. It took Don to stamp his foot down for the RFU to finally relent. 'I tell you what I'll do,' he said. 'I'll send the RFU a bill for my services and then give you the money.' A few days later, I received a letter from the RFU asking me to submit my travel expenses. What a surprise.

The rehabilitation was painstakingly slow. Every day I would sit in this chair with a strap underneath my neck and a hoist on a pulley above, which would stretch it. Day after day after day. The time away from the game should have been a great opportunity to work on other aspects of my game or conditioning, but frustratingly I didn't make the most of it.

Throughout my career I don't think I was ever treated harshly by coaches or selectors. When I got dropped from teams, it was because I wasn't good enough. I'm comfortable with that. What angers me now is that I know I could have been better. Sometimes when I do talks to schools or businesses, my advice is to ask more questions and seek out experts to pick their brains. I never did that myself. It was not the done thing. Instead, I kept quiet as I didn't want to come across as pretentious.

If I had been a bit more proactive during my time with Don, I could have identified specific areas to improve my game so that I was ready to go as soon as I was able to play again. Instead, I just went to the local gym to do some pointless exercises and used matches for Northampton to try to get fit again, which was a disastrous policy. The rehabilitation also meant that I missed the visit of the All Blacks to face England at Twickenham, and it did not make for easy viewing seeing Nigel Redmond play so impressively in my place in the 15-9 victory.

At least I was able to get my own back on the RFU. While rugby union didn't officially become a professional sport until 1995, that didn't stop the players benefiting from the odd financial perk here and there when the game was amateur by selling tickets on the black market. England players in the 1990s used to get three free tickets for internationals at Twickenham and the right to buy 10 more.

Everyone would buy their full allocation and we would have to pay dear old Colin Herridge in cash. Before we had even paid the RFU, we had already received a bundle of cash from the corporate hospitality guys, so when we queued up to play Herridge, everyone paid him with crumpled £50 notes, which only made him more suspicious. The RFU were always warning us not to sell them on the black market and that there would be spot checks, but there was always a rumour that some Twickenham grandees had once sold their tickets on and the black-market guys had kept them in a safe as an insurance policy.

I became the point of contact for the ticket sales as I had a good relationship with one of the hospitality people. Before one of our games in Paris, I was made an offer for our tickets and so I booked out a car from Greyfriars Police Station in Bedford and drove to Yardley Hastings, a village near Northampton, where some of my team-mates were sharing a house. It was an old stone farmhouse and, with the likes of Tim Rodber, Ian Hunter, Paul Grayson and Matt Dawson living there, it was a proper party house.

I knocked on the door, standing there in full uniform with envelopes of cash, ready to pick up the tickets. There was no answer. The door was unlocked, so I went in and saw the detritus of a major party – it looked like a scene out of the film *Animal House*. There was Hunts, lying on the floor with very little on. When he looked up, he didn't register that it was me and saw this giant figure standing there in a police uniform. I thought he was going to have a heart attack.

'Hunts, it's me. It's Bayfs,' I said, trying to calm him down.

'Bloody hell, Bayfs. I thought it was the Old Bill.'

'It is. I just need your match tickets . . .'

Even though I was injured for the New Zealand game, I was allowed my allocation and it was a big earner, with the corporate hospitality guys offering £800 per pair. I think we each pocketed around £4,000, which wasn't a bad sum for the early 1990s. The players could also go around the hospitality tents after the game and get around £300 in their hands for beer money. Given how tight the RFU were, we felt it was our just reward.

I finally made my comeback in a club match against Nottingham. Someone took a picture of me and I look ridiculously massive. I had bulked up in the gym but was too muscle-bound and the ill-advised conditioning would catch up with me.

On the plus side, Ulster and Ireland hooker Allen Clarke had joined the Saints and before the match he asked me where I liked the ball in the line-out. Imagine, just for a minute, in today's game having such a discussion with a hooker before a match, knowing that you have never even trained together. We talked it through but inside I feared it could be a disaster.

At the first line-out, Clarkey threw the perfect ball. It was that lovely one I liked where you just have to stretch a bit more to get to it and I flicked it down to our scrum-half. I looked at Clarkey. 'You and I are going to get on famously!' I boomed. But soon I was puffing and panting. I had lost the mobility that had previously defined my loose play, yet just a few weeks later was picked to play against Scotland at Murrayfield in the opening game of the Five Nations. It was a ridiculous decision. You're never going to turn down the chance to play for your country, but I knew I wasn't ready. We won 15–14, but I was desperately short of match fitness.

When we lost our second game 13–12 against Ireland at Twickenham, when Simon Geogheghan scored his try, I knew the writing was on the wall.

There is a narrow road from the Petersham Hotel, where the England team stayed, to the Richmond Gate Hotel, where the England B team stayed. It was like a walk of shame. Nigel Redmond remembers looking out the window of the 'River Room' in the Petersham and seeing me trudge on by, and saying 'Yes, he's been dropped!'

Geoff Cooke had come up to me with the reassuring words that I wasn't playing against France but remained 'in our long-term plans'. So instead of playing against France at the Parc des Princes, where Rob Andrew kicked all the points in a 18-14 victory, I was off with Jack Rowell's England B team to the Stade Jean Bouin, where at the time the long-jump pit alarmingly encroached onto the pitch.

We were soundly beaten and I didn't play well at all, taking a knock and coming off. I couldn't wait to get home. It was during that game that I imagined what it felt like to be one of the Scots players on the Lions tour in 1993. I really didn't want to be there. It's a mental weakness; I shouldn't have felt like that. But it was a new experience. No one prepares you for being dropped.

Looking back now, I realise I was being an arrogant sod. I was playing for my country (at whatever level) and I could have laid down a marker straight away and said: 'Right, I'm coming back.' But I didn't. The rest of the championship passed me by.

The light at the end of the tunnel, however, was the tour to South Africa in the summer. I returned to England determined to replicate the training programme that had prepared me for the tour of Fiji three years earlier. I concentrated on losing the bulk I'd gained, dropping a stone to around 18st, while retaining the strength and working on my running and endurance. By the time the squad was selected, I was ready to go. I was fit, but I was also hungry again because I had to get my place back.

South Africa in 1994 was such an amazing place to tour. Nelson Mandela had just been elected president, the country was gearing up to host the Rugby World Cup the following year and we were facing teams we had never come across before because of the sports isolation during the apartheid years. But behind the exhilarating sense of a new nation emerging from a troubled past, it remained a country blighted by violence.

When we arrived in Durban, myself and Deano, who was also a police officer, spent a night with the local regional police. They showed us the work they had to do, along with security videos they had shot and an incident list from the night before. We were asked what would be on a typical list in England.

'There will usually be a pub fight, a couple of domestics, someone will have had their car nicked, a bit of criminal damage and a couple of reports of noisy neighbours,' we told them.

'Really?' said our host. 'Last night we had five murders in one small area.' They took us around a township and explained that they had to use underpowered weapons because they could not take the risk that if they fired a bullet and missed it would travel on through several other shanties. Instead, the bullets had to drop within 50 metres.

We were then shown a video of people on a march. They were dancing and singing before three little dots suddenly appeared from the bottom right of the screen and landed in the crowd. The screen bleached out and then slowly, when the colour returned, it revealed absolute carnage. Three hand grenades had been dropped into this crowd, killing 20 or 30 people. I looked at Deano aghast. 'Bloody hell. That doesn't happen in Bedford.' It was simply horrific to watch.

The scenes put our challenges on the tour into perspective. That had begun when Stuart Barnes took Will to task when we arrived, after he had tried to order a boycott of the travelling press pack. Will had received some critical coverage and said to us: 'Right, we are going to blank the press. No one talks to them.'

But the reaction was far from the unanimous response Will had hoped for. Barnesy challenged him. 'If this had happened to one of us, would you be saying the same?' It immediately created an atmosphere, but was a very astute question from Barnesy. The moment crystallised the feeling in the squad that there was a superstar element within the team and then the rest of us. Sponsors were only interested in a small number of players. These days everyone has a social media outlet to push their name and brand, and everyone gets the same match fee. Back then, if your club appeared in a televised game more than twice a year, you were doing well.

It was quite a tour for Barnesy, who was never one to shy away from controversial issues. I got to know him quite well from the Lions. He's incredibly intelligent and a deep thinker, but he also wants to be a hippy at heart, with his love of Bob Dylan and red wine. He had a great tour on the pitch and was unafraid to challenge racial tensions off it. We had been aware from the start that there was a focus from some quarters on the racial make-up of our team. We were proud of the diversity of our squad and there was one post-match event in Bloemfontein, when Barnesy was the midweek captain, that he walked the England team out of as soon as he could because of the racial undertones.

It was a difficult time for South Africa as a country and most of our games were quite lively. We were the first team to tour the country after the free elections. I remember playing in Kimberly against South Africa A and jumping for the ball at a line-out, and wondering whether I should go for the ball or the 20 oranges that were being thrown at me. Some supporters would sing the old national anthem. There was a real edge to the place.

At the World Cup the following year, Jerry Guscott, who had missed the tour in 1994 because of injury, claimed that Jason Leonard and I had saved his life one night. We were playing this silly childish drinking game where you take a sip of your beer and spit it into the face of the person standing next to you. Jerry took a swig of beer and someone shouted: 'To your right.' Jerry turned to his right and spat his beer into the face of this big Afrikaner standing beside him. The guy did not see the funny side of the game and opened his jacket to reveal a gun. Everyone froze for a second before Jason stepped over and took him by one arm and I then took the other. We just picked him up and marched him off, dropping him down out of danger. When we got back, Jerry said: 'You guys saved my life.' Jase and I looked at each other. 'We should have let him shoot him . . .'

In a rugby sense, I was thriving. Jack Rowell was on the tour as manager for the first time and he knew just which buttons to push with me, a bit like Dick Best. He could wind you up and you just wanted to rip his head off. During one of the dirt-tracker training sessions, he shouted across at me.

'I can see why Geoff dropped you, Bayfs.' For the next ten minutes, I ripped into everything that moved. Then, at the end, came the kind of look that Besty would give me as if to say: *I knew you could do it.*

I liked Jack. He reminded me of my dad in a lot of ways: physically, mentally and character-wise. Ultimately, though, I think the England team ended up marking time under Jack until Clive Woodward came in. We all know what happened then.

I just loved the challenge of trying to win my place back in the team. It made me realise that I operated best when I was out of my comfort zone. When life gets a bit comfortable for me, I can take my foot off the gas. I didn't have the mental strength of the likes of Johnno. I also thrived when there were no other distractions apart from rugby – for example, on tour in 1991, the Lions in 1993 and now South Africa. It would be the same during the World Cup the following year. My head can quite quickly get full of weird thoughts and I can so easily be thrown off track. But when I'm on it, I am absolutely on it. It's just that it didn't take much to knock me off. Adversity is what I respond to. I was fit, hungry and a little bit angry at losing my place, and what followed was probably my best sustained period of performances, right through to the 1995 World Cup.

When the team was being read out for the first Test, Will turned to us and said there were no changes to the team that finished the Five Nations.

So I piped up. 'Well, there is one change.'

'Who?'

'Er . . . me.'

'Oh yeah, sorry.'

It was nice to be wanted.

*

The highlight of the tour came ahead of the first Test, in Pretoria, when we got to meet President Nelson Mandela for a brief handshake before kick-off. Yet, once again, we were reminded of the challenges the country still faced.

Johnno had not been selected because he had suffered concussion in the defeat by Transvaal when he was punched by Johan le Roux, so Nigel Redmond started alongside me. We stood beside each other for the anthems. When they played 'Nkosi Sikelel' iAfrika', the new national anthem, no one in the stadium knew the words. There was just music.

'Ollie' Redmond turned to me and shouted: 'Look at these fuckers, they don't even know the words to their own anthem!' Then, seconds later, all hell broke loose as they played 'Die Stem', the old Afrikaner anthem. Helicopters which had been below the level of the stand suddenly took off and circled the stadium, showing off the old and new flags of South Africa while security dogs were barking and snarling. I turned to Ollie. 'You and your fucking big mouth!' The place was rocking.

But so were we. Our back row was outstanding, with Ben Clarke and Tim Rodber dominating the Springboks, and we absolutely smashed them, winning 32-15. It was a shattering blow to their pride in what was meant to be the start of the build-up to hosting the World Cup the following year. Afterwards, we learned of a rumour that the Springboks team had refused to play until about 15 minutes before the kick-off because of a dispute with their union, which may not have helped their mindset.

I was up against a guy called Hannes Strydom. With five minutes to go, he was at the bottom of the ruck when he turned to me and said: 'Bayfs, this has not gone to plan.' It was one of those moments of dry humour I loved in the heat of battle, and I enjoyed chatting with him and sharing a beer after the game.

It was also the first time any of us had come across the young Springbok captain Francois Pienaar, who was winning just his eighth cap. Here was an unknown blond, blue-eyed flanker and you can only imagine the banter that we directed at him. Sometimes it was necessary to ridicule an opponent like that so you could dismantle them in your mind. It was a defensive mechanism, so when you saw them on the pitch, you would almost chuckle to yourself because of all the stupid things you had said about them. We had no idea what a great leader he would turn into. We just thought that if we could have a laugh and lampoon him, then great. So we did.

Our performance was so emphatic that it was reprised in the opening scenes of the film *Invictus*, prompting the rugby authorities to rethink their plans for the World Cup. The director clearly hadn't brought in a rugby advisor because we are all shapes and sizes. The props look like second rows and the centres look like flankers. But I am proud that that's where the film starts, with President Mandela and his officials watching the Springboks get dismantled by England. We had left our mark.

Three days later – and just four days before the second of the two Tests – we travelled to Port Elizabeth to face an Eastern Province team that was notorious for kicking lumps out of their opponents. It would become known as the battle of Boet Erasmus.

It seemed apparent that they went to target Rodber when he came on after just 12 minutes thanks to Dean Ryan suffering a broken thumb. Up in the stands, we started to get threats from the supporters near us so we moved down to watch the match from the sidelines as the atmosphere turned nasty. Before the first half was up, Jon Callard had his face sliced open by the boot of Elandre van der Bergh. It was a sickening act. Jon needed 25 stitches and could have lost his eye. But van der Bergh merely received a telling-off. Rodber, who had taken over as captain, approached the referee: 'Sir, what do you have to do to get sent off in this game?'

When it all kicked off again 10 minutes later, he would find out. The South Africans went after him and there was no way that the Brigadier of the Green Howards Infantry was going to back down. He became only the second England player to be sent off, after pummelling Simon Tremain, son of All Black legend Kel, who was also dismissed.

One of the journalists covering the game wrote that when Rodber landed the first punch, he must have thought he might be cautioned. When he landed the second punch, he must have thought he might be getting a red card. When he landed the 20th punch, he must have wondered where he would be sitting on the flight home.

But this was when Jack Rowell came into his own. He was a guy who didn't like conflict, but he laid down the law, acting like a ruthless businessman just when we needed him to be. He basically told the South Africans that if they banned Rodber, who had clearly been targeted, from the second Test, we were going home. It worked.

He stood up for us in press conferences too. We had an official function at Kings Park at which Louis Luyt, the obnoxious and boorish president of the South African Union, welcomed us by telling us they were going to host the greatest World Cup, the first proper one, and they were building the best stadiums in the world. Jack stood up and thanked our hosts for the lovely hospitality, but then turned to Luyt. 'Louis, you've missed a trick. I see that you're trying to get more capacity here but if you simply open your mouth a bit wider we could get 15,000 seats in there.'

Rodders was cleared to play in the second Test, but that didn't stop the South African antics. At our training sessions that week to prepare for the second Test, a helicopter circled our training ground every day. You could tell they had a camera and were filming all our moves.

The Springboks made some changes to their starting XV, bringing in Mark Andrews for his debut. And they also appeared to debut some new laws, as out of nowhere they started lifting at line-outs. I mean proper lifting, not the cheeky little shoulder lift I used to get from Jason Leonard sometimes. I remember the first line-out jumping at the front against Andrews and, as I went for the ball, all I could see was his shorts. *'What the fuck? Is this guy Superman?'* Lifting was not allowed in those days but the referee said it was a fair jump. He seemed to be refereeing an entirely different game.

The Springboks claimed their revenge, winning 27-9. If you aggregated the scores over the two Tests, they finished one point ahead. But we knew we should have won the series and felt we had laid down a marker ahead of our return to South Africa the following year. The World Cup was in our sights again.

13

Deep Heat, Old Farts and Tackling Jonah

Rugby players of a certain age will remember a pre-match routine that effectively involved a lot of bear-hugging, squeezing, screaming and running on the spot, banging the tiled floor of the changing room with your studs on.

Well, you will be glad to know it was no different with England. The forwards would be sent into the showers to do their grunting, leaving the backs the space for a more refined warm-up. This was fine until the new West Stand was built at Twickenham and our changing room had showers with sensors rather than taps. So, just at the crucial moment when we were stamping and shouting to psyche ourselves up, someone would nudge the shower sensor and we would all be sprayed with cold water.

The late Roger Quittenton would often provide some pre-match hilarity to the matches he presided over. Roger was the referee who awarded the controversial match-winning penalty to New Zealand when Andy Haden jumped out of the line-out against Wales in Cardiff during their 1978 tour. Roger used to wear ridiculously tight shorts and sported a perma-tan.

He would come into the changing room and always ask what colour of shirts we were wearing. One day someone asked him why he always wanted to know. 'I don't want to clash,' he said, revealing that he had five or six shirts with him to ensure that he always looked amazing.

Before one of the English divisional matches, I remember us attempting to work ourselves up into a rage. 'Come on lads, we are going to fucking smash them, COME ON!' Just then there was a knock at the door. And there was Roger. 'All right, boys?' he asked, at a pitch just high enough to ensure we once again burst out laughing, the moment of serious intent lost with just three words.

On another occasion before a game, Victor Ubogu trod on a tube of Deep Heat and the cream spurted out all over the wall and up Brian Moore's blazer. We all start pissing ourselves laughing and Carling is shouting over the din: 'For fuck's sake, lads!'

Victor had quite an impact during our Grand Slam campaign in 1995. After routine victories over Romania and Canada when we returned from South Africa, there was a sense of confidence and expectation in the squad ahead of the Five Nations. We travelled to Dublin, wary of what had happened two years previously, and this time ready to meet fire with fire.

It also gave us the opportunity to wind up Mooro. A young hooker by the name of Keith Wood was making his Five Nations debut for Ireland, having made an impressive start to his international career on the tour of Australia in the previous summer.

'What do we need to focus on?' asked Jack in our final team meeting on the Friday night. 'Just remember what happened in 1993,' said Will. 'They're going to come at you with hammer and tongs. Absorb the early pressure and there will be something done to throw you off your game. But whatever you do, you must keep an eye on this new hooker, Keith Wood. He looks like an incredible talent; he's big and fast and has great hands.'

Will handed over to Deano. 'Yeah, lads, let's get stuck in from the off. We have to go hard. Remember the chaos they caused in the line-out two years ago. This is our time to maul them off the park. And Will's right: whatever we do, we have to watch out for Keith Wood. He's more than 17st and 6ft tall, but so mobile with it.' By this stage, the steam was already bellowing out of Mooro's ears. 'He's not 6ft, he's 5ft 11ins,' he barked. 'And he's only 16st.'

Dewi and Rob were next up to talk about the game plan and back play. Hilariously, both finished, entirely deadpan, with a similar pay-off: 'And let's keep an eye on Keith Wood.' Mooro completely lost it. 'Okay, lads. I fucking get it. I fucking get it!' And stormed out of the room.

In the end, Mooro needn't have worried. I was up against Neil Francis and he had one of those weird games. He was a big boy and smart too. He could read a line-out really well and started the game brilliantly. But then he seemed to have one of his moments and lost interest, going off and being replaced by Gabriel Fulcher.

Ben Clarke also made history by becoming the first player to receive a yellow card, which had just been brought in. At that stage, you didn't leave the field but it was a warning, which earned him a lot of piss-taking afterwards. We were on song and won the game comfortably, winning 20-8 with tries by Will, Clarke and Tony Underwood.

Against France at Twickenham, I remember looking at their line-up just before the kick-off and thinking, *This is going to be tough.* They had Abdel Benazzi, Lauren Canbannes and Oliver Roumant in their pack and, for some reason, we had Dewi Morris calling out line-outs that day. It was hilarious. Our calls were far from complex, but Monkey managed to mess the first one up. He got so confused he just mumbled out a series of letters and numbers that made no sense. We all stood there gaping at him as the crowd roared.

'Come on lads, for fuck's sake, help me out here!' he shouted. Mooro just rolled his eyes and said: 'Don't worry, I'll take over.' We ended up going back to old-school signals. If the scrum-half's right foot was pointing towards the touch-line, the throw went to the front. If his feet were parallel, it went to the middle. And if his left foot was pointing to the back of the line-out, it went to the tail. And this was meant to be international rugby.

Yet despite our shambles, I felt reassured when I looked at my opposite number, Oliver Brouzet, and saw him looking around the stadium at the crowd. He looked intimidated. Happy days. *He's not ready for this. Let's get stuck into this one.* I had felt like him once, but by 1995 I was playing the best rugby of my career. I was fit, strong and mobile, and had grown in confidence about my role and influence on the side. I would love to be one of those players who could say they had a sustained period of excellence over four or five years. Instead, I could pin it down to that short period in 1995. Oh well. It would have to do.

We smashed France 31-10, with Tony Underwood scoring twice and Jerry gliding over for another to make amends for our defeat to them in the World Cup. As we were about to leave the Petersham Hotel in Richmond for the next game, against Wales in Cardiff, the plan being that we would drive separately in our own cars, Will Carling came up to Jason Leonard with a smile on his face.

'Jase, I've got Jack Rowell's keys,' he said. 'Why don't we hide them for a bit of a laugh?'

'I can do better than that, Will,' replied Jase. He stepped outside and lobbed the keys into the meadow that slopes down from the entrance to the hotel, into the long grass. Will was just standing there, looking alarmed. 'Jase, what have you done?'

When we got to Cardiff, Les Cusworth, the assistant coach, gathered the squad together. 'Okay, lads, Jack's going to be a bit late. He can't find his car keys.' Queue hearty sniggers in response. It was so childish but there we were, chuckling away. He had no chance of finding them so he must have got a spare set. I am sure the keys are still lying hidden in the meadow to this day.

The atmosphere was so different from my first visit to Cardiff in 1993, when there'd been a sense of hesitancy in the air. This time, I knew we would be fine. The tour to South Africa had given us an inner confidence and even though we had lost the second Test, we felt that was down to some poor refereeing. Wales didn't stand a chance and it was in Cardiff that Victor came into his own again, getting us up and running by scoring the first try. Despite never having done so, I imagine every player must be elated to score a try for England, but Victor went absolutely crazy in his celebrations, to the point when someone shouted 'All right Vic, steady on.'

We romped on to a 23-9 victory, with Rory Underwood scoring two more tries and Rob Andrew, who kicked everything that season, landing a couple of penalties and a conversion. That night we were out in Cardiff and Victor, who is normally very good at spending other people's money, was in a generous mood. 'Champagne for everyone!' he shouted.

'Hang on Vic, steady on,' came the reply for the second time that day.

'Don't worry, it's on me. I was 20-1 to score a try today.' He said his mate had seen the odds the night before and Vic had asked him to put £100 on it.

We were piling into the champagne when Victor's mate suddenly appeared. 'Here comes my friend!' boomed Victor. But his mate was looking very sheepish.

'Hi Victor. Sorry mate,' he said. 'When I saw that the bet was for you to score the first try, I thought you had absolutely no chance, so I didn't place the bet.'

Victor's face dropped, and we were the ones celebrating now, having just spent all his money. And his mate? Well, he was instantly our new best friend, of course.

It was back to Twickenham for the Grand Slam match against a Scotland side that was also going for the clean sweep, but it was another comprehensive 24-12 victory for us, with Rob Andrew kicking seven penalties and a drop-goal. Graham Rowntree, the former Leicester prop, made his debut off the bench that afternoon. Jason Leonard had to go off with about 15 minutes remaining and Rowntree had been in such a hurry to get onto the pitch that he forgot to tie up his shorts. So when we went down for the next scrum, I ended up grabbing hold of everything that I didn't want to grab hold of as I reached my arm through to bind on his shorts. 'Do your fucking shorts up, would you, Wig?' I yelled at him. 'That's disgusting.'

With our third Grand Slam in three seasons, we felt unstoppable ahead of the World Cup in South Africa that summer. We had beaten New Zealand and South Africa since our World Cup final defeat by Australia four years earlier, and many of the squad had the experience of a Lions tour under their belt. There was a feeling of confidence across the squad that we could finally get our hands on the Webb Ellis Cup. It was an arrogance that would prove to be our undoing.

For all our talent and experience, it now seems unforgivable to think that we were undone by our lack of preparation and planning. These were the last days of the amateur era after all, and we did not disappoint.

Before we had even left for South Africa, the squad had been plunged into turmoil when, just ten days before the start of the tournament, Will was stripped of the captaincy after his infamous '57 old farts' jibe. It had been a throwaway comment that had been picked up on a microphone after an interview with Greg Dyke had finished. Dyke was making a Channel 4 documentary, turning the spotlight onto the tensions created by the final days of amateurism. 'If the game is run properly as a professional game, you do not need 57 old farts running rugby,' Carling was heard to say, referring to the RFU committee.

A couple of days after the broadcast, we were at Twickenham on a baking hot day in May to watch the Pilkington Cup final as Bath thrashed Wasps when we were told that Will had been stripped of the captaincy for his comments. You couldn't make it up. The players got together to hold an impromptu meeting to discuss our reaction and it was decided that we would tell the RFU that Will was our captain and no one else was going to accept the captaincy.

The message was relayed to the RFU's president, Dennis Easby of Berkshire, a former referee, via the late Terry Cooper, who at the time was the rugby correspondent of the Press Association. After Will apologised, Easby was able to turn the committee around and Will was reinstated just a few days before we departed for South Africa. It was another classic case of the RFU misreading the room, but I could understand why there was an element of friction. The committee had a lot of people who did amazing work for the junior game, but sometimes their understanding of the elite game was lacking. I remember one of the presidents of the RFU telling me that Lawrence Dallaglio would make an excellent prop, which was obviously ridiculous.

The game was moving so far and so fast. Ultimately, the right result was reached and I don't think it had any lasting effect on our preparations. But safe to say we gave Will plenty of stick about it.

By this stage, my relationship with him had changed. Now that I had been a senior player in the side, I think he came to expect more from me. He could see that Martin Johnson had arrived as his 'for ever' player and young guns like Garath Archer were starting to knock on the door. I felt he looked at me to say: 'Come on, Bayfs, we need a bit more from you.'

But I always liked Will. He has a very dry and dead-pan humour. When I first got on the 1991 tour to Fiji and Australia, he didn't have a clue who I was. I'm sure he would have been looking at his incumbent second rows – the big and aggressive Paul Ackford and Wade Dooley – and then seen this skinny bloke. *Who the hell is he?*

But our relationship over time improved and I have huge admiration for what he achieved with England. I think he was a really good player and a great captain. There were alternatives. I think Rob Andrew could have been a brilliant captain. Mooro? A fierce leader but maybe a bit bonkers. Rob could have captained that team without a doubt. But Will was the right captain at the right time.

I'm not sure if this was a way of thanking us for backing his captaincy, but before we left for South Africa, he had arranged for all the players to have these ridiculous-looking 'atmosphere suits' that we were meant to train in before we left. The idea was to recreate the heat and the humidity of the Highveld, but most people used them for decorating. I can remember turning up to a running track at Bedford wearing it. They were made of very heavy fabric with a hood and a plastic visor so we could see out, like a rather embarrassingly tight-fitting hazmat suit. I think everyone who saw me ran for the hills.

Our opening to the tournament was hardly convincing, scraping past Italy and Argentina before a reasonable win over Samoa. But by the time we reached the quarter-finals to face Australia, there was a growing sense that momentum was building, helped in part by some dastardly espionage.

Someone came up with a masterplan to dress up our sports psychologist, Austin Swain, as a backpacker and sneak him into the Wallabies' training session. His instruction was simply to get us any information that he could. The smallest nugget would have done, but instead he came back with a treasure chest overflowing with stolen intellectual property.

We listened with laughter as he recounted his James Bond-style mission.

When he rocked up at the stadium, the groundsman thought he was a tourist. When the Australia players and coaches arrived, they thought he was a friend of the groundsman. Swain could not believe his luck and kept the deception going brilliantly. He ended up watching the entire Wallabies' training session while drinking beers out of their cool box. He eventually slipped away with every single move the Australians used.

Swain had been a decent rugby player himself and was also a coach, so he knew what he was looking for. He wasn't able to pick up their calls, but memorised everything else. I remember Jack Rowell asking him to stand in front of us all and tell us everything he could remember. Almost an hour later, we were sitting there with our jaws on the floor. 'Wow, you really did watch the whole training session!'

His reward? A new nickname. From now on, he was known as 'Neidermeyer', as in sneaky little shit, from the film *Animal House*.

Our reward for Neidermeyer's subterfuge was to be able to anticipate every Australian move, culminating in a 25-22 victory in Cape Town, avenging our defeat by the Wallabies four years earlier in the World Cup final.

The victory did not pass without a moment of humiliation for me, however. Early in the game, with adrenaline pumping, I lined up David Campese, the legendary Wallaby wing, and brought him to the ground. It was one of the great moments of my career. Sadly Campo didn't see it that way. 'Aw, mate, that is just embarrassing,' he berated himself, incredulous that he had allowed himself to be tackled by a lump of a second-row forward like me.

My main role that day was to neutralise the threat of the great John Eales at the line-out. Eales was by far the best line-out operator in the world and in the pre-match line-out meeting, we devised our masterplan.

'Bayfs, we are basically going to just use you as a decoy and throw the ball somewhere else,' I was told. The boys knew how to make me feel important. But it actually worked. Eales marked me, freeing up our other jumpers all afternoon. Yet despite all our advantages, it turned out to be a ferociously competitive game. Rob Andrew and Michael Lynagh traded penalties before we took what looked to be decisive advantage with a brilliant breakaway try by Tony Underwood.

Yet barely a minute into the second half, the Wallabies hit us with a classic Aussie Rules ploy. Lynagh launched a high ball and Damian Smith jumped all over Mike Catt to collect the ball in the air and score. The aerial battle is commonplace in today's game, but back then it gave the Wallabies a real advantage. In those days, the catcher stood his ground and turned his body a bit so the ball would go backwards if he dropped it. In contrast, the Australians would fly in because they had done it since they were kids playing Aussie Rules.

Our forward power told in the end – just. As the game went into extra time, in the final minute Mooro finally threw the ball to me at a line-out and thankfully I caught it and trundled forwards. Dewi threw his usual pass to Rob – it must have bounced three times before he caught it – before bisecting the posts with the winning drop-goal.

There was another bizarre twist to the tale of our victory when, in a conversation years later with Eales, it turned out that we had both been using exactly the same line-out codes during the match. I remember thinking, when they made their call, that the ball was thrown to where I expected, and it turns out they were thinking the same about us. Even more remarkably, we had changed our codes at half-time, and it turns out they had done the same, and made the exact same changes as we had!

The elation of our victory was short-lived, however – and we only had ourselves to blame. Neidermeyer was dispatched to the New Zealand camp, but this time was sent packing. We, meanwhile, headed to Sun City for three days of 'R&R' just before our semi-final. What could possibly go wrong?

It is impossible to imagine a team in the professional era preparing for a World Cup semi-final by going on the beers for three days, but in these final days of amateurism, it seemed an entirely logical thing to do for all of us, including for Rowell and his coaching team. We had been away from home for a long time and the feeling was that we would benefit from a break. But it turned out to be the maddest and craziest thing we could have done.

Celebrations on the night of our quarter-final win had been relatively calm as some players had their families with them. As the boys got on the team bus on the Sunday to depart for Sun City, waving goodbye to their wives and girlfriends, Jerry said with a smile: 'Right, now the tour can begin!' It was probably the first indication of how the remainder of the tournament was heading for us.

At Sun City, there was no sign there was even a World Cup on. We took full advantage. There was a lot of drinking, a lot of messing around. Stories started to make it back to us that the All Blacks were preparing for the game with brutal training sessions that left hooker Sean Fitzpatrick requiring 30 stitches in his head. Meanwhile, we were playing cards, drinking beers in the sun. Our attitude was simply: 'We'll be fine.' Instead of devising a special plan to combat the explosive talents of Jonah Lomu for what, for many of us, was the biggest game of our lives, we partied as if we were on a massive stag do.

None of us realised then just how good Lomu was. But there was an issue of pride at stake too. Devising a plan to stop him effectively meant you had to say to a player, 'I don't think you can tackle him on your own.' And none of us would have admitted to that anyway.

We'll be fine. We are Grand Slam champions, we have some of the best players in the world, we are British Lions. We'll be absolutely fine.

Scotland had just lost to the All Blacks in the quarter-finals and were saying they had never seen anything like Lomu, but we simply weren't listening. He was barely mentioned during our stay in Sun City, bar the odd low-key comment: 'Let's just make sure we keep an eye on him ...'

When we returned to Cape Town for our first session on Thursday, we were barely fit to drive, never mind train. But our capitulation was not solely to do with the physical after-effects of our jolly, rather the complete lack of a strategy. I didn't go onto the field thinking that I'd had too much to drink. That wasn't the problem. It was the lack of preparation, of tactical preparation. We should have come up with something – I don't know what, but something completely different. Our training should have been the toughest, hardest training to get us ready for that. We weren't ready for Lomu.

We just weren't ready for him. In the final, South Africa committed three defenders to Lomu, and filled in the gaps left elsewhere as best they could. Plus, New Zealand were poisoned, but that's another story!

We knew our fate after just four minutes. The All Blacks pack rumbled forward to within 25 metres of our line. They hit up in the midfield first, with Frank Bunce, and as the ball was recycled we were short on our right side. It was clear that New Zealand had only one aim – get the ball into Lomu's hands. Graeme Bachop fired a wild pass beyond full-back Glen Osborne and over Lomu's head.

The giant wing had to turn to collect the ball on the bounce but once he gathered it, it was immediately obvious we were in trouble. Having handed off Tony Underwood and burned off Carling, Mike Catt was left stranded as the last line of defence. Will somehow managed to tap-tackle him but all that did was to send Lomu stumbling at full force into Catt, who had no chance of stopping him. It was a brutal demonstration of Lomu's power and our inept preparation.

The 45-29 final scoreline flattered us, even though Will had spearheaded a gutsy rear-guard action in the second half. The defeat would serve as a chilling revelation as to just how far we had fallen behind the southern hemisphere. New Zealand had effectively prepared as a professional side. While everyone remembers Lomu's four tries, the moment of ridiculous skill came when All Black No. 8 Zinzan Brooke, running back a skewed clearance kick by Carling, banged over a drop goal from just inside our half. It was freakish and they were taking the piss. We resorted to gallows humour. Someone shouted to Deano: 'Why can't you do that . . .?'

I look back now at the 1995 World Cup with massive regret.

To get to a World Cup is amazing. Some guys are lucky enough to get to two or three World Cups. But even one is special. So special. And to get to the semi-finals with such a talented group of players and be within touching distance of the final left me with such an overwhelming feeling of remorse.

We got it horribly wrong. The teams that were genuinely competing for that World Cup title were almost operating at a professional level at that stage, just in their preparation alone, whereas we were still miles behind. Our coaching staff, like the players, were still amateur and had to juggle the demands of international sport with their day jobs. The consequence was that there was simply no joined-up thinking as to how we would turn this all-conquering English Grand Slam side into a World Cup-winning team.

As players, we weren't always receptive to new ideas either. I remember one day when Dave Alred appeared. Nowadays, he is revered as a great kicking coach who worked extensively with Jonny Wilkinson. If it wasn't for him, England wouldn't have won a World Cup in 2003. But we just wondered: *Who is this fucking idiot?*

He tried to get us to do this weird stuff during a recovery day in the swimming pool and you can only imagine how guys like Deano responded. *I don't think so, mate.* We were caught up in our own bubble in the northern hemisphere. Winning a Grand Slam meant everything to us, but absolutely nothing to the southern hemisphere, where the game was changing at great pace as it surged onwards to professionalism. We should have realised that, to win the World Cup, we were going to have to beat Australia, New Zealand and South Africa. But we fell spectacularly at the second hurdle. And that's not to diminish the task in hand.

There is a reason why England have only ever won one World Cup. Even in 2019, when Eddie Jones' side managed to beat Australia in the quarter-finals, followed by an unbelievable performance against the All Blacks in the semi-final, they still fell flat in the final against the Springboks. But what I know is that we had a brilliant collection of players, and we did not do ourselves justice when the heat was on.

If you look at South Africa's World Cup wins, they've been helped by other teams being taken out of their way. We beat Australia in 1995 (although they had already beaten the Wallabies in the opening game so could argue they weren't a huge problem) and New Zealand, for whatever reason, were not themselves in the final. In 2007, the big boys had been removed when France beat New Zealand in the quarter-finals, and England beat Australia, and then France, to reach the final. And even though they were held together by sticky tape by the end, England almost won. It was the same in 2019. New Zealand would have smashed South Africa in that final in Yokohama.

Our problem in 1995 was that we had this amateur way of thinking. In many ways, we England players hadn't learned our lesson from the Lions tour in 1993, where the next game was always the hardest and your opponent's threats evolved. On that Lions tour, we felt we should have won the first Test, and we did really well in the second Test. That's when we should have knuckled down and taken our game to another level. But we were knackered and some of us were probably a bit homesick, so we didn't prepare as well as we should. Nowadays, you wouldn't even think of hitting the sauce before a semi-final. It was a sign written in big letters that if this England team wanted to become world champions, it would have to go up another level. And we had another level there. I think that, if you sat any of that 1995 crew down and asked them, 'If you could rewrite history, would you go to Sun City on the lash?', I am certain they would say: 'Probably not.'

Having said that, if you look at that All Blacks side, it was a phenomenal team. They should have won the World Cup. Yes, they lost the final, but they went on to have a tremendous run of wins the following year. Indeed, if you talk to Fitzy, he will tell you the highlight of his career was winning the tour series against South Africa in 1996.

Our humiliating exit for us was made worse when we lost to France in the third/fourth play-off game that no one wants to play in. The French players were convinced that they had beaten South Africa in their semi-final and that it had been an absolute stitch-up. There had been a deluge of rain before kick-off and if the match had been cancelled, France would have progressed to the final under tournament rules because of the Springboks' inferior disciplinary record. Kick-off was postponed by an hour as groundskeepers attempted to sweep the water from the surface, including five women with scarves around their heads and brooms. Remarkably, the game went ahead in the most atrocious conditions and the French players were convinced that Abdelatif Benazzi scored a try near the end that would have won the match.

The one upside of our match against France is that we ended up having a massive night on the beers with the French players afterwards. It probably broke the mystique of the fixture that we had dominated since the 1991 World Cup, but also brought to an end a lot of the tension and edge to it. It was an epic night and great to get to know them better.

Louis Luyt did nothing to quell the sense that South Africa were never not going to reach the final by attempting to give

Derek Bevan, who had refereed the semi-final and was a touch judge in the final, a gold watch and ironically describing him as 'the most wonderful referee in the world' and the 'outstanding referee in the World Cup'. It was an incredibly awkward moment.

To be fair to Bevan, he and the other officials present simply walked out of the dinner in disgust at the false insinuation. But Luyt was only just warming up. He then went on to assert that New Zealand and Australia, winners in 1987 and 1991, couldn't call themselves world champions because they hadn't had to play South Africa. This, he said, was the first proper World Cup. Mike Brewer, the All Blacks back-row forward, wanted to storm the stage and punch him. He had to be dragged back. Of course, we were sitting at the back of the room, shouting: 'This is brilliant!' It was a madcap finale.

An adventure that had begun with the controversy of Carling losing the captaincy and then regaining it again would end in an even more bizarre fashion for me. When the Springboks were crowned champions, our local security team, who were made up of hardmen who I am pretty sure had seen some action back in the day, were in tears. And as we packed up to go home, one of them gave me an emotional embrace and handed me a box as a gift.

'Open it when you get home,' he said.

'No, I'm going to open it now,' I replied. There was a nine-millimetre pistol in it. *Good God.*

'That's for you,' he said, on the verge of welling up.

'Er, I don't know how things work here but I can't take that!'

'What about if you just take the bullets?

'No, I can't do that either. But I appreciate the gesture.'

Not long after we got home, the game faced the over-whelming challenge of coming to grips with the brave new world of professionalism. And my England career was heading for an abrupt end.

14

A Change of Perspective

I am not a religious man in any shape or form. But I can still remember that feeling, an indescribable sensation that something was not right. I slammed down my knife and fork. 'Where is Polly?'

To this day, I cannot explain why I had a subconscious surge of concern for my daughter at that precise moment. We were having breakfast at our villa during a family holiday in Majorca after I had returned from the World Cup in South Africa. Polly was the youngest of my two daughters at the time, just 18 months old. Rosie, her big sister, was three. Me and my then wife Helena had decided to go away with another family for a few days to the Balearic island. Our villa shared a swimming pool with three other properties. As there was no fence around the pool, we had decided to keep the doors of the villa shut as a precaution. *But where was Polly?*

I dashed out the back door to where the pool was and that knot in the stomach that every parent knows was tightening. 'Polly! Polly! Where are you?!' But there was no sign of anyone. I ran on, towards the driveway where Polly had enjoyed playing on a pile of gravel nearby, chucking stones around. But still no sign. 'POLLY!'

Then, as I headed back to the villa, I saw a sight that will never leave me. An inflatable lilo was in the pool, and there, floating up from underneath it, were strands of hair.

I have no memory of what happened next. But those who witnessed it in the surrounding villas said they heard my guttural scream as I dived into the pool to scoop Polly out. My beautiful Polly. As I laid her down beside the pool, she was already blue and had stopped breathing. I couldn't pick up any pulse. I tried to resuscitate her and my heart leaped when she finally began to cough up water and started to cry, but she was still drifting in and out of consciousness.

My mate Andy arrived at the scene and we carried her into his car and drove to the local town to find a hospital, but without mobile phones or sat navs we were desperate. Andy spotted a police car driving down a one-way street and to catch their attention turned the car and drove up the street towards them in the wrong direction.

The police officer was ready to take his gun out, but thankfully saw the situation straight away and took us to a local medical centre. There the doctor, dripping with sweat, tried to put an intravenous line into Polly's tiny little arm. Eventually she was moved to Palma Hospital, travelling with Helena in an ambulance.

We followed in the car and when we got to the hospital there was Polly, pink and alive, yelling and screaming and very much back to full health. The doctor, with a grim face, told us that if we had left it another 20 seconds, she would have been dead. He said that what had saved her was the fact that she had not breathed in any water because, as she was so young, she hadn't struggled. She had swallowed water but he said if she had breathed it in, it would have wrecked her lungs and that would have killed her.

We were so relieved to get her back that the rest of the holiday passed with a strange veneer of normality. At the end of the holiday, she was even presented with a certificate for winning the 'hold your breath' competition.

But it was when I got home that the nightmares, the worry, the doubt, the guilt and the fear began to eat me up inside. I kept thinking we could have returned home with this tiny little box with my daughter in it. It absolutely side-swiped me, but in true fashion I bottled up all these corrosive emotions. I have never spoken publicly before about this incident, but looking back now I know it has had a significant effect on me.

Consumed by the bouts of guilt and angst, I lost all interest in rugby and it was a contributing factor in losing my place in the England side. During matches, little flashes would come into my head and I would lose my concentration. In my head, just for a moment, I was holding my dead daughter in my arms, a recurring nightmare that stayed with me for years. I should have spoken to someone about the impact it had on me, but I never saw anyone. I just did what I've done with everything else. I put my feelings in a box and closed the lid.

There will be people who wonder what I was worrying about. I know I am an extremely lucky man. Polly recently turned 28 and she is a fantastic daughter and person. So is Rosy and my third daughter, Lucy. But even now I will occasionally wake up with a night terror about the incident.

I am man enough now to say what happened that morning scared the shit out of me.

The psychological impact coincided with my inability to cope with the transition to professionalism. The 1995 World Cup had proved to be a watershed moment for the game. The southern-hemisphere teams had been driving for the game to become fully professional and major decisions were being made in shambolically amateur environments. Just two months after Joel Stransky had landed his drop goal at Ellis Park in Johannesburg to defeat New Zealand 15-12 in extra time of the World Cup final, Vernon Pugh, the chairman of the International Rugby Board, announced on 26 August that the sport was 'open to professionalism', the most seismic shift in rugby since it had split into two codes a century earlier.

The decision seemed to catch the home unions by surprise. Or perhaps they were still in denial. While the three major southern-hemisphere unions, New Zealand, Australia and South Africa, were immediately able to contract their leading players, having signed a $555m television deal with Rupert Murdoch's News Corporation, the RFU announced a moratorium on payments.

As Twickenham dithered, the Premiership clubs moved swiftly to sign up all the players, which proved to be another landmark moment for the English game, the impact of which is still being felt today. I have still got in a box somewhere in my attic a contract for the 'World League' that was proposed in 1996. We were told to sign it and hand it in to a solicitor.

Yet there was no way I was going to sign anything which would end up in a safe somewhere else. I would only sign it when I knew what was happening. I just didn't trust anyone. We had a meeting at the Holiday Inn at Crick service station near Northampton to discuss what our futures would be. I was told that, for £75,000 or £150,000, we could end up playing in the North America league. The first reaction was amazement. But it was then followed by a dose of realisation. *Really?* It would have been great for the first month, but I was sure that very quickly we would all be left wondering what on earth had we done. It was a mad, mad time.

While the RFU had insisted on a moratorium on payments, we all signed up for our clubs anyway. That is where many believe the RFU made a huge mistake. They could have signed up the top 45 players in the country, there and then. Many have since argued that this would have put in place the foundations for England to dominate on the world stage. But, having experienced the transition, I think it would have been the death of English rugby. There is certainly no way we would have won the World Cup in 2003 because the RFU would not have had a clue how to run the professional game or professional clubs when the game opened up. And in that first year there wasn't much money around. It wasn't until Sir John Hall took over Newcastle and started splashing the cash that it began to take off.

I didn't have an agent then. Dick Best came to the house to talk to me about potentially joining Harlequins and I remember Phil de Glanville asked if I would be interested in going to Bath. But they were just tentative enquiries. When I retired, Dick came up to me and said: 'You were the best signing I never made!' I ended up going to see Keith Barwell in his office at the Saints. He said: 'This is what we can offer', and I just said: 'Great.' That was it. I was a professional rugby player. The contract was worth significantly more than I was getting with the police, but it wasn't life changing. When the Five Nations got underway later that season, we started to receive the odd cheque for playing for England via the Rugby Players' Association, but it was pennies in comparison with what the players get nowadays.

The biggest impact of the opening-up of the game for me was that I had to resign from my beloved day job with Bedfordshire Police in November that year. Guys like Tim Rodber were still able to remain in the army, but police regulations would not allow me to have two jobs. It absolutely derailed me. I found the training as a professional rugby player boring and missed the kudos and comradeship of being in the police. I had loved being able to play rugby one day and then completely forget about it and submerge myself in police work. Playing for the Met also represented some of the happiest times I experienced in rugby. Suddenly I was sitting at home thinking: *What I am going to do?*

I felt like I had completely lost my identity. The training was all over the place. We were trying to introduce professional elements into what was still effectively an amateur sport. There was no real thought about how it would work. No one knew what to do as a professional. The answer seemed to be train more, train harder, train every day – train *three* times a day. People kept telling me I was too skinny and had to get bigger. I should have gone to an established professional sports coach and asked, 'How can I get better?'

Instead, it was simply a case of eating more, training more and lifting heavier weights, which I did without any control. As a consequence, I suffered injury after injury after injury. I needed to identify my strengths and weaknesses. One of my strengths was I could move around the pitch pretty fast and I could get up in the air quickly, the reason being that despite being 6ft 10ins, I weighed only around 18st. My frame was similar to that of Dodie Weir, the Scotland and Lions lock. I should have persisted with training that suited my frame, but instead the emphasis turned to bulking up. That meant eating loads of food, which was great fun, and going to the gym.

The result was that I was strong but I couldn't play rugby. I reached 20st and then started picking up successive injuries. It was not a good weight for me and my body was not ready for that. I was still carrying my neck injury and needed a far more scientific approach than just going to the gym. It didn't do me any favours. I was doing it the wrong way and it was actually counterproductive.

An insecure streak left me looking at the new breed of second rows coming through, like Garath Archer, Simon Shaw and Danny Grewcock, and thinking that I had to be like them. With more confidence and advice, I should have stayed the same size and weight. If it was good enough to get me in the England team, then fine. But all I could think about was getting bigger.

Northampton's relegation to the second division did not help. When I was a player on the rise, their season in the second tier had allowed me to develop my game away from the spotlight. But now I needed the spotlight to maintain the levels I had reached. With Northampton romping to high-scoring victories every week, it was far too comfortable an environment for me at the very point in my career when I needed to be stretched more than ever. The struggle for me was that others seemed to be thriving in the new professional era.

I remember reading an article on Tony Underwood being

one of the first professional rugby players. But I was the first person to give up a job – to properly give up a job – to become a professional rugby player and I missed it. I know it must sound strange as you imagine being paid to play rugby must be the dream job. But I found it boring as hell. I missed my mates and I missed knowing exactly what I needed to do. I also missed how, when you go to the police station, they don't really care if you play rugby. They're only interested in whether you can do the job. I was comfortable in my routine when combining training with my day job. Of course, you got a few questions about playing for England or the Lions or my club but, ultimately, you were a police officer for this eight-hour shift and I missed that.

I worked with some brilliant police officers who were also incredible characters and human beings – people who, without overdoing it, would give their life, and I would for them, if something really kicked off. And we had some fairly hairy moments at times. It also gave you a sense of purpose. Being a police officer was so much more important than being a rugby player, even if I was playing for England.

Turning professional meant that I lost all that. I was still with great individuals in the changing room, but now we were rugby players and that was it. Our identities had been blurred. I used to love looking around at my team-mates and seeing fellow police officers, farmers, lawyers, doctors, soldiers, students and businessmen. Suddenly, all the colour was gone, replaced with one broad brushstroke of grey. For some, going professional was the best thing that could have happened to the game, while others walked away from the elite game, preferring to concentrate on their careers. I was left in some sort of motivation-sapping rugby purgatory.

The relationship with the game changed too. Being dropped when you were an amateur was painful, but it didn't mean you could lose your job. I never played a game thinking that my family's future depended on it. I just played because I loved the game and loved being involved with everything that went on around it.

In the amateur days, a small grassroots club might open a new clubhouse by inviting the England team to play against their first XV. Everyone would turn up, get a couple of hundred quid to cover their travel expenses and some free pints of beer. Can you imagine that now? Yet that was the world the England team were in back then: shit kit, questionable sponsorship deals, a Twickenham stadium where they would cut the lines into the grass because it was so long, and holding fitness sessions in the old Rose Room. It was just insane. But I also loved every second of it.

Now the brave new world of being professional, coupled with the mental struggles I was experiencing after almost losing Polly, left me unmotivated and at a loss. The memories of the high-octane experience of the World Cup in South Africa were now distant. I had lost my mojo. And I would never get it back. But at least, thank God, I still had Polly.

15

Take That, Bayfs

The thirteenth of February 1996 is a day that will be for ever etched in history. It was the day that the legendary boy band Take That announced to the world that they were breaking up, sparking an outpouring of grief from their fans across the globe. It was also, of course, the day that I was dropped from the England team.

Peter Jackson, the rugby correspondent of the *Daily Mail* at the time, reported my reaction, which would later be recorded as the paper's sports quote of the year.

'Being dropped by England and Take That splitting up on the same day is more than any man can take,' I told Jacko, with a wry smile.

And while Take That would go on to reunite in various guises, as I packed up my stuff, got into the car to return home from the England camp in Marlow and travelled back up the M40, I knew that I was most likely going 'Back for Good'. I had returned from the World Cup feeling at the peak of my game. By the end of the year, I was named in some pundits' world XVs and thought I had played pretty well in the autumn games – a defeat by South Africa and victory over Western Samoa at Twickenham. But the struggles I had been dealing with on and off the pitch were finally starting to catch up with me.

I was picked for the opening Five Nations match against France at the Parc des Princes and it was then that I realised how key the relationship between the hooker and line-out jumper is. Brian Moore had retired, and Mark Regan had succeeded him. I would never diss Mark Regan; I let other people do that. But I had played pretty much every England and Lions game with Mooro at hooker. Suddenly there was a new guy and the timing wasn't quite there. We were not quite on song.

A late dropped goal by Thomas Castaignède condemned us to a 15-12 defeat, perhaps a consequence of the Entente Cordiale that had broken out following our session together at the end of the World Cup. Wales were up next at Twickenham and although we won 21-15, once again I lost two or three line-outs and just wasn't making any impact on the game. With a weekend off, we assembled in Marlow for a training camp to prepare for the Scotland game.

Want to know what it's like to be dropped by England? Well, it goes something like this. We were assembled in the changing room, waiting for Jack Rowell to announce the side to travel to Murrayfield, where, just four years earlier, I had made my Five Nations debut.

That felt like a lifetime ago. Jerry Guscott turned to me. 'Ah, Bayfs, this will definitely be your last England training session,' he said. 'You're definitely out of the team.' He was joking. At least, I *think* he was joking. But then, seconds later, Rowell read out the team. I wasn't in it. The young tyro Garath Archer was starting with Martin Johnson. I was out of the squad.

'Fuck! I am so sorry mate,' said Guscott. 'I didn't know.'

'Yes, you did, you bastard!'

But he didn't know. It had just been banter, the banter that I had loved when I had been at the heart of this England squad.

Just to compound my humiliation, Jack came over to me. Except this time, there was no mention of me still being in their long-term plans.

'Bayfs, Garath is stuck in traffic. Do you think you could run with the first team until he arrives?' he asked. *Jack, you are really taking the piss now.*

But of course I did it. And when Archer arrived, I said: 'I was just keeping the place warm for you mate. Good luck.'

Still reeling from the body blow of my being dropped, there was more humiliation to come. England beat Scotland at Murrayfield and the next home game at Twickenham was against Ireland, where victory would ensure that Rowell's side (no longer my England) would win the championship for the fourth time in six years.

The twist in the tale was that Allen Clarke, my new best mate at the Saints, had been picked for Ireland, replacing Terry Kingston at hooker. And, for the first time in a long time, I found myself going to the match as a fan. I suspect most England players who have just been dropped would be in the same bizarre situation: wanting England to win, but for the player who's replaced them to have an absolute shocker (sorry, Garath). I was surrounded by England supporters in the stand, all of whom were absolutely pissed and took it upon themselves to try to cheer me up.

I don't think Archer, who was up against a young Jeremy Davidson, the Ulster lock who would go on to become the players' player of the series on the Lions tour of South Africa the following year, won a ball all afternoon. England still won comfortably, and I could at least take some solace from the fact that I had played in two games of another championship-winning campaign.

But, as if I was being punished for my negative thoughts about Archer, I ended up missing the last train back to Bedford after a night on the town with some of my mates and found myself sitting at King's Cross station like a vagrant, waiting for the trains to start up again about 4.30 a.m. on Sunday morning. When the first one arrived, just as I stepped onto it, a pigeon dumped its load all over me. A bloke on the platform looked across at me. 'That just about sums up your weekend, Martin.' *Thanks, mate.* But he was right.

What angers me most now was my reaction to being dropped. In 1994, it ignited an absolute bonfire inside me. But two years later, I almost felt a sense of relief. I just didn't feel up for it any more. I guess I was feeling a little bit sorry for myself, but that mental weakness had been revealed again. It was a horrible feeling because I knew I was done. I was tired, mentally tired, and my focus and application had gone.

It didn't help that Saints were playing in the second division and it was hard to get up for fixtures against the likes of Blackheath or Wakefield. Even the Saracens boys found that difficult when they were playing in the Championship and then struggled with England in the Six Nations and Lions in 2021.

But a good player would rise above it, instead of using it as an excuse. Rodders didn't lose his place, and Matt Dawson and Paul Grayson made their way into the England team from the same position. Instead, I felt tired. I don't know what was wrong with me, but my body wasn't working as it should have. I have subsequently found that I have a strange condition called peripheral neuropathy, which I may have unknowingly been suffering from back then. It's effectively poor nerve conduction into my legs and it means I can't put any strength or size into them.

When I was growing up, I could walk over stony gravel or baking-hot sand without any sensation, so I have probably had it all my life and it just deteriorated.

I cannot be certain, but I found within a very short period of time that what I used to find easy became increasingly more difficult. Physically, it was harder to get fit and to train effectively. My diet probably didn't help, nor would doing the wrong sort of training.

If I had sorted out some expertise, I might have been able to find some solutions, but instead I found myself going to England training sessions and struggling to hang on in, even though I was running and training. *Sweet Jesus.* I was only in my late twenties, but was starting to feel old. I didn't know what was going on.

My mindset would get worse. That summer, a mate of mine sent me an article from one of the local newspapers in Bedford after Will Carling gave a speech to open a car showroom. In the question-and-answer session, my mate Dave Twigden asked Will if he thought I would ever play for England again: 'No, he won't. He'll never play for England again.'

I remember reading that and thinking, *Fucking hell, Will!*

But he knew what he was talking about. And inside I knew he was probably right.

Later in the year, the players involved in the Five Nations Championship-winning squad were presented with a book written by the journalist Frank Keating to chart our year together and tell the behind-the-scenes story about our triumph. As I was driving up the M40, in a fit of petulance, I flung it out the window. *That'll show them*, I thought. The silly thing is, I wish I'd kept it now. It's probably still there, in a grass verge somewhere, a rotting relic of my England career that had burned brightly but was extinguished far too quickly.

So too did my club career. When I started at Northampton Saints, I wanted to be like our tighthead Gary Pearce. He was by far the best tighthead in England, but for some reason was not getting selected for the national squad by then. (Gary won 36 caps, making his last Five Nations appearance in 1987. His last selection was on the bench for the 1991 World Cup final.)

If my international days looked over, I at least wanted to get myself to a level where I could then play for the Saints, week in, week out. In my head – almost like Dan Cole, the Leicester prop, has experienced now he's out of the England squad – I always wanted that period of time, that sense of playing for your club and not worrying if there's an England selector in the stands, the knowledge that when the season ends, there's no summer tour to consider. Instead I would be going on holiday with my family. And when the season starts up again, I'd be playing, like Gary Pearce did at Saints, 30 games for my club.

I would have loved to have said to Saints, *I've had four or five years with England, I'm done now, I'm yours. It's payback time.*

We were about to play in a new stadium and a fresh European competition was starting up.

But I never got the chance. I would never play for England again. And within two years, my playing career would be over.

16

Falling Down

Somewhere in a drawer in my garage is a bag containing the boots, mud and all, that I wore for my last-ever rugby session. It was a nondescript training session in February 1998 where I was attempting to prove my fitness to play for the Wanderers, Northampton's second team.

But instead of proving my fitness, it was during that session that I suffered the neck injury that ended my playing career. After the session, I took my boots off, put them into the bag without even cleaning the Franklin's Gardens mud off them, and stuffed them in the drawer. There they have remained ever since.

I haven't looked at them in years but I can still remember the make and style: Nike Tiempo. I'm sure the laces are now rigid and who knows what state the boots themselves are in. The only other thing in the bag is the peg I used to hang my clothes on. When they redeveloped the stadium, a fan cut the peg off the wall and sent it to me. He told me he knew it was my peg because he used to work in the stadium and knew that

I always changed in a particular corner. It was a nice touch.

I don't know why I've kept the boots because I'm not the type for memorabilia. I've got three shirts from my playing career up on the wall in a study that my wife has now kicked me out of. I don't know what I'll do with the boots, but I don't think I'll ever clean them. I'm sure my kids will be delighted to be left with them when my time is up. No one really knows I've got them. Occasionally my wife will say to me that we need to sort the garage out, but I always find an excuse.

Perhaps they serve as a reminder to me of what could have been, an object frozen in time, a nagging remnant of a career I am proud of but deep down would now admit that I should have made more of, particularly in my final year. For the truth is that opportunity did knock for me again in 1997, even if my form and resilience were not what they should have been. I could even have made another Lions tour, and what a send-off that trip to South Africa would have been, if only I had sorted my head out and knuckled down.

I had been troubled by injuries throughout the 1996–97 season, but I was still selected for England's summer tour of Argentina and Australia. Jack Rowell had come to watch me play in a game against Newcastle and I delivered a decent performance. It was during an all-too-rare run of games when I avoided injury.

By now I was playing a different game. I had turned to guys like Tim Rodber in an attempt to make my game more physical and aggressive. I would come off the training pitch unable to lift my arms. 'Shit, you do that every game?' I asked Rodders. 'That's insane. Can't I just run and jump?'

I was aching after every game, but felt I was evolving. I was invited to the NEC in Birmingham for an initial Lions meeting around Easter time to get things like measurements done. I drove up with Matt Dawson, Tim Rodber and Paul Grayson. At that point something should have been ringing in my head to say: 'Bayfs, you're not far off. You're in the conversation for the Lions and England again.' Yet I lacked the focus.

The run of form was far too late for me to be considered for selection for the original Lions squad, but it was still enough to convince Jack I was worth the risk for the England tour. Then, one fateful afternoon towards the end of the season, I was doing hill runs in a local park when I pulled my calf. It was in pretty bad shape. I saw Phil Pask, our physio, but didn't stick to the rehabilitation plan.

I guess I just thought it would be all right if I eased off a bit. Of course, it wasn't. The touring party would leave without me. Years later, I saw another physio about something else. 'Jesus, there's a big old chunk of scar tissue in your calf,' he said. And I just sighed. It's a little reminder of my idleness and the fact that I was never inquisitive or resilient enough.

Throughout my career, I had reached peaks but I wasn't able to maintain them in a way that Martin Johnson could. I found it difficult because I just got sidetracked, mentally, emotionally; I lost my focus and drifted away. I suppose it might suggest I didn't have enough of a selfish streak to retain that level of commitment outside of the hot-house environment. I played my best rugby when it was just me, away from my family and friends, on tour or on a Lions series or at a World Cup. But when I had to try to fit in family life and work, I became distracted – not because I thought I'd made it, but because of my character.

There was also the stark reality that the second rows who

were coming through were better than me. I initially lost my place to Garath Archer, who was a very good second row, but in his slipstream came Simon Shaw, Danny Grewcock and Ben Kay, who all were phenomenal players. I wouldn't have been able to hold those three off for very long, not very long at all. Physically, Shawsie was unbelievable. And Danny Grewcock. You talk about me not being a fighter, well, that's all Danny wanted to do. And Ben Kay has a brilliant rugby brain. Working with him at BT Sport showed why Clive Woodward chose him for the 2003 World Cup team ahead of Danny and Simon; his grey matter is working all the time. Yet still I know I could probably have eked out a few more games for England.

Until I came to write this book, I had blanked out those final months of my career. I had come to accept the reasons for being dropped by England and everything falling apart before it. But now, with the benefit of hindsight, I feel like such an idiot for not grasping that chance to get back into the England team when it was still there. I let myself down and it's hard to accept.

I should have been able to sort myself out. I had been selected for England again. All I needed to do was just get fit again. It's the most basic thing, isn't it? Getting fit. That was it. I don't know all the imponderables, but what I do know is that in the summer of 1997, allowing myself to wallow in self-pity and laziness was probably not the right thing to do. *What an idiot.*

Instead, Northampton asked me to go on tour with the youth team to the United States. There were some great players on that trip, including Steve Thompson and Ben Cohen, who just six years later would be winning a World Cup with

England, and Ali Hepher. And some of the antics on that trip made me think the game was in safe hands. You can't drink in American bars until you're 21, so at least two-thirds of the touring party were not allowed out. Or so we thought. One night the coaches went for a drink and some guy recognised our kit. 'Hey, there are a lot of your friends in the bar next door.'

It was a fetish bar. As we walked in, we could see one of the lads being whipped behind the bar. There was a hen party there too and the girl had a dress with sweets on and a sign saying 'suck for a buck'. If you paid her a buck, you got to suck the sweet off. I gave the lady $50 and it was like a feeding frenzy.

Then another lad came into the bar beaming. 'I just went into a shop next door and they were cleaning the floor and I slipped and fell. I was taken to one side by the owner, made to sign a form and given $1,500 as long as I didn't sue them. Happy days!' Next thing they were all heading to the shop, flinging themselves to the floor, but there was now a warning sign up and the owner was telling them all to get out.

The tour was great fun and it gave me an insight into coaching. I wondered whether it was something I should move into at the end of my career, but I concluded that I was just not analytical enough to be a full-time coach.

Then, the hammer blow came, underscoring everything I had got wrong that year. A call came in from Jack Rowell.

'Bayfs, are you fit?' asked Jack. 'The Lions have been in touch. They want you to go out to South Africa because Doddy Weir is injured.'

'Jack, I am currently in America, two stone overweight with a torn calf.'

'Oh, okay then. We'll have to send them Olly Redman

instead.'

So not only had Olly taken my place on the England tour, he was now going on a Lions tour. And he did a great job, captaining the midweek side as the Lions won a famous 2-1 series victory. Yet it could have been me, if only I had been more dedicated. What a career swansong that would have been.

I had one final push when I got back from the US. Clive Woodward took over from Jack and I was called to a meeting at Loughborough for all potential England squad members. Back in the enlarged squad, there was still a glimmer of hope. I can remember we were due to play against Newcastle early in the new season. I was going to be up against my new rival, Garath Archer.

I read an interview with Rob Andrew, who was now director of rugby at Newcastle. Rob said he was interested to see how I was going to get on because he had heard I had put on more than a stone. I read it and thought that Rob probably was genuinely interested because he had been my fly-half for pretty much every game with England and the Lions, apart from a few when Barnesy was in there. But the game never took place. We woke up to the tragic news that Princess Diana had died and the game was postponed. When we eventually did play the rearranged fixture, I was injured. Of course I was.

England lost 25-8 to New Zealand at Old Trafford that autumn, but I wasn't involved again. I was briefly heartened by a surprise phone call from Wade.

'Hey, Bayfs, keep at it lad, you're better than those guys.'

It was a lovely touch from the big man, my hero and old

second-row partner. It meant so much coming from him. But it is remarkable how quickly people move on.

And the end, when it came, came quickly, and was mired with controversy. After the game had turned professional, we had been inundated with representatives from insurance companies. A lot of them were cowboys, but one came to give us a presentation at the Saints. Geech, who was our director of rugby at the club, said we should listen to them as they were a reputable company.

During the presentation, the representative said they would cover any previous injuries. At which point Ian Hunter and I looked at each other and said: 'This sounds promising!' It sounded too good to be true so I asked for more information.

'What do you mean by that?' I asked.

'Well, if the doctor passes you fit to play in a game, then you're covered.'

That was good enough for me. I signed up there and then and wrote them a cheque for the premium. The problem was that I got injured before the cheque had even cleared. I had signed the form on the Friday and then injured my neck in training on the following Tuesday when Gary Pagel landed on me in a contact session.

The insurance company argued the toss, insisting that it was a pre-existing injury. When I told them at the presentation we had been told that we would be covered if we were deemed fit to play by the doctor, they also denied that. Thankfully all the players signed statements to say that they had been in the meeting and this is what had been said, but the company continued to argue.

The RPA, the players' association, was still in its infancy then, but one of the benefits of membership was £25,000 legal insurance cover. My solicitor was the brother of the former England team doctor, Terry Crystal (one of the Crystal brothers got the brains, the other was Terry). His advice was to push it all the way without telling them about our legal cover.

The insurance company kept coming back, warning us that we did not want to go to court because it would cost us a lot of money. But we held our nerve until the last minute and then told them we would be happy to go to court and revealed the size of our cover.

It did the trick. The next day I got a phone call asking if I would come to their office in Bristol to negotiate. I ended up being offered 40 per cent of what I was covered for and my solicitor told me to take it. It was a small triumph but it did nothing to ease the pain of my career coming to a premature end.

I had undergone an operation to try to fix the damage to my neck but, although it was successful, by May the medical advice left me with no option but to retire. I had played just five games for the Saints all season.

'Despite having had a successful operation, there is danger that a further injury to my neck could be more serious,' I said at the time. 'I felt that it would be too great a risk to my health if I were to continue playing.'

I had been Northampton's first full-time professional. Now I was the club's first professional retiree. By then, I had already stuffed my beloved boots in that bag in my garage. And I did so filled only with bitterness and despair. My love affair with the game seemed well and truly over.

17

Broon Frae Troon

What on earth was I going to do with myself now? I was just 31 years old when I was forced to retire and found myself in a pretty dark place, hanging around Northampton with little to do and with the weight gain of my final playing year showing no signs of abating.

I started working with another former Saint, Brett Taylor, to set up Northampton's academy. Brett, a former teacher and army man, was brilliant and really switched-on. While working with him, I started thinking: *I actually could become a coach*. The problem was that I was so angry with the world because I couldn't play any more. I was overwhelmed with frustration watching my mates getting ready for the next game when I couldn't play. I have no doubt that, given the bitterness within me, I wasn't a very nice person to be around at the time.

Looking back, what I should have done was go to another club, go somewhere else, reinvent myself and start from scratch in a different environment. Instead, I tried to make it work at Saints. I started coaching the youth teams in the academy, the Under-16s and Under-18s. It was a mistake from the outset.

I went in thinking that I was 'Billy Big Bollocks'. I was a former England and Lions player coaching a bunch of kids. But I quickly discovered that being a coach is something entirely different and requires a very different skill set. I found myself surrounded by well-meaning volunteers or former players, good guys who had years of coaching experience behind them. They didn't have any of the international experience I had; some of them didn't even have first-hand playing experience. But they were much better coaches than I was because it was what they wanted to do.

My approach, like many other former players who went straight into coaching after the game turned professional, was to tell the players to do what I had done, because it had worked for me and it was all that I knew. Zinzan Brooke, the former New Zealand No. 8, no doubt did something similar at Harlequins, where he had taken charge, going through the entire All Blacks playbook until it was done. And when it was done, he had nothing left to give.

Years later, the Saints hooker Steve Thompson reminded me of my first appraisal with him. 'I was expecting you to say that I had done okay,' said Steve. 'But you told me that if I played like that again, I would never play for the Saints again, never mind for England. You said that I needed to sort my life out!'

Andy Newman, who went on to win the Heineken Cup with Saints in 2000 before going on to play for the Ospreys and Glasgow, also reminded me of my halcyon days of coaching. I think I told him something along the lines of: 'If you spend as much time in the gym as you do the pub, you'll be a great player!' Andy could have played for Wales in the second row but he was one of those hugely talented players who would rather have a pint in his hand than a dumbbell. I had a point. But when I bumped into him a few years ago, he told me a few home truths.

'Bayfs, you were my hero at Saints but when you coached me, I just didn't get from you what I needed,' he said. I could understand his frustration. It was mine too.

'Yeah, I just wasn't in the right place to do it,' I told him. 'I let you down.'

I am happy to admit that now.

The Saints had been really kind to me and offered me an opportunity to embark on a new coaching career, but I wasn't cut out for it. When I get things right is when I get under the skin of something, right to the heart of it. I managed that fleetingly during my playing career when I only had rugby to focus on and I was living and breathing it. My foray into coaching was another example of experiencing mental walkabout when I was not committed to something. My coaching career was over before it had even begun.

Thankfully, the club then offered me another opportunity – to work on the corporate and fundraising side of things as they looked to develop Franklin's Gardens. But once again, almost immediately, after a couple of presentations I knew it wasn't something I was cut out for.

I knew it was time to start looking elsewhere. The job at least gave me a little bit of money to ease the pain when I stopped playing, but with little interest in the day job at Saints, I began to do some public speaking to bring in some extra income. Not for the first time in my career, it would lead to a sliding doors moment. And one that would rekindle my love for rugby in the most extraordinary of circumstances.

My public-speaking journey had begun many years earlier. It was while I was recovering from the neck injury that I had sustained on the Lions tour in 1993 that I got my first gig, when I was unable to play against New Zealand at Twickenham. I was sorting out one of the hospitality guys with tickets and he asked me to do a short question-and-answer session in one of the marquees after the game. It went well and my name started to get around the booking agency circuit. Requests started to come to do other events at junior rugby clubs and sportsman's dinners. But what was I going to say? Would people really be interested in anything I had to say?

The lightbulb moment came one long afternoon at Liverpool Airport while I was waiting to fly to the Isle of Man for a sporting club event. The comedian I was working with sat with me and, during the five-hour wait, we started telling stories and I shared some of the madcap moments of my rugby career.

'Why don't you use those in your speech?' he asked.

'No one will be interested.'

'Of course they will.'

Those hours together in that fog-bound airport produced the structure and backbone of a speech that I still use to this day for after-dinner events. With the raw material, I was confident that I could become a storyteller like my father. I may have fallen out of love with rugby, but the game was quickly helping me back on my feet.

I started working with a guy called Paul Terry, whose

company was called Events International, and started doing speeches and Q&As after matches. Paul would become like a member of my extended family. He's known my kids since they were small children, and Polly, when she turned 18, started working for him in his hospitality facility. It became an important network of support for me when I was going through tough times, such as when I was dropped by England and when I was going through my divorce from Helena. When I went to Twickenham or abroad with them, I knew I would have a great time.

Even now, when I go back to Twickenham, I look at the old storage facility at the back of the East Stand, where they would set up their marquees, and get an incredible feeling of affection. They were great days. All the hospitality is in-house in the stadium now and it's pristine and shiny, but in those days there was a delightful rawness to it. You would have a tent full of 800 people – chief executives of blue-chip companies wearing rugby jerseys, singing songs, spilling beer down their front and staggering home. Wonderful.

But the biggest influence and impact came from Gordon Brown. No, not the former prime minister but Gordon 'Broon Frae Troon', the late former Scotland and Lions lock forward. He would become integral to my story. Broonie was a force of nature, a great raconteur. He was also a very generous man and became my champion on the after-dinner circuit.

It was after one event in Leamington Spa that we did together that he gave me a golden piece of advice. My speech had gone fine. I had some little cue cards with me with little instructions on them – 'do this' and arrows to the next story and the next joke. It did the job but was all very formulaic.

Then Broonie got up and gave a whirlwind performance. He was telling jokes, sharing stories, forgetting punchlines, repeating jokes – but no one cared because it was so hilarious, thanks to the enthusiasm and the energy he put in.

'Mate, that was brilliant,' I told him afterwards.

'Bayfs, you'll be a really good after-dinner speaker, but what you have to do is lose the notes. It's all in the head. Be natural and react to the audience. Just let yourself go.' And so I did. It was a great piece of advice.

He would have a much bigger impact on my post-playing career than I could ever have imagined. One morning in early 2000 my phone rang. It was a speaking agency. Gordon had been due to speak at an event in London but had fallen ill. Could I stand in for him? I jumped on the train. I couldn't make the lunch in time, but was able to make it for the speeches.

Little did I know that in the audience that afternoon was an executive from Warner Brothers. My speech had gone down well and the following morning I received a phone call that would turn my world around. It was an invitation to try out for a role in a new film they were about to start production on. I was convinced it was a wind-up; it had to be one of the Saints boys. Eventually he persuaded me that it was genuine and two weeks later I drove down to Leavesden film studios to do a screen test, which involved walking around on decorators' stilts for most of the afternoon.

My stumbling around somehow impressed the right people and a few days later I was offered the job of being the stunt double of Robbie Coltrane's character Hagrid in a new film called *Harry Potter and the Philosopher's Stone*. The contract would be far from life-changing, but the opportunity was.

Tragically, I would later find out that Gordon's illness was much more serious than I had thought. He had been diagnosed with cancer and he died not long afterwards. I was interviewed on BBC Radio 2 a couple of years ago and was asked if there was anyone I would like to thank for my career. I told the story about Broonie and, unbeknownst to me, his daughter was listening to the show. Afterwards she got in touch to say thank you for what I had said about her dad. It was the least I could have done.

18

A Pain in Robbie Coltrane's Arse

I'll never forget the look on Keith Barwell's face when I told him that I was going to be a movie star. The Northampton Saints owner had been the heartbeat of rejuvenating the East Midlands club and was a great supporter of the game, and he looked at me like I was talking out of my arse. Little did he know that my first starring role was in fact to play the *arse* of Robbie Coltrane. Well, his body double, if we're being technical.

Barwell thought I was mad. He has this silver-headed riding crop and he slammed it on his desk. 'What are you thinking of?' he said. 'You want to be a movie star? Come on, Bayfs.'

Inside, I thought I was being mad too. It would have been so much easier to stay in the corporate job that I was doing with the Saints. I was earning around £20,000 a year and had a degree of security at the club. I wasn't a man known for taking risks, but even with all the turmoil of finding my feet in the early days of my retirement, there was something inside me urging me to go for it. It was time to roll the dice.

The gamble paid off. To those who have not played at an elite level, this feeling may be hard to explain, but working on the set of the *Harry Potter* films would be the closest thing that I experienced to a rugby environment, and it gave me the opportunity to move on with my life. The whole experience put a smile back on my face and the old me kicked in. I loved the excitement and tuned into the team ethic of the production. I felt alive again.

A guy called Nick Dudman was head of special effects on the film and he would effectively become my boss for the next ten years. Greg Powell was the stunt coordinator and had also worked on the James Bond films. His uncle, 'Dinny' Powell, was one of the charioteers in the Hollywood classic *Ben Hur*. I was blown away by working with professionals with such a remarkable film heritage.

My foot was through the door, but what I didn't realise is that I was on a two-week grace period. If they didn't like me, I could have been travelling back up the M1 with my cap in hand to see Keith to get my old job back. The first big hurdle was another screen test, this time alongside Robbie Coltrane. Robbie is around 6ft and Hagrid had to be 7ft 6ins tall.

Nick had originally been told that they were going to have to digitally put Robbie into every shot and it was going to be one of the most expensive parts of the whole movie. Nick's idea was that shots of Hagrid's back – and those of when he was with the kids, who were only halfway up his body – could be filmed using a double. That's where I came in.

The special-effects team calculated that to make the costume work, they needed someone who could get to 7ft 6ins on stilts. But they also required the right shape and measurements for the elbows and knees to match where the elbows and knees were on the costume.

Apparently, proportionately I was perfect for it. They constructed a big flexible body suit and what was called a 'dead head' – a mixture of fibreglass and silicone to look like Hagrid's head. But, intriguingly, it was all done in secret. Chris Columbus, the director, said he didn't want to see me until the costume was ready. 'He doesn't want to see what you can do,' I was told. 'He just wants to see you and Robbie walking together in costume and then he'll know straight away if this works.' No pressure.

I was dressed behind a big screen and they put Robbie in full costume, including the beard, so that we could walk out together. There's a clip of the moment on YouTube when the two Hagrids were finally unveiled for the first time as Robbie and I held hands and stepped out. The reaction was a mixture of gasps and laughs as Robbie and I walked onto set in full costume. 'That's it,' said Chris. 'It's brilliant, it works.' And that was it. I had a job. I signed a contract, although it was nothing special and involved no royalties.

I may have rediscovered my sense of worth, but at the start I made a lot of mistakes. I didn't know any of the terminology and didn't know what was going on. And I got used to hearing the dreaded word 'cut' in the early days of production. However good the suit looked, it would only work if I got the performance right.

I felt as if I was back in Fiji, trying to make my way in an England squad that barely knew who I was, trying too hard to prove to everyone that I could do it. How could I add value when I was feeling far from my comfort zone?

And there was that feeling again. *What am I doing here?*

It was the meeting with Richard Harris that gave me the sense of value and esteem that I needed to settle into my new role. For Harris, who was playing Albus Dumbledore and being treated like the Hollywood royalty he was, to recognise me from my rugby career gave me a status on the set that I would never have had without it.

There I was, on a film set with Richard Harris, about to get into a giant fat suit, and the reason I was there was the game of rugby. It's just another crazy place that I've found myself in because of rugby. And at least if the crew knew that Richard knew me, I must be okay.

Yet to heap the pressure on my now very broad shoulders, they wanted to use me on the very first day of filming at a railway station. Up on the hill above us was a row of paparazzi photographers, so I was given this huge umbrella to ensure that my identity remained a secret. One of the first things I was asked to do was to walk along the platform and peer into the windows of the train that was packed with children, just to see how they would react to seeing this giant. When they looked up at me wide-eyed and gasping, it was the natural reaction that Chris wanted.

The final shot of Hagrid waving goodbye to the train as it departs the station in *Harry Potter and the Philosopher's Stone* is me. The challenge was to be able to replicate Robbie's movements, but over time I came to be able to mimic him and that enabled them to use me more often.

To that end, I also had a little bit of unintended medical

assistance. One of the early shots took place on a Sunday at Leadenhall Market in London, which was filmed out of sequence because one of the children had fallen ill. As I hadn't expected to be needed that weekend, the previous day I had gone to have a vasectomy and when I got home, I received a call from the studio.

'Martin, we need you to do some filming tomorrow. Is that okay?'

'Okay ... Of course, of course,' I lied, already feeling extremely tender down below. I didn't tell a soul how I was feeling and turned up at Leadenhall the following morning. The problem was that my costume included a foam yoke, like a bicycle saddle that came up between my legs and then everything else was clipped onto that like a Sumo wrestler's belt. So, on that very first day of filming, I was walking through Leadenhall Market and Chris the director shouted over, 'Martin, you've absolutely nailed Robbie Coltrane's walk!'

I was walking so gingerly because of the operation. I then had to remember how I walked. *Walk as though your balls are the size of oranges!* After the filming, I let on how I was feeling.

'Why did you not tell us?'

'Because I thought you wouldn't let me do it.'

How very method of me. In fact, as I became more experienced in the role, my imagination would get the better of me and I would totally immerse myself in Hagrid's character, even though I was just his double.

I even managed to blag myself a speaking part (of sorts). Early in the filming, I was in a scene with Daniel Radcliffe, who played Harry Potter, and Hagrid's line would be spoken by someone else just off set. Daniel was just 11 years old in the first film and I noticed at times his attention could be drawn to where he was hearing the voice from. It happened with some of the other child actors too.

So I suggested that if I learned the lines too, I could speak directly to him so he could focus on me, rather than on the voice coming from the side of the set.

'Do you think you can do it?' asked the producer.

Well, I thought to myself, *it couldn't be any harder than trying to decipher one of Dewi Morris's line-out calls.* So I spent the whole night learning the lines for the next scene, staying up even later than on a typical night out with the England squad. It worked like clockwork the next day. I mumbled the lines through the costume to Daniel and he was able to look straight at me as he delivered his lines.

'Great job,' said the director.

It was about to become even greater. As I was ready to leave for home at the end of the day, I got a message to call in with security on the way out. There was a big South African guy on security who I always used to chat rugby with on the way in and out.

'I just need your security pass,' he said to me. I handed the pass to him, which on it described me as 'Martin Bayfield: (Extra)'. The security pass to work on a movie set was my prized possession, but being an extra meant that I had to drive myself to the Leavesden studios in Watford every day, pay for my own food and share a big caravan, which was called the 'three-way' because it was split into three compartments. It was absolutely fine because it was all that I knew.

But when the security guard returned to his desk from the back office with a new card for me, everything was about to change. 'Here you go, Martin,' he said. There it was. In big, black, bold writing: 'Martin Bayfield: (Actor)'.

It turned out being an actor was so much more fun.

'What time do you want the car to come to pick you up in the morning, Bayfs?' added the security guard. 'And let me know if you ever need to stay in a hotel.'

When I got to the studio the next day, I was guided to my own Winnebago and was offered a menu with delightful food to choose from. 'Okay, I could get used to this,' I said to myself as the door shut on my Winnebago. All because I had offered to learn some lines to help out Daniel. My fellow extras were less impressed. 'You smart-arse,' one said to me. Guilty, your honour. Colin Herridge at the RFU would have been proud.

What was even more encouraging was that after the end of filming for the first film, I went to see Nick to see if he thought they were going to want me to work on the sequel.

'I have to tell you, in the strictest confidence, Martin, that when we had a planning meeting for the next film, the first thing that came up was the director saying that we have got to have Martin in the film because it doesn't work without him.'

Sod you, Barwell. I was going to be a movie star, after all!

My links through rugby would also provide a helping hand in sorting out my contracts. I was at a rugby event at Grosvenor House in London when I found myself beside a hotshot City lawyer called Simon Goldberg. I told him about my new occupation and he asked who had done my contract for the first film.

'I did it myself,' I said, feeling a bit naive. 'I just signed it.'

'Okay, I'll take this on,' he replied. 'Just sort me out with a couple of tickets to Twickenham every so often.'

He did all my contracts right through to the end and each time improved the terms.

In 2003, I was asked by the BBC to travel to Australia to work at the World Cup. I was going to be based in Canberra with the Ireland team. But they were about to start filming the third film, *Harry Potter and the Prisoner of Azkaban*, and Simon asked if I would be released to do the World Cup. Warner Bros, not unreasonably, said 'No way'.

The BBC were not that impressed, but Simon sensed an opportunity to improve my contract, telling Warner Bros that I had been forced to give up the opportunity to further my burgeoning rugby broadcasting career (yeah, right, Simon) to do the next *Harry Potter* film.

'Er, Simon, you do know they only wanted me there as a reporter?' I said.

I remember one of the producers saying to me: 'I don't know who your lawyer is but he's doing a good job for you.'

Simon phoned me. 'Do you still have your rugby boots, Bayfs?'

'Why?'

'Given the roll I'm on, I reckon I could get you back into the England team!' He had got me a phenomenal deal. But, a bit like playing for England and the Lions, acting was not always as glamorous as you might have thought.

We worked 12-hour days, on set for 7 a.m. every day for pretty much 25 weeks. After a quick bit of breakfast, I would get into my costume, pulling on this all-in-one bodysuit, which was very fetching. I had the help of a crew that became known as 'Team Hagrid', made up of a couple of dressers and an animatronics specialist who could connect all the wires to the back of my head. The costume was incredibly heavy and awkward to move around in and would get extremely hot. Sometimes I would be used straight away, on other days I would be sitting around for hours. They built specially oversized director's chairs for me to be able to sit in while I was in the costume. I'd stay in it until lunchtime and then get back into it for the afternoon session, not leaving to go home until 7 p.m.

The people working with me had worked on big films like *Star Wars* (more of that later) and the advice they gave me was to allow myself to get hot in the costume and then stay hot. Trying to cool down and then heating up again would only end up with me getting a cold, I was warned. The head was air-cooled and, with the body suit, I wore a waistcoat that was filled with rubber tubes through which I could have cold water pumped.

I only ever used the waistcoat once, when we were under lights for a long period and it became really hot. But the rest of the time I would just get into the suit, sweat like an idiot and get hosed down at the end of the day. My ability to learn lines and deliver them meant they were able to use me more and more and, by the second movie, the technology behind the suit had improved.

Hagrid's head had become animatronic, which meant with a remote control they would move the eyes and open and close the mouth. I could even blink. By the third movie, it had improved again, with a voice-recognition system installed so that when I said the lines, the lips of the mouth on the head would move.

There's a scene in the third movie, which we filmed on a hillside in Scotland. The kids were running in front of me into Hagrid's hut and I was plodding behind. When I got to the doorway, I stopped and looked behind me to see if we were being chased.

Chris Carreras, the assistant director, turned to me and said: 'How did you do that? No one told you to do that and it really looked good.'

'The problem is, Chris, I actually think I am Hagrid and I reckon he would want to be sure the kids were safe.'

Robbie and I got on well together. He was very cheeky and great fun. In *Harry Potter and the Goblet of Fire*, the fourth movie, I even had to learn to waltz, which was as embarrassing as it was hysterical. Like my rugby days, I ended up making some great friends. Each film would last for 25 weeks and while sometimes I would sit for two days without being used, I was pretty much on duty every day during that period. I could invite friends and family onto the set at times and, one day, Keith Barwell's son Leon, who has since sadly passed away, came to see me with his wife and family.

'We all thought you were mad when you left the Saints,' he said, 'but seeing all this, it was the best decision you ever made. Rugby is always going to be there for you, but this is something special.'

It became even more special when we managed to mix rugby and *Harry Potter* together. After my request had been turned down to be released to cover the Rugby World Cup, one day I arrived at the studios to find that huge plasma screens had been installed in the sound sets.

'Wow, what's going on?' I asked.

'That's for you, so that you can watch the rugby,' said one of the crew.

Every time there was a break in filming, they flicked the rugby on and everyone started watching the games with me as the drama unfolded and my old mucker Martin Johnson led England to their World Cup triumph in Sydney.

The gesture really touched me. I just remember thinking: *Who would do that? Just for the tall guy in the Hagrid suit?*

But that is what it was like to work on those films. They were special people. I can remember being stuck in Scotland one night because of the weather and finding myself having dinner in the hotel with Sir Michael Gambon (who replaced Richard Harris, following his death) and Robert Hardy. We were staying in the beautiful Isle of Eriska Hotel on the west coast and it turned out to be one of the most remarkable nights of my life.

I love to tell stories and I also love to listen to them, and as the wine flowed, these remarkable actors started regaling each other, with me spellbound as I listened on. Michael Gambon started by telling this story about having lunch with Al Pacino in Los Angeles; Pacino was fascinated with his knighthood and wanted to know what perks came with it. As quick as a flash, Gambon had pulled out his hotel key card and told Pacino, 'You get a Knight's card', before quickly returning it to his wallet. 'The card means that you can approach four women each year and they cannot refuse you or they are thrown into the Tower of London.'

By this stage everyone in the restaurant of the Eriska is listening in because these guys just don't tell stories, they act them as well. Gambon said that seconds later a good-looking middle-aged woman walked into the restaurant and sat at a table nearby.

'Here, I'll show you,' he told Pacino, standing up from his

table and approaching her. 'Go with me on this,' he told her. 'I am trying to wind up Al Pacino. Will you walk with me out of the restaurant?' Gambon said the woman obliged and he took her around the corner for coffee and a bagel. A little later, he and the woman returned to the restaurant. 'I was doing up my trousers and she was tucking in her blouse,' said Gambon. 'And I sat back down at the table and said to Pacino: "I've got two left this year."'

Pacino's response? 'I've got to get me one of those knighthoods!'

It was one of those nights when I had to pinch myself. If only the England boys could see me now, wining and dining with these legendary actors. Harris was one of those special characters I was blessed to meet. One night, he managed to get a special round of applause for wangling an extra £40,000 when the filming went beyond the end date on his contract. For any filming that went beyond that date, he would be paid around £5,000 per hour.

We had to do a reshoot during the summer and, as it was a night shoot, there were fewer hours available to film. So they whizzed him into Leavesden. After an hour of travel and an hour of make-up, Harris was already £10,000 up. He only had to deliver about three lines, so it wouldn't take long – at least, so we all thought. But then one of the guys shouted that there was a problem with a camera. Another hour gone. Another £5,000. Next thing, the lighting guy shouted out that there was a problem with the lights. Yet another hour. Yet another £5,000. It became quite clear that he was paying people to mess things up. Then daylight broke, meaning we'd have to stop filming and return the following night. When we eventually finished, the director announced: 'That's a wrap. And I think we can all agree that Richard Harris deserves a special round of applause!' And he just took a bow and shuffled off. What a guy.

The first time we watched the first *Harry Potter* film was another unforgettable night. The day before it was to be officially released to the public, there was a 'cast and crew showing'. The studio took over every cinema in Leicester Square so that everyone involved in the production, from the leading lights to the caterers and drivers, could go and watch. What was so memorable was that when you're in production, you're only aware of the bits of the movie that you're involved in. Seeing it come together on the big screen for the first time was emotional and fun in equal measure.

Everyone was waiting for scenes in which they had been involved, causing pockets of cheers across the theatre. Or if there was an amazing special effect, the whole audience would applaud. It was an incredible feelgood moment. I was up at the back with my bucket of popcorn, thinking: *I am actually in this film. This is nuts.*

It was also the only time I had been to the cinema when everyone waited for the credits at the end of the film and, as each person's name came up, there was a little cheer. I was sitting watching it with my children, waiting and waiting for my name to come up. Eventually it appeared under 'Stunts' because they didn't know quite where to put me and I got my own special cheer.

Several months later that year, I did a speaking event at the Hilton Hotel in London and the *Harry Potter* film was available to watch on the televisions in the hotel rooms. We had all got very drunk and piled back to someone's room, and, because I was there, we decided to watch the film. Someone mysteriously produced an old car aerial and I had to stand by the screen, holding the aerial, and point when I appeared in the film. Each time I appeared on screen, we had to drink. I don't think we made it to the last scene as we were all obliterated by then. And so the Martin Bayfield/Hagrid drinking game was born.

If you are interested to know the first scene I am in in the first film, then look closely when Harry is first brought to the Dursley house as a baby. As the motorbike flies in, they use a stunt man and then, when Hagrid gets off the motorbike, that's me. As for the rest, well, I'm afraid you're on your own if you want to play the Hagrid drinking game.

19

A Wheezing Darth Vader

With an equity card now among my prized possessions, it felt like my days as PC546 in the Bedfordshire Constabulary, and the unhappy sojourn as a professional rugby player and academy coach, were truly behind me. Having played my *big* part in a £100 million Warner Bros movie, my sights were now on Hollywood.

'In rugby, I hit every one of my goals and had a wonderful time doing it,' I said in a newspaper interview before the first *Harry Potter* film came out. 'Now I want to do the same with acting. It may be a bit of a laugh for my rugby friends, who insist on calling me "Luvvie" and "Darling", but being involved in the *Harry Potter* film was such a great experience that it has sparked something in me. My ambition now is to become a serious actor. I don't have a clue whether I will ever achieve it, but I will have failed myself unless I try. What I did in the film I think I did very well. I want to do more, and I have the utmost confidence that I can.'

Yeah, yeah, of course I did. I look back at those words now

and wince. Back in those naive days, I think I did genuinely believe that I could make the transition from rugby player to Hagrid's double and then a mainstream actor. I got myself an agent and awaited news of calls from Steven Spielberg about the next big blockbuster. Instead, I got an offer to do panto – *Jack and the Beanstalk* at the Royal & Derngate theatre in Northampton. I was Fleshcreep, the Giant's henchman, because the Giant didn't actually exist. He was just a sound effect. Oh well.

But I kept the faith and, in 2005, I thought my big break had come. I was invited to audition for the leading role in a new independent film called *StagKnight*. What do you mean you've never heard of it? Well, the reason you haven't is because it was never released. And, more importantly, I never got paid.

I should have realised from the audition, which was a weird experience, and maybe from the fact that I was offered two parts in it. When the script arrived in the post one day, I ripped it open and read the brief instructions. One of my parts was going to be that of 'William'. Fantastic, I thought. This is it. I have finally made it, and if my character is in the script then that must mean I have lines to say. Not just behind the animatronic head of Hagrid, but me, Martin Bayfield, the *actor*. I poured myself a large gin and tonic and scanned through the script looking for dialogue involving 'William'.

My excitement soon faded, however, as I realised that 'William' did not seem to be involved in many of the opening scenes. And my heart sank when I eventually found him. The script read something like: 'Enter William – a tall [yes, I can do that], powerful [just give me a couple of weeks in the gym] DEAF MUTE'! Brilliant. Just brilliant.

The alarm bells also should have rung at the fact that it looked like there was only one proper actor among us – Sandra Dickinson, the American with the squeaky voice who used to be married to Peter Davison when he was Dr Who. And she was probably most famous for TV adverts in the early 1980s. Those of a certain age will remember her catchphrase 'Put the dinner on, I'll be home in 20 minutes!' to Davison in an advert for non-stick pans. Not exactly a Hollywood A-lister.

The rest of the cast, including me, were wannabees, desperate for a big break. One of the actors called himself Joe Montana, without realising that a much more famous Joe Montana already existed. The director was a guy called Simon Cathcart, who decided to make *himself* the star of the film. He used to tell us to radiate two things during production: anger and joy. Joe would snipe back to him: 'Hey Simon, why don't I radiate my foot up your ass?!'

The plot involved a group of mates who knew each other from school. They were washed-up 40-year-olds – each one had their own problem – and they went to a paintballing centre together in the middle of nowhere, which was run by Dickinson. I think the blurb described it as 'a homegrown comic tale about sex, drugs and a killer night out. A stag weekend gets out of hand when the paintballing and partying finishes and the summoning of a vengeful Templar Knight begins.'

The script, in the right pair of hands, could make for a very funny film. It could have been a bit like one of those zombie comedy films like *Shaun of the Dead*. But, unfortunately, it wasn't. It was a crude awakening for me and my silver-screen ambitions, but also provided a hilarious insight into the world of budget filmmaking.

There were often times when we found ourselves sitting in a forest at around 3 a.m. thinking: *What on earth are we doing?* As well as playing William, who helped Sandra run this paintballing centre, I also played the Knight who was brought back from the dead. I think it was filmed on the grounds of a mate of Cathcart's in Surrey, and whereas the *Harry Potter* films took 25 weeks to complete, this was done and dusted in around four.

Part of the sales pitch for the paintballing was that the participants were treated to a weird barbecue, for which they had to get dressed up. They were then instructed to say an incantation, which released the Knight from Arthurian times. He then ran around the forest killing everyone. My costume was hilarious. They produced a helmet they bought off eBay that didn't fit and the rest of the armour was made from shin pads that were sprayed silver and tied to my body. My shoes were labourer's boots by a brand called Dewalt, which were also sprayed silver. This was all fine until the scene where I had to stamp on a guy's head and crush it. After the shot, the cameraman said: 'Yeah, slight problem. We could see the branding of the boot.'

And so, from then on, my nickname was 'Sir Martin Dewalt', which at least sounded appropriately medieval. But it is safe to say it never made it to your local cinema. Trust me, that was a good thing. And I'm still waiting for my cheque.

My next big opportunity came in the BBC police drama *New Tricks*. My agent called me to say he had got me a part in an episode. Fantastic. Mainstream television, here we come. But when I turned up at the set, my hopes of a big breakthrough sank. The part I was given was 'Rugby Player 2'. So, not only did I not have a named part, but I was also not even 'Rugby Player 1'.

Well, at least it felt like a step up from *StagKnight*, but unfortunately this wasn't a speaking role either. All I had to do was stand in a shower with four other blokes in a fictional rugby club. Okay, I had done that many times before.

In the rehearsal, we were told that because of the camera angle, it was fine for us to wear swimming trunks in the shower or a towel around our waists. But when it came to the actual shoot, the director had a change of mind. 'Sorry guys, but we need you to be naked. Is that going to be a problem?'

No, all good, I replied. I had stood in many showers, many times, naked with big ugly rugby players. Three of the other guys were fine too, but the fourth had a bit of a problem.

'It'll be fine, mate,' I tried to reassure him. 'They're only going to show the back of you.'

'But I want to look good.'

'Well, do some push-ups and a few sit-ups and you'll look great.'

'No, I want to look good, you know . . . down there.'

'Don't worry, mate. Just find a quiet corner, put some wind in your sails and you'll be fine.'

A few minutes later the director walks in. Everyone ready?

'Yes.'

'Yes.'

'Yes.'

'Yes.'

'Er, no,' yelps my friend. 'I think I may have overdone it.'

Despite the disappointment of *StagKnight*, I finally made a return to film in 2012, two years after the end of Harry

Potter, when I played one of the three cyclopes in the production *Wrath of the Titans*, the sequel to Jonathan Liebesman's
2010 film *Clash of the Titans*. It was great fun, even though it
didn't lead anywhere either. This was a motion-capture role,
similar to the one that Andy Serkis did when playing Gollum
in the *Lord of the Rings* films.

The filming was at Pinewood Studios and my part was
shot on a huge soundstage, with a big, suspended rig that had
cameras all the way around it. Everything was filmed within
the rig and from every angle. I was wearing a black bodysuit
with reflective markers all over it so that the cameras could
pick up my movement. I then had to pretend I was fighting,
running, chasing or jumping over things – all the movements
needed to create the character – and then they put the camera
right in my face to get all the expressions so that they could
map it and bring it to life as a rendered CGI creature.

In the centre of the set was an Action Man figure on a stand
that I had to focus on. After three days of filming, during
which I did all the movements for all three cyclopes, at the
end I said: 'Could we just film this as if it was real?' Bearing
in mind I was supposed to be this 30ft creature, I picked up
my club and smashed poor Action Man to bits. 'There you
go, there's your film,' I said. It was the last image we shot,
the real ending.

Meanwhile, my work as a summariser for BBC Sport and
Radio 5 Live, and appearances on *The Weakest Link*, *Ready
Steady Cook* and, of course, *New Tricks*) opened up opportu-
nities for me in television. I joined a new agency at the end
of 2011 and, by a stroke of luck, one of the producers on
Crimewatch had searched on the internet for a 'police officer +
TV presenter' to see if anyone out there who had experience

of both the police and broadcasting. Up popped my name. As I'd already done work for 5 Live, he contacted me and it went from there.

Like working on the *Potter* films, it was a high-pressure opening. I can still remember the countdown to my first live show. 'Thirty seconds to go to live,' said the producer in my ear. 'Twenty seconds to go ... ten seconds to go.' Then he said: 'Good luck, Martin. Just remember there will be around *eight million people* watching the show tonight ... Five seconds to go.' No pressure mate, thanks.

Presenting *Crimewatch* was also the first occasion I was the subject of trolling on Twitter. I had replaced Rav Wilding and a lot of people liked Rav. He is a great guy. He was young and good-looking. As my mum might say: 'Me, not so much.' And so, inevitably, when I took over, a lot of people were asking: 'Who the hell is this guy?' One of them took to Twitter to ask that very question. 'What qualifies you to do this job?' some guy tweeted me. I replied back: 'Well, I was a police officer for ten years and I am a TV presenter.' His reply? 'Oh, okay, fair enough.'

I ended up presenting on the programme for five years and it was an amazing thing to do. Obviously I had experience of police work, but what the programme reminded me of was the incredible effort that police officers put in to crack cases and get people in front of courts and receive justice. And I just loved working with Kirsty Young – she is an exceptional broadcaster. It had become quite a high-profile job since the tragic murder of presenter Jill Dando in 1999, when she was shot dead outside her home in London. I was respectful of what had happened to Jill, but even though we did some very big stories, including re-examining the case of the disappearance of Madeleine McCann, I never felt in any danger because of the job. We all just got on with it.

It wasn't long after I had started with *Crimewatch* that the opportunity for another film role came my way. *Game of Thrones* had already established itself as a huge TV hit when a casting agent got in touch with me to ask if I wanted to audition for a new character by the name of 'Mountain'. I went to his home in north London, a lovely three-storey townhouse, and once again it shone a light on the remarkable way business is conducted behind the scenes of these hugely successful productions.

He invited me upstairs to the top-floor attic room, which was obviously his children's playroom. I didn't have to learn any lines, but I had to pretend that I was in a sword fight – using one of his kids' plastic lightsabre toys from *Star Wars*. Then I had to pretend that I had been killed but then suddenly grab hold of the head of my opponent, who thinks I am dead, and push his eyes out with my thumbs. He handed me a prop for this – another toy, like a mannequin's head that you put make-up on and style their hair. Perhaps trying to impress him, as I pressed away at the eyes of this thing, suddenly there was a bang and it came apart under the pressure.

'Er ... That's really good stuff, Martin, but now I'm going to have to buy a new toy for my daughter,' he said, with a look that suggested he would have to do a bit of acting himself later.

A few days later, I got a call to say I had got the job. We had about six weeks until the filming started over a weekend in Croatia. They were going to pay me a sum of money to go to the gym for six weeks to train hard to bulk up a bit. The problem was that all they could guarantee me was one scene in one episode of the series and the offer came just as BT Sport was launching at their studios in Olympic Park. I asked the bosses if I could get a release for *Game of Thrones* but was told that they needed me. I had a guaranteed four-year deal with BT, so in the end there wasn't really much of a choice. I think it's safe to say that I am probably the only person who has turned down a role in *Game of Thrones*. The guy who subsequently got it was the world's strongest man, Hafþór Júlíus Björnsson. I doubt he needed six weeks in the gym to bulk up.

What was frustrating was that, about a year later, I was in conversation with the top guy at BT Sport and mentioned this story. 'Oh, mate, if you had told me I would have let you go and do it. It would have been great publicity for the channel.' I love *Game of Thrones* and sometimes, when I flick through it and see the scene that I would have been in, I think: *That could have been me.*

However, it wouldn't be my biggest regret or disappointment in my acting career.

I have always been a huge fan of the film *Star Wars*. Even now, as a very tall grown man who should know better, I have a *Star Wars* poster hanging on the wall of my office at home. Indeed, I am such a fan that when my agent contacted me to say that someone wanted me to audition for a film, but wouldn't say what it was, I think it must have been the Force that enabled me to work out, when I read through the script, that the part they wanted me to play was that of Darth Vader, one of the greatest fictional villains of all time.

I went onto YouTube to watch the performances of David Prowse, the former weightlifter who played the part in the first three films. Prowse also spoke the dialogue during the filming, before director George Lucas insisted that his jovial Bristolian accent didn't quite fit the bill and hired the actor James Earl Jones to do what became a legendary voice-over. I wasn't sure what they would make of my Bedford twang either, so I concentrated on studying his movements and learning my lines. So far, so good. The trip to Pinewood Studios was even more mind-blowing for this oversized *Star Wars* groupie. I was first taken to a little caravan and then onto the main Pinewood area.

It is a remarkable place, a maze of little sheds filled with lots of independent businesses all connected to the film industry – lighting, electrics, plasterers – and then there was the big brand-new James Bond soundstage. My eyes couldn't have been wider, at least not until I was taken into one of the workshops, and then into a dressing room. There, hanging up on the wall, was the Darth Vader costume. The *original* 1977 Darth Vader costume.

In the three prequel films, made after the first three, Darth Vader had been made to look quite shiny, new and smart, and there had been a consensus that they'd got that wrong. For this film (I later worked out it was *Rogue One*), a return to the original costume and design had been decided upon, making him look rougher around the edges and more authentic. It wasn't as flashy and it had a more homespun look, as if it were an outfit made from clothes and items from a charity shop – and made me even more excited to be pulling on the original costume.

It didn't quite fit. I couldn't see out of the eyes and the helmet smelled of a cross between air freshener and mould. It was the same when I was in the *Harry Potter* films. I was told that the outfits weren't washed because they'd lose their colour and fade so, instead, they were just sprayed and wiped down, which is pretty gross if you think about it for too long.

One of the costume guys came up to me.

'Well, have you done it?' he asked.

'Done what?'

'The breathing.'

'Of course I have. I've been walking around breathing like an asthmatic Darth Vader.'

As part of the move to return to the soul and rawness of the first *Star Wars* films, all the original props were being used, including a full-sized X-wing fighter, which I embarrassed myself in front of when I saw it. I don't know what came over me but I walked across to it, gave it a hug and started to cry, not exactly showcasing my Dark Side acting ability. It was pathetic.

'Are you okay, mate?' asked the casting agent. 'Can we get on with this?'

'Oh yeah, sorry,' I blubbed back.

The scene I had to act in was one where the baddie character Director Orson Krennic visits Darth Vader in his castle to explain that the Death Star weapon had not been compromised and Darth Vader, after a lot of pointing (he doesn't get to do much else), ends up doing the choking movement with his fingers to demonstrate his displeasure with poor Krennic. I went through the scenes, but didn't get a good vibe. I got in my car and drove home and phoned my agent. 'I don't think I've got this.'

I was right. They contacted me a few days later to tell me the audition had been unsuccessful. I think they had already used another actor for previous scenes in the film and perhaps they decided to stick with what they had; I'm not sure.

All I was left with were questions. Had I prepared for it properly? There were people I knew there who had worked on the *Harry Potter* films and they would have given me the inside track on what exactly they wanted. I don't know what it was: maybe I didn't move as they wanted me to, maybe I could have drilled down deeper into the role. Either way, I don't think I've been that disappointed since I was dropped by England. I was absolutely heartbroken. I'd have played the part for free because it would have been such a cool thing to have done.

But the Force definitely wasn't with me that day. I didn't get much help from the Dark Side either. My *Star Wars* dreams were sadly dashed. It took me years to be able to watch *Rogue One* and I think it's the best of all the *Star Wars* films. I watch it all the time now that I've got it out of my system. But at least I can look back at my career and say: 'Do you know what? For one hour I was Darth Varder on the set of a *Star Wars* film.' And that's a memory that's priceless to me.

In the mad world of public speaking, films and TV work, sometimes it's important to remember what really matters. It's easy to get carried away, as I had done in my *Star Wars* audition. But the moment that I lost touch with reality came not long after I had reached the final of the BBC cooking show *Celebrity MasterChef* in 2018.

My wife Jane had been diagnosed with thyroid cancer and the date for her operation coincided with the broadcast of the final. That night I had already been booked for an event at The Brewery on Chiswell Street in central London, but Jane told me not to cancel it. 'Don't worry, I'll be fine. The operation is late in the evening and I'll still be in post-operative recovery when you're finished.'

So I went to the hospital to make sure she was comfortable and that everything was in place for the operation, before I went on to the event. My broadcasting colleague and former player David Flatman was also speaking and not long after I arrived, I turned to Flats and said: 'I shouldn't be here. Why am I here? What am I doing here?'

I had to go. I told the organisers, who were good as gold, and I left the event to return to the hospital, sitting in the reception of the Royal Marsden looking like a gentleman burglar in my black tie attire. A few hours later, Jane came out of the operation, looking very poorly with tubes coming out of everywhere, and I just remember thinking I had very nearly got this so badly wrong. Of course, she was right, I would have finished the gig by the time she came out of the operating theatre, but my place was here, waiting for her and then being by her side. Without a doubt, I was the smartest visitor to the Royal Marsden that night.

As I walked out of the hospital a few hours later, still in my black tie and feeling fraught about what Jane had gone through, my head was down with worry when a group of drunk lads walked past. 'Oi, it's the bloke out of *MasterChef*!'

I had forgotten all about the final. Instead I had reconnected with what was important to me.

20

Poacher Turned Broadcaster

I was never punched by Sean Fitzpatrick, the legendary All Blacks hooker, on the pitch, but I can reveal that we almost came to blows in an ITV studio during the 2007 World Cup. Well, when I say 'blows', I'm pretty sure the punches would have been coming from only one direction.

It was my first presenting gig at a major tournament. Actually, it was my first presenting gig at *any* tournament. I had been plunged into it without any training whatsoever, but thought I had been doing a pretty good job in bluffing my way ... until the moment that New Zealand sensationally crashed out of the tournament at the quarter-final stage with a dramatic and controversial 20-18 defeat by France in Cardiff. The All Blacks had been heavy favourites to win the tournament and the game in Cardiff was seen as little more than a colourful sojourn ahead of the business-end games in Paris.

Yet Les Bleus had shocked New Zealand with a thrilling victory before most of the Kiwi fans had even arrived in Europe, having presumptuously only bothered to book match tickets and travel for the semi-finals in Paris. The controversy in Cardiff was provided by Wayne Barnes, the English referee, who had critically missed a forward pass by Frederic Michalak in the build-up to Yannick Jauzion's match-winning try.

The drama made for fantastic television and the atmosphere in the studio was electric too, until, that is, I found it hard to contain a giggle just after we had cut to a commercial break following the final whistle. It was just an instinctive reaction. I thought the whole thing was absolutely astounding. I wasn't smiling because I thought it was funny, but because it was so remarkable and unexpected.

The French had done it again, just as they had so famously when they defeated the All Blacks in the semi-final at Twickenham in the 1999 World Cup. Let's just say, in *sharp* contrast, Fitzy did not appreciate my reaction. 'Mate, if you don't take that smile off your face, I'm going to punch it off,' he growled at me.

To say there was a bit of tension when we went back live after the break was an understatement. To be fair to me, I wasn't laughing *at* the All Blacks. I had just found the match and finale an amazing experience and one of those days when you could say: 'I was there.' But I thought Fitzy was going to kill me. Thankfully, a bit like the All Blacks' World Cup hopes, the frisson in the studio came to nothing.

It was a remarkable tournament to cover. Several years earlier, I had begun the transition from ageing player to broadcaster by doing bits and pieces for the BBC, who were amazing to work for. They gave me the opportunity to do a bit of punditry, a few interviews, some reporting and then live commentary on the radio.

I made plenty of mistakes, but it was a great learning experience and great fun.

My *Harry Potter* commitments meant that my sports broadcasting career stalled until my big break came earlier in 2007, when Mark Sharman, who at the time was ITV's controller of sport, had seen me host a sport industry awards dinner. Afterwards, he came up to me and said: 'What you've basically done there is TV-presenting, Martin.' Not long after, I was offered a role on the World Cup team as the second presenter, working on the less glamorous matches, aside from that quarter-final at the Millennium Stadium.

I was off duty for the final at the Stade de France between England and eventual champions South Africa, and there were pockets of grim-looking All Blacks supporters on the concourses around the stadium, just off the plane from New Zealand and dressed in funereal black. It was a fascinating spectacle. If Australia had lost to France, I reckon most of their fans would have just sold their tickets and gone on the piss in London or Paris. But there was no way those All Blacks fans were giving up their tickets. It was almost like a sign of protest at Barnesy's howler.

Among our party was the now-retired Francois Pienaar, the young pup I had faced on the tour of South Africa 13 years earlier. He was now a legend of the game, the 1995 World Cup-winning captain who had famously shared the embrace with Nelson Mandela and done so much to help change attitudes and build bridges across communities in the new Rainbow Nation. But what he didn't have on that balmy late afternoon in October was his media accreditation to gain him entry into the stadium.

The officials at the Stade de France are traditionally sticklers for the correct documentation for media wishing to enter the stadium, usually including a passport. It's not an uncommon sight to see a red-faced journalist attempting to speak pidgin French to explain they had left their photographic ID back in their hotel. Security was even tighter for the World Cup final, but there was no sense of panic from Pienaar.

Hanging from the side of the Stade de France were these huge banners of previous World Cup-winning captains: David Kirk of New Zealand, Australia's Nick Farr-Jones and John Eales, and England's totemic leader and my former second-row team-mate Martin Johnson ... and Francois. As the French official stopped him to ask for his full documentation, Francois simply turned and pointed to the huge banner of himself, fluttering in the evening breeze.

'There, my friend, is my accreditation,' he said, with a smile, and walked on by. No wonder you are such a great leader, I thought to myself. What a true legend.

I love my work reporting and presenting with BT Sport and ITV, not least because it keeps me young. My playing days are now so far behind me that the game is nothing like the one I played. I had one season of lifting in line-outs. If you asked me to explain a modern-day line-out, I wouldn't have a clue.

For the same reason, I just love going into the England camp. It's exciting. I have huge respect for the players and the work they put in, but in truth I am as probably as envious of them as I am impressed. I remember doing an interview with Jonny Hill, the Exeter Chiefs lock, during a recent England Six Nations campaign and I just wanted to talk to him for ever. It's such a different world. But the element of fun is still there too. I can go down to Sandy Park, the home of Exeter

Chiefs, stand on the touchline and hear the supporters chant at me: 'We want Flats, we want Flats,' declaring their preference for David Flatman. As someone who dished it out, I don't mind the ribbing.

But picking up the microphone and interviewing my former team-mates was not always an easy transition to make. I'd got up to enough hijinks in my time as a player off the pitch and made many more mistakes on it, so it was only natural to have a sense of empathy with them once I had turned from poacher to broadcaster. The first big television interview I did was with Martin Johnson, when he was England manager at the 2011 World Cup in New Zealand. At that stage, ITV didn't have any rights for the Six Nations, so this was the first time I had come across him in my new professional guise.

The interview took place in their hotel in Dunedin on South Island and I found it a surreal experience interviewing a guy who I had played alongside in the second row for 18 Test matches. He came across impressively and I was left with the feeling that Johnno could do something really special with England, just as he had done as a player and captain. But, ultimately, he didn't have enough support around him. Not that he probably wanted any.

I would soon be presented with the biggest dilemma I would face while reporting on England. After that encouraging start, the tournament quickly descended into a traumatic experience for Johnno and his team. England would go on to crash out at the quarter-final stage, also at the hands of France, in a campaign that was tainted by a string of off-field misdemeanours and controversies. And I would find myself unwittingly at the centre of the biggest scandal of the lot.

England had struggled in their victory in a pool match

against Argentina in Dunedin before travelling to the magnificent resort town of Queenstown for some rest and relaxation. As the team had an eight-day gap between matches, the players took full advantage of a night off. So did most of the media pack. I was not alone in waking up with a stinking hangover the following morning.

Booking a trip on a jet boat followed by a helicopter ride had seemed like a good idea at the time, but on that foggy Monday morning, it felt like purgatory.

But it was nothing like the hell that Mike Tindall and Co had found themselves in, following an even bigger night on the tiles. Some of the players had been pictured at a dwarf-tossing event in a backpackers' bar in Queenstown and video footage of a very drunk Tindall with a mysterious blonde was about to emerge. Not only would this plunge Martin Johnson's squad into disarray, but it would also leave me facing a journalistic quandary.

As we jumped into our minibus to head back to Dunedin ahead of England's next match, my mobile phone rang. It was a New Zealand number.

'Is this Martin Bayfield?' said the caller.

'Yeah.'

'I'm from the Cowboys bar in Queenstown.'

'Oh ... okay.'

It's one of the moments that you dread. I didn't remember any Cowboys bar in Queenstown. In fact, I didn't remember very much at all about Queenstown. *Oh no, what have I done now?*

'Mate, I got your number from my dad. You worked with him during the 2005 Lions tour of New Zealand. We've got a video, mate. We've got a video of some of the England players doing stuff that they shouldn't have been doing.' I quickly told our producer to pull over and the guy started to give me the details of the video. *Holy shit,* I thought to myself. *This is serious.*

'Okay, we've got one of two options,' I said. 'We have either got the scoop of the tour and we go with it, but never get any assistance getting access to England players ever again. Or we phone up the England media team, tell them there's a shitstorm coming their way, give them the number of this guy and tell them: "It's over to you."' It didn't take us long to work out that the second option was the path we were going to go down.

Will Chignell, who was in his first gig in charge of the RFU's media team, and Dave Barton, the England manager, knew nothing about it. They didn't have a clue. It was the first time that I felt real conflict between the rugby player I had been and the media person I was becoming. This was an amazing story. I wasn't a trained journalist and yet I had been handed an earth-breaking story. It made me realise what my responsibilities were. I just couldn't do it. My gut feeling was to let someone else sort this out and I still think what we did was the right thing to do. And, unsurprisingly, we got every interview request we wanted for the remainder of the tournament!

Yet it did nothing to ease my concern for Johnno. I was alarmed to see him effectively hung out to dry. Johnno, being Johnno, was always going to protect his players, particularly given the fact that he had played with some of them, including Tindall, who initially refused to apologise for his behaviour. What Johnno needed at that precise moment was an experienced older head to put his arm around him and say: 'Don't worry, I've got this. You look after the team preparations.'

The RFU had already endured a summer turmoil of political strife that had led to my former Saints team-mate John Steele, one of the stars of the England B tour to New Zealand that I'd been part of in the summer of 1992, being dismissed as chief executive. Rob Andrew, who was the RFU's professional rugby director at the time, should have been the man to take the pressure off Johnno in New Zealand, but from the outside at least, it appeared that all he was interested in was going off to do kicking sessions with Jonny Wilkinson and Dave Alred, England's kicking coach. Johnno needed more support.

The players didn't do him any favours either, and that was a surprise given what an iconic leader he had been as England captain, having won a World Cup eight years earlier with some of them.

Another incident soon followed that also rocked the RFU. The England players had a day off and 11 of them took part in a Land Rover sponsors' day. It created friction because the players assumed it would be a fun afternoon driving along on Muriwai Beach near Auckland and a bit of 'R and R', including surfing and finishing with a barbecue and a few beers.

I'm not sure what was lost in communication between the RFU and the players but, for Land Rover, it was an opportunity to film a promotional shoot, which involved driving at 20 miles per hour along a beach. It's safe to say the players were not amused. I had first-hand experience of that because I was in one of the Land Rovers with my producer and a cameraman, with James Haskell, the England flanker, driving. Haskell can be a bit of a character at times and he decided to put his foot down, literally, as we bumped and crashed around in the back. There were a few tasty exchanges between the players on the radios.

Land Rover afterwards lodged an official complaint about the players' behaviour, to great embarrassment to the RFU, and the details of the day came out when the post-World Cup review was leaked to the press. What didn't come out, however, was the fact that Haskell ended up being stranded on the beach after the party left him behind. He'd just finished doing an interview with us and, when we looked around, all the cars had gone. We were stranded in the middle of nowhere, with no taxis around and not even a phone signal to call for help.

We eventually flagged down a farmer's truck and asked him to drive us to the top of a nearby hill so we could at least get reception. 'You might want to do a headcount,' I told the RFU press guy. 'You're a man down.' It would be almost two hours before a taxi eventually turned up. Haskell had every right to lose his shit in that moment, but despite the frustrations of the afternoon, he was great fun. We found an old bottle and put it up on a post and tried to knock it off with some stones and had a laugh. In the 1990s, a day off certainly didn't involve several hours doing a photoshoot with a sponsor.

The legacy of that controversy-ridden campaign, which culminated with Manu Tuilagi being arrested for jumping off an Auckland ferry the day after England had lost to France, would be far-reaching. Stuart Lancaster succeeded Johnno as head coach and, from my vantage point of covering the team, spent the next four years trying to present the England side as whiter than white – one that never got drunk, never put a foot out of line – and I believe they lost their identity and lost their edge.

I remember speaking to Dylan Hartley after the final Six Nations match at Twickenham before the 2015 World Cup and he said he was going out for his first-ever social night out under Lancaster. It had taken four years. Watching from afar, all I could think to myself was that these were young men: let them be stupid, let them be daft. But the RFU was so scared of upsetting sponsors. Lancaster frequently made the point of the players reconnecting with the fans, but that should have just taken one season. All it takes to reconnect with the fans is to win games. Do that and they love you. In the four seasons under Lancaster, England finished in second place in the Six Nations each time; that tells you all you need to know about the side. They were a really good team, but in my perception they were just being held back.

At times Stuart cut an isolated figure at the team's base at the Pennyhill Park Hotel in Bagshot in Surrey. We used to call it the 'Gilded Cage'. Everyone was there, but often Stuart would be sitting on his own, writing his notes or whatever. It was quite sad to see because he's an amazing guy. He had assembled most of that squad during his time as the development coach, but again, like the Johnson regime, they needed someone else in that set-up, albeit for different reasons – an older head as a manager, but that person wasn't there.

It was painful watching the whole thing in freefall at the 2015 World Cup. Again, I was working for ITV during the tournament and we were staying at Pennyhill Park on the opening night of the tournament when England struggled to secure a bonus-point victory over Fiji at Twickenham. It had been a late kick-off and when I got back to the hotel around 1 a.m. with my producer and cameraman, Jonathan Joseph, the England centre, was walking across the reception with his arm across his body.

'Are you okay?' I asked him.

'No, I think I have torn my pec [pectoral muscle],' he said and walked on.

I turned around to my producer. 'That's England stuffed,' I said. 'That only leaves them with Sam Burgess as midfield cover. They are stuffed.' Burgess had been a fantastic rugby-league player in Australia, but had only just switched codes earlier in the year and had been a controversial selection in the World Cup squad ahead of Luther Burrell.

England went on to lose to Wales, with Burgess in the midfield in the next game at Twickenham. With Australia still to come, everyone knew the game was already up. England were on course to make history for all the wrong reasons as the first hosts not to qualify from the pool stages.

Wales had every right to gloat about their 28-25 victory, having overturned a ten-point deficit in a comeback that was capped with a brilliant late try by Gareth Davies. Yet I was impressed by the reaction of Wales captain Sam Warburton and centre Jamie Roberts. There was no sense of triumphalism; instead, they appeared to have empathy with England's pain. Both said they were delighted to win but that they felt for England and the players because they knew what they were going to have to go through now and it was going to be horrible for them. My respect for them both went through the roof. Of course, as they walked off down the tunnel and into their changing room, you could hear chaos was kicking off. But their public reaction was pure class.

After Bernard Foley inspired Australia to an emphatic 33–13 victory to confirm England's humiliating exit, the tournament would end in embarrassment for me too. After England had long since packed their bags, Australia refused to stay at Pennyhill Park after reaching the final, so instead New Zealand moved into the plush hotel, which was great news for my wife Jane, who's a massive fan of the All Blacks captain Richie McCaw.

She was staying with me at the hotel the night of the final and good old BT Sport had thoughtfully scheduled me to work at Welford Road the following day for the big game between Leicester Tigers and Worcester Warriors. Who said this job was all glamour? It was an early start for me, but in the meantime Jane bumped into McCaw and had her photograph taken with him in front of the hotel. You can imagine the scene. She has her arm around him, he has his arm around her, there's a Mercedes car and a beautiful country house in the background. It looked like the perfect husband–and–wife photograph. And, unbeknown to me, Jane got it framed and then put it on one of our bedside tables. It took me about two weeks to notice it.

'What's this doing here?' I asked.

'Well, you can only dream,' replied Jane.

The RFU's reaction to yet another World Cup crisis was to lurch again in a completely different direction by bringing in their first-ever overseas head coach and hiring Eddie Jones, who'd been in charge of Australia when England won the World Cup in 2003.

Eddie is a fascinating, enigmatic figure. He can be brilliantly funny at times, but also equally crass. His tenure opened with victories against Scotland and Italy in the 2016 Six Nations, when he first revealed his confrontational style by suggesting the parents of Ireland fly-half Johnny Sexton, who had gone through a period of sustaining concussions, would be worried about his long-term health. The public backlash came not just from Ireland supporters but also embarrassed England fans. Yet it was the edge that Jones brought that was enough to turn England from a decent side to Grand Slam champions with just a little bit of tweaking. It was effectively Stuart Lancaster's side but with added bite. Being at Pennyhill Park became much more relaxing for the players, at least in terms of the freedom to socialise again. It was a different story during training, however.

England won the championship again the following season, despite losing to Ireland in the final match, after which Jones's attitude to being outspoken appeared to change. Ahead of the return fixture 12 months later, when Ireland were going for a Grand Slam at Twickenham, footage emerged from a speech he made at a corporate event in 2017, where he referred to 'the scummy Irish' and Wales as a 'little shit place'. I think he felt after that storm he should keep his powder dry, although sometimes he just cannot help himself.

I didn't go to the World Cup in Japan because Jane was undergoing cancer treatment, but despite reaching the final, England have stumbled along since then, never quite replicating the intensity of those opening two seasons.

Nowadays I never quite know what kind of Eddie I am going to get when I conduct a post-match interview with him. The only consistent thing is that he never looks at me when he is speaking. He always looks directly into my chest. No doubt some media professional has told him to do that so that he doesn't look small (Jones is 5ft 8ins, more than a foot shorter than me). I'm quite tempted to put a sticker on my chest with a little smiley face, or a pointer saying 'I'm up here, Eddie'. On second thoughts, maybe it's better if he doesn't look up.

21

The Ostrich, the Goat and the Golf Club

I should have known there was going to be trouble. As I drove up the driveway of the golf club in Gloucestershire, it was hard not to miss the ostrich running around a makeshift pen, an arresting aberration in such plush and manicured surroundings.

Uh-oh, I thought to myself. *This looks like it's going to be a long night.*

One of the joys of speaking at sportsmen's dinners at grassroots rugby clubs is meeting such a wide variety of people – although not, it's fair to say, usually animals. The junior rugby club from Bristol that had booked me to speak at their end-of-season function had not mentioned anything about an ostrich, who seemed to be charging around like Manu Tuilagi in his pomp.

With a sense of trepidation, I slipped into the clubhouse to be greeted with an atmosphere already reaching similarly high-octane energy levels to the ostrich's. It was only 7 p.m. and everyone was already plastered.

'Great to see you, Bayfs. Did you see the ostrich in the way in?' asked one of my reception committee. *Of course* I had seen the ostrich. 'We're holding a sweepstake for the first person to ride it!' *Dear God. This one is going to be lively.* 'Tell them to get their money in. We're already up to £500.' *Will do, I am at your service tonight.*

As the ostrich sweepstake swiftly soared past the £2,000 mark, I was on my feet with the microphone to announce the first awards of the night. I read out the winner of the 'clubman of the year'. I forget the winner's name, but let's call him Bill. He was elated to hear his name called out, but his award was not universally well-received, particularly by his mate 'Dave'.

'How the fucking hell has Bill got clubman of the year?' shouted Dave. The pair promptly started fighting and moments later were thrown out of the clubhouse. Five minutes after that, they returned to the function room, arms around each other. 'I love you, Bill,' said Dave. 'No, I love you, Dave,' said Bill. How sweet. With order seemingly restored, the club president finally introduced me ahead of my speech to an increasingly raucous audience. 'Anyway, this is our speaker, Martin Bayfield,' he said.

I stepped up onto the stage and was on high alert. These guys were roaring. There was only one thing for it. I swore and swore and swore again. I have never used so many swear words in a speech, but it was all I could do to get their attention. But just as I started to get control of things, the doors burst open and this young lad staggered in. His blazer was ripped to shreds and he was covered in blood and mud. But rather than being met with concern from the audience, a huge cheer went up. It turns out he was the winner of the sweepstake and had tried to ride the ostrich. The compère grabbed the microphone from my hand and went straight over to the poor sod, like a TV reporter scrambling to cover some breaking news.

'So, I got on it, but you bastards didn't tell me there was a goat in there with it,' lamented our rodeo hero. 'The bloody thing tried to protect the ostrich and butted me all over the pen!'

Welcome to the weird and wonderful world of after-dinner speaking at junior rugby clubs. You can never quite be sure what to expect at these gigs, but I love coming across the characters who form the backbone of our great game and hearing their tales.

I remember speaking at one club and noticing that all the memorabilia on the walls was of French origin. *This seems a bit odd*, I thought to myself, and asked the club chairman. 'Last year, we invited the chief constable to our dinner and during my speech I remarked about how all the memorabilia on our walls had been stolen from other clubs,' he recalled. 'The chief constable made us return it all! So, this year we have put up all our French stuff because he doesn't have any jurisdiction in France.'

At another event, the club's 1st XV captain stood up to give his review of the year. Now, although my job is to try to give a (hopefully) entertaining and witty speech at such events, typically each club has their own comedian, some of whom are far funnier than I am but maybe just don't have the confidence to get up and do a routine in front of an audience. This club was no different.

'The season started well,' reported the captain. 'Everyone turned up at training twice a week and we were winning all our games. Then Christmas came. After Christmas, attendance at training dropped off, results started going against us ...' Then this voice at the back of the room shouted out: 'Oi, you can't blame it all on Santa Claus!'

Navigating the verbal killing fields of junior rugby club dinners was a fantastic way to learn my trade as an after-dinner speaker. I've had some brutal experiences and things have gone horribly wrong, but the great thing is that normally the audience is too drunk to remember.

Some players attempt to go straight to big corporate gigs without having put the hard yards in first and they struggle. I can understand why. When I started out, I would do jobs for £50 and could experiment and say whatever I liked. I remember a speech for Nottingham Law Society, and after my first joke, three tables of women got up and walked out. Oops, sorry. *Okay, a lesson learned there.* The key thing I picked up from those early days was not to rely on gags. At the first few speaking gigs I was offered, I felt under pressure to force some jokes into my story to make sure the audience were entertained. But as I gained more experience, I realised that what people want to hear are not generic gags, but stories and anecdotes. And I love telling stories. Through the experience of people walking out and tumbleweed moments, I also learned the importance of getting to know your audience. You're there to entertain them, so the very least you can do is understand what type of content they're expecting to hear. I don't want to offend anyone. I just want people to have a laugh.

One of my best traits is my ability to get under the skin of a project when I'm engaged with it. It was like that with the police, the *Harry Potter* films and, at times, during my rugby career when I was in the zone and free of distractions. Whether it be dinners at grassroots rugby clubs or big corporate events, I believe the key to successful speaking is really getting to know the people you're speaking to. A lot of speakers will sit in the 'green room' and tell their hosts to call them when they're ready. But I always insist on attending the dinner first. There are two reasons for this: I get a free meal out of it; and I can understand the heartbeat of the event. Once you have that, you can tune into it and give yourself a greater chance of delivering a well-received speech.

With the *Harry Potter* films, I had a tiny role. But I just *got* it. I understood what it was about and said to myself that I was going to maximise everything about it. It's the same with my speaking. When I stand up to do a speech, I want to have fun and I want the audience to have fun. I can genuinely say that I love it.

The key thing is to remember that the audience don't know your speech (unless they have been to too many rugby dinners or been at those where other speakers have ripped yours off). They don't know when you have missed a line out or mixed up the order of the stories. But most audiences are good at sensing whether you're genuine or not. If you're trying to entertain them by being yourself, by being natural, you'll get a bit more slack.

Often that can mean going off your script. I once did a speech for the Confederation of International Logistics and Transport, which went by the wonderfully verbally challenging acronym of CILT. Just before I stood up, a joke came to mind which broke the ice.

'Ladies and gentlemen,' I said. 'Thank you for inviting me here to your dinner tonight. I must admit I have never been so nervous about getting an acronym right ... [Long pause] ... And to be honest, I am surprised that so many men here tonight managed to find it.'

One of the awards that night went to Hermes, the delivery company. I'd just watched a documentary that had investigated the company's practices and included footage of Hermes couriers mishandling parcels. Hermes had insisted the programme was not a fair reflection of their business and had taken action to prevent such incidents happening again. Whatever, it was worth a gag.

'Guys, don't bother coming up to receive your award,' I said to the Hermes table. 'I'll just throw it to you!'

If everything is written down, you can't be spontaneous like that or ad lib. So rather than use notes, and remembering the advice from Gordon Brown (still not the former prime minister), I spend many hours when I'm on my own muttering away to get the speech right in my head and recounting stories to myself. It's the same when I'm working for BT Sport or ITV. When the cameras are off, I spend those minutes getting the script into my head. This may sound a bit weird, but sometimes when I have a big 'opener' when I'm presenting for BT Sport, I'll sing the lines in order to get them into my head.

I think I've only ever had one session of public-speaking training. It was from Rob Nothman, the BBC Sport broadcaster and producer, and his key piece of advice was not to worry about getting your speech right word for word. All people want to know, said Rob, is what you're trying to tell them. Just get the words out. Don't hang your hat on everything having to be word-perfect. Just get the spirit of what you are trying to say out there and it'll work. It was a really good piece of advice.

When modern-day players ask me for advice about public speaking, I give them the same message. For me, it's also about telling stories. Don't worry overly about jokes. The people in the room want you to place them in a scenario that they've never been in. They want to know what it's like on the pitch at Twickenham playing for England, in the dressing room at half-time, or on the beers afterwards. It's about the characters and the situations we found ourselves in, on and off the pitch. Those stories are priceless. The finishing touch is about giving them a little twist at the end to overcome any sense that 'you had to be there' to get the joke, to enable the audience to really appreciate the anecdote.

Don't expect everything you say to be funny. Sometimes the audience just don't hear what you've said. You might think it's funny, but they might not get it. Or you might say something which you think is just run-of-the-mill and the audience roars with laughter. And don't let silence stump you. The key is to keep going. You'll be fine. Don't tell in-jokes about your own team because that excludes people. Instead, you must invite the audience into your world and entertain them while they are there.

In my experience, it's also important to expect the unexpected, as invariably things quite often happen out of the blue to test you. I can remember being at an event at Wanderers Rugby Club, which had their clubhouse inside the old Lansdowne Road stadium in Dublin. It was the night before an Ireland–versus–England match and I was with Dick Best, my old England and Lions coach. I was sitting beside a woman whose husband was the other side of the table and Besty was in the middle.

Besty was being his usual pompous self. 'What on earth is this wine they are serving us?' he taunted. 'They should stick to Guinness!' The guests on the table were lapping up his pantomime villain performance until a waitress came along with a tray of piping-hot bowls of soup. Just as she approached our table, she tripped and the soup went all over the woman, who was wearing a beautiful low-cut dress. She screamed with pain and rushed away. I thought that was the last we would see of her. But sometime later she returned, draped in wet tea towels to cool her down. 'I wasn't going to miss this,' she declared.

But the drama was not yet over. Moments later, there was a huge thud and I turned to see her husband lying face down on the table and wine spilled everywhere.

'Is he all right?' I asked Besty. 'Is he drunk?'

'I think he's had a few but I don't think he's *that* drunk.'

Seconds later, blood began to ooze from the back of his head. It turned out a speaker had fallen off the wall and knocked him unconscious.

Bestie looks at me. 'Only in Ireland, Bayfs, only in Ireland.'

So, off the husband went to get treatment. As with his wife, I thought we wouldn't see him again. But, incredibly, he also returned to the table, sporting a tea towel wrapped around his head. Good job there were plenty of tea towels on hand.

When you witness events like this before you deliver

your speech, you never forget them. So, yes, always expect the unexpected, even if it involves an ostrich. And a goat.

22

To Rugby, with Love

When I look back on the impact that the game of rugby has had on my life, the things that stand out for me are laughter, fun, a huge amount of pride and honour. The game also gave me an element of family life that I didn't have because of having an older father and that fact that I didn't have a brother providing the rough and tumble that other kids would have had with their families.

Rugby gave me another family, too. Father figures at certain times, brothers too, and a ripple effect that resulted in my sister moving to New Zealand, living a life there that she loves. It was because she came out to watch me play for the Lions in New Zealand on the 1993 tour that she ended up emigrating there. If I hadn't played rugby, she might still be in England.

Nowadays, rugby helps keep me young – and in gainful employment – through the broadcasting work I do with BT Sport and ITV. It keeps me in touch with today's game and the heroes who play it. I think I still get it (just). I get genuinely excited for the modern-day player and what they can do.

When I do TV work, I never take for granted where I am or what I'm doing. I recently did an interview with Jamie George, the Saracens and England hooker, and I just loved the guy. I thought he was brilliant. It's a privilege to hear from players like Jamie to find out what makes them tick, what's going on in their heads, and sometimes even how scared they can be. Some of them have no idea where the game is going to take them or where they will end up.

Jamie is sorted with a good business already set up for when his playing career comes to an end, but I find it fascinating to speak to players who are on their rugby journey, the same journey (albeit from a different world) that I was on many years before them. I know the day will come when I will be regarded myself as an 'old fart' and, when I get there, all that I ask of the players of that time is to indulge me. I know the old alickadoos can drive you mad. And I know they talk rubbish half the time. They certainly did when I was playing for England. But give me 20 years (I guess some might argue I reached that point years ago) and I'll also be no doubt talking utter rubbish to the next generation of players. And no doubt they'll think: *What is this idiot talking about?*

But I hope the players will allow me to wallow in that moment – because, at the time, my England team thought we were doing the best that we could and that we were elite sportsmen. Compared to the England team of today, we might have been a shambles. Put me up against someone like Maro Itoje or Courtney Lawes and, even in my prime, they would have eaten me for breakfast. They are so much better than I was. Some of it is genetics, but mostly it's the training, nutrition, sports science and the standard of rugby they're playing.

When I first started playing, there were no leagues. There was only the John Player Cup. You played all the big teams and then clubs like Askeans and Vale of Lune. How do you get yourself geared up for games like that? You can't. But at the same time, the modern game wouldn't allow someone like Wade Dooley to play for Fylde or West Hartlepool and then for England.

When George Martin was first selected for England in 2021 from relative obscurity at Leicester, people thought something like that had never happened before, but it had. Wade was elevated into the national side from a far more obscure place than the fringes of Leicester's Premiership squad.

The modern-day professional may be a different breed to the players of my day, but what I hold most dear is the thread that links them to us, and us to those who went before us. I love the history – I think that's due to the influence of my father. But my fear for the modern game is that that thread which stretches back to the black and white photographs hanging in clubhouses across the country is in danger of being cut.

The future of the game concerns me. The game has arguably never been in a greater sense of flux. Private equity has taken a share of the club and international game, there's pressure for new competitions and more law changes, and concerns continue to grow about injuries, particularly concussion.

While the professional players are creating their own experiences, the links with the past – via the old farts – are weakening. It's now rare to see an England player attend the official post-match dinner at Twickenham. Recently they've used the risk of Covid-19 as the reason, but that has given them an easy out. They don't want to be there anyway. They have recovery work to do, they've been in camp for a long time and they want to see their families. It's hard work for them.

It's all a far cry from the nights when we used to have more than 900 people at the Hilton Hotel celebrating Grand Slam victories in dinner suits. Nowadays it's a small gathering, which sometimes I speak at, in the Spirit of Rugby function room in the west stand at Twickenham. I would urge the modern-day players not to turn their backs on these events because in that room will be many people who have achieved something in the game and who are being rewarded with a big day out at Twickenham. These people give up their weekends to run junior rugby clubs, which in some areas are the heartbeat of a village or town.

The volunteers may not have a clue about modern professional rugby, but they shouldn't be judged on that. Going to Twickenham to watch England is their reward for all the hours given up so that 300 kids can play mini rugby every Sunday, or because they've played 400 games of rugby for their club. Some of these volunteers are also successful business people who provide financial support or sponsorship. You never know if you'll need the support from the rugby family and it's these people who can provide a safety net for them when their playing careers come to an end.

When I was briefly the academy coach at Northampton Saints, I asked all our players to go into the old Sturtridge Pavilion to look at all the old black and white photographs of former Saints. I wanted them to build a connection with the past and what it means to play for the club, to recognise that the guy who helped park the cars on a match day had once played for England and the British and Irish Lions. Our old groundsman, David 'Piggy' Powell, won 11 caps for England and represented the Lions on the tour of Australia and New Zealand in 1966. I wonder how many of our players knew of his outstanding past as a player?

Rugby remains an amazing game, but if change is coming, it's critical that the thread is not cut between the professional game, the grassroots and its amateur past. And I would also urge the administrators not to constantly think that this great house of rugby needs an extension. They should just make what we have work really well and be proud of it.

There has been talk of South Africa declaring an interest in joining the Six Nations. Well, I don't want to see the Springboks in the Six Nations, and I don't even want to see their franchise sides playing in the European Champions' Cup. I know that bigger brains than mine are making the decisions and the nature of the game is that it is ever evolving. I also don't want to come across as a rugby dinosaur or like one of the old farts I have criticised. It may work and if it does, we will live with it. But if you were to ask me right now, I don't want it. Given what the world has been through with the pandemic and climate change, can we really justify a 9,000-mile trip for an 80-minute game of rugby? I really don't think so.

South Africa will say that they must travel thousands of miles to play in any Rugby Championship, and I do feel sorry for them in that regard. There's no doubt they also feel they're propping up southern-hemisphere rugby with the size of their broadcasting deals. And I can understand why they are looking north. Most of their players play their club rugby in the northern hemisphere anyway.

On this, there's an irony in the fact that English rugby actually did South Africa a huge favour in preparing their players for the 2019 World Cup and their victory over England in the final. Look at how the likes of Faf de Klerk developed at Sale Sharks. I think we deserve at least half a star to indicate that we kind of won the World Cup by training all those players in the Premiership! But I don't want to see them in the Six Nations. I'm not saying it would devalue the Six Nations, but I think we would quickly get bored of playing them every year and it would diminish their mystique. And what would become of Lions tours to South Africa if they were playing against the four home unions every year? And the autumn Tests? There's no point playing South Africa at Twickenham in November if they have already played there earlier in the year.

The Six Nations is a European competition. To make it a trans-hemisphere competition would not only completely alter its dynamic and culture, but also add extra pressure on the club game and the players at a time when talks about the future structure of the global season are supposed to have player welfare at their core. There's also the impact that South Africa's departure from the Rugby Championship would have on New Zealand and Australia, who in particular have been struggling financially and in terms of playing numbers.

There's an argument that promotion and relegation should be brought into the Six Nations, given how Italy have limped along over the last decade. But the second tier in Europe is not yet strong enough for that to be considered. In many ways, it's similar to the debate about promotion and relegation in the Premiership, where many sides in the Championship simply do not want promotion to English club rugby's top flight. My view is that Italy fit in the Six Nations. When they first came into the tournament in 2000, they had a lot of great players and, with the right investment and coaching structures, they will come again.

There is this constant push to create the perfect tournament, but I believe we already have it. My only wish is that we could find a way for the coverage to be on one broadcaster, so that a narrative can build throughout the Championship and year after year.

My love for the Six Nations and the history of the Championship is why I find it difficult to warm to manufactured competitions. It takes 50 or 60 years before you can talk about them in the same breath as the Six Nations or the Bledisloe Cup match between New Zealand and Australia.

As much as I love rugby, the game is simply not as big as some would like to believe it is. There's a constant drive to grow the sport, to chase new audiences and commercial revenues. But why can't we just appreciate what we have and nurture it from the bottom up?

We must accept the reality that other countries in the world will never be powerful enough to really compete at the top end, simply because they do not have the playing base or a sufficient number of athletes who are physically big enough. They should be encouraged to play, compete and have fun, but we have to be realistic about the ability to broaden the base of countries who can challenge for the World Cup.

Rugby is a niche sport. It's like cricket. It only has a few countries who play the game very well and who are well supported. Outside of that, I think World Rugby has to define what its development needs to be. I love to see the growth of the game in new areas, but they are so far off competing with the established unions.

There has only been one World Cup winner from the northern hemisphere – England in 2003. France have yet to win a World Cup, while Ireland are still to even reach the semi-final stage. It's a tough competition. They say rugby is growing in Malaysia. Great, but they are never going to win the World Cup. And look how many millions have been thrown in trying to grow the game in the United States, but it's still like watching a pub team. However, we have allowed Canada, who were almost ready to play at the very highest level, to fall completely off the rugby map.

When I was playing for England, Canada were a serious side with brilliant players. They were ready to step up. World Rugby already had a major presence in North America, yet look at Canada now, a pale shadow of a side that once contained legends such as Gareth Rees and Norm Hadley. The problem is that there was no money in Canada. The money was in the US, but the rugby was in Canada.

To the RFU, my warning would be to not just focus everything on the England teams, the Six Nations Championships, the World Cup or the Lions. That is for the elite, those fantastic players who reach the pinnacle. But the real heartbeat of the game lies underneath all that.

I find it just as amazing to see local clubs across the country with 200, 300 or 400 kids out playing. I'm a huge admirer of the enthusiastic amateur and so it's really concerning to hear reports of clubs no longer able to field the same number of teams as they used to, of fixtures not able to be fulfilled because of declining participation.

One of the reasons that I enjoy speaking at grassroots clubs is I love meeting the club alickadoos, but increasingly they appear to be like polar bears standing on an ice-shelf that is slowly melting. There are fewer and fewer places for them to go. Clubs that used to put out six teams might now only be putting out two. There are societal reasons behind the fall in participation in team sports, but I don't think we're helping the clubs enough. I'm not sure the national league structures are helping. Clubs just want to play against their local rivals. They don't want to get on a coach and drive the length of the country to play a game.

And I think we have lost that connection between the lowliest grassroots team and the national team. Somewhere along the way, someone has built a bloody great big wall. Clubs are told that if they want to get over that wall, they can, but they're going to have to buy their own ladder, that the authorities are not going help.

When I meet characters at the RFU after games at Twickenham, they are lovely people, but some of them don't know anything about the professional game because it moves at such a pace. They see a full Twickenham and an (occasionally) winning England team and are seduced by that. But the mass of rugby people underneath just want someone to play on a Saturday and Sunday, somewhere for their kids to play, somewhere safe to play, and for the game to be safe. I would scrap all payments to players at grassroots level and I would scrap promotion and relegation, because what does it really matter? The joy of promotion can be quickly replaced by the angst of having to recruit and pay a load of journeymen players for a club to avoid coming back down again, only for the money to run out and to be left with no option but to sell their ground.

I would suggest all most clubs really want is a full clubhouse and a thriving playing section that's having fun. I'm sure it's working for some, but it's almost like everyone is hanging on to this idea that a club can emulate what Exeter Chiefs did, rising through the leagues to be eventually crowned English and European champions in 2020. But Exeter were unique, and when they went into the Premiership, it was nowhere near as competitive as it is now. When London Welsh went up a few years later, they found it much, much tougher and the financial strains ruined the club.

So don't judge success on the England team, for beneath that, success is about 200-odd thousand who want to play the game for fun every Saturday. And if you don't give them the stage to perform on, or that stage is crumbling, then they'll start to say: 'Thanks very much, but I'm going to do something else.'

When I go to a home game at Saints, there's always a junior competition taking place on the back pitches. Some of those kids will be looking across at Franklin's Gardens and thinking: *One day I want to play there*. And that's great. But most are likely thinking: *I know I am never going to be good enough to play there, but don't stop me playing. Let me have my fun.*

I think we look for obstacles at the top of the club game too. I would love to see an amalgam of the Premiership and the Championship, including ideally clubs in Cornwall, Yorkshire and East Anglia, to create two divisions of 10 clubs in an NFL style. This way local derbies would be maintained, while the top four or five clubs from each division would go through to play-offs. It's a system that would also free up the number of players who can't get a game for a Premiership club to develop and showcase their skills, which would ultimately increase the supply line to the national side.

We need to bring clubs together, not disenfranchise them. Some clubs may never want to reach the Premiership, but they're unhappy when they see clubs like Ealing Trailfinders, the winners of the Championship in 2022, denied entry on minimum criteria grounds. Fairness is important to them. And a shiny stadium with a big capacity only takes you so far. I would much prefer to see derby matches like Saints against Bedford at Goldington Road, where my rugby journey began.

It's because this game has given me everything that I care so much for its future. It's dominated my life, made me who I am and given me some of my best memories, along with a career in film (well, for a bit at least) and sports broadcasting.

It gave me an identity, first at school, and then led to my initial job with the police when Brian Baister embarrassingly flirted with my mum. When I joined the police, it was rugby that enabled my skinny, scrawny beanpole self to grow up and gain some status. I learned how to have a laugh, a beer and find my voice, discovering who I was after a childhood of being constantly told not to throw my weight around and not to show off. Instead, I found myself in an environment where the message was: please throw your weight around and we kind of like it when you show off.

But more than anything, rugby has given me so much fun. To all my former team-mates and coaches, a huge thank you. It was quite a journey, and I loved every minute (apart from being dropped). To the future players I may interview or commentate on, please bear with me as I slowly edge towards my 'old fart' years (that includes you too, Carling).

To the game of rugby, thanks for the experiences and all the memories: I simply would not be the same person without them. Very tall or not.

ACKNOWLEDGEMENTS

The seed of an idea for this book was first planted in the early months of Lockdown 1. That time when on the face of it we were all a bit giddy with thoughts of a few weeks off work, home schooling, Joe Wicks workouts and cubic yards of sourdough bread.

Sadly, we all know the reality. People were hurting and those weeks would turn into long, painful months.

During this time requests started to trickle and then roll in. Requests from concerned relatives asking for a personal message for their mum or dad; for Grandpa and Granny. Heartfelt requests simply asking us rugger chaps to record a message wishing the recipient well, to keep their chin up and keep going. I have no idea how many of us did it; quite a lot I'd guess, and I'm sure it wasn't limited solely to current and former rugby players; all sports can conjure a touch of magic and awaken the senses.

With rugby off our pitches and screens for what seemed an eternity, we turned to the archives to get our fix of high-powered, energetic 'egg chasing'. We reminisced, we giggled, we bathed in the nostalgia, and it made us feel good. It made me feel good. It made me realise how much I love this crazy game of ours and I got to thinking. Dangerous, I know!

Thoughts became a conversation with my agents and before we knew it plans were afoot for *A Very Tall Story*.

Left to my own devices this would have remained a thought, but with the encouragement and gentle cajoling of my agents we have words on paper. So, huge thanks to Richard Thompson, Chairman of M&C Saatchi Merlin, and Tory Finch for backing me on this. Over the past 11 years you have helped guide, nurture and develop my career, pushing me into areas where my self-doubt screamed 'No'. The laughs have come thick and fast and when there have been bumps in the road you have smoothed them out to make the journey a far more comfortable ride. Thommo, you're a crazy man, a giant of a character and one of the finest human beings I know. Tory, your patience knows no bounds and, wow, you have been tested. You are simply remarkable and a joy to work with. Thank you both.

Gavin Mairs is the remarkable soul who has put these words on paper. Gavin is a very fine and hugely respected sports journalist, who clearly had nothing better to do. Gav, I will be eternally grateful for your patience and skill. Through numerous visits to the Spotted Dog in Flamstead and fuelled by gallons of cappuccino you expertly decoded my ramblings into something that has made sense. As the book developed so did a great friendship which makes this whole process doubly satisfying. Thank you just isn't enough.

I am so grateful to Ian Marshall and his team at Simon & Schuster for backing this idea and taking it to print. To have such a heavyweight in publishing behind us and to have been so supportive throughout the process has been a real boost.

A huge, collective thank you to the amazing men and women I served with in the Metropolitan Police and

Bedfordshire Constabulary. Within your ranks I grew as a man and will forever be indebted for your friendship. Thank you for covering for me when I was off playing for club and country; your support was never taken lightly.

To the host of storytellers and bon viveurs who have illuminated my life: cheers! To my 'Twickenham Saturday' family Paul, Becks, Cooch, Tricky, Sarah and the never to be forgotten Peter, when life without rugby started to hurt you guys scooped me up and got me going again.

To Joe, Gemma, Chris, Nick and all of the Creature Effects team for *Harry Potter*. What a journey we all went on with the Boy Wizard. The best of times.

The biggest thanks, though, goes to my family. For the love you have given me, for the joy, the laughter and the stomach-churning roller-coaster excitement, I cannot imagine this journey without you.

INDEX

Ackford, Paul ('Ackers') 3, 10, 44, 51, 55, 69–72, 81, 147, 169
All Blacks 10, 65, 106, 110, 115, 118, 120, 129–33, 135–45, 159, 173–9, 208, 243–6, 254
  World Cup (1995) 4
Alred, Dave 175
Andrew, Rob 2, 58, 83, 101, 120, 129, 152, 163, 166, 169, 171, 204
Andrews, Mark 160
Animal House 150
Archer, Garath 168, 187, 193–4, 202
Argentina 10, 169
Arms Park 100
asthma 10, 43, 239
Athletic Park ground 138–43
athletics 67, 95
'Auckland Bay' anecdote 144–5
Auckland dinner incident 20–1
Auckland 135–7
Aunty Ruth's 68–9
Aussie Rules 171
Australia 2, 10–11, 47, 89, 136, 170, 175, 178, 245, 248, 253–4
  Grand Slam 1984 tour 49
  Lions 1989 tour 80, 106, 144
  London Division 1988 victory 61
  Midlands tour 48, 49–60, 64, 70, 71
Austria 22

Bachop, Graeme 174
Back, Neil ('Backy') 33, 54
Baister, Brian 43
Baldwin, Dave 98
Bank of England ground 47
Barnes, Stuart ('Barnsey') 47, 101, 154–5
Barnes, Wayne 244
Barton, Dave 249
Barwell, Keith 185, 215, 221, 224
Barwell, Leon 224
basketball 34–5
Bay of Islands, New Zealand 114
Bayfield, D. S. (ancestor) 133
Bayfield, Helena (first wife) 75, 96, 181–2, 211
Bayfield, Jane (second wife) 240–1, 254, 255
Bayfield, John (father) 88, 210
  education and career 26–8
  Martin's England selection 15–16
  Martin's relationship with 27–9
  OBE awarded to 27
  Ursula meets and marries 24
Bayfield, Karen (sister) 107
  birth 26, 29

Bayfield, Lucy (daughter) 183
Bayfield, Martin ('Bayfs'):
  academy coaching 229, 270–1
  acting career 1–2, 4–6, 212, 215–
    41, 245, 260, 261
  after-dinner speaking 86, 210,
    210–12, 257–65
  at Bedford 10–11
  birth and early life 26–9
  broadcasting career 20, 42, 130,
    202, 222, 234–7, 240, 243–
    56, 262–3
  caps totals 3, 43
  career choices 43–4
  commendations for bravery 19–20
  cover star 147
  daughter's pool accident 181–4,
    189
  divorce 211
  education 17–18, 28–30, 33–9, 43
  England B team pick (1990) 9–10
  England Schools 14, 39–44, 42–3,
    100
  Five Nations debut 73–5, 76, 82
  Grand Slam winning sides 3
  hero-worship 79–81
  humour as defence 30, 158
  ill health/injuries 63–4, 67–8, 114,
    148–9, 150, 186–7, 201–2,
    210, 218–19
  last-ever rugby session 199
  'Lazarus' sobriquet 120
  Lions Test debut 14, 107–33
  at Met Police 10, 11, 42–5, 48
  at Midlands Schools 47–60, 95,
    131
  nicknaming penchant 118–19
  at Northampton Saints 4, 65–6,
    71, 91
  in panto 230
  peacemaking ability 29–30
  police career 229
  in police force 11, 19–20, 43–7, 51,
    91, 109–10
  retirement 179, 191, 207–13
  Rosie's birth 95–6
  self-doubt 33, 183
Bayfield, Polly (daughter) 181, 189,
    211
Bayfield, Roseanna ('Rosie')
    (daughter), birth and early life
    95–6
Bayfield, Ursula (mother):
  autobiography 24
  birth and early life 21
  honest nature 25–6
  John meets and marries 24
  Martin's England selection 15–16
BBC 44, 213, 222, 232, 234, 240,
    244, 262
Beale, Nick 65
Bedford Athletics 67
Bedford Blues 52–3
Bedford Colts 37, 41–2
Bedford 10–11, 11, 12, 34, 37–9, 42,
    65, 94, 169
Bedford School 14–15, 36–8, 41
Bedfordshire Constabulary 19, 52,
    65–6, 91, 110, 186, 229
Bedfordshire on Sunday 110
Beechwood Park School 17–18, 28,
    35, 37, 39
beer-mat flipping 42–3
'Behind the Badge' interview 42
Ben-Hur 216
Benazzi, Abdelatif 164, 177
Berbizier, Pierre 83
Bergh, Elandre van der 159
Berlin Wall 24
Best, Dick ('Besty') 47, 55–7, 61–3,
    70, 96, 98, 103, 112–13, 124,
    155–6, 185, 264

Bevan, Derek 177–8
Bisham Abbey 80
Björnsson, Hafþór Júlíus 237
Blyth, Andy 69
Botha, Naas 95
boxing 12, 42
Brain, John 53
Brain, Steve 51
Brewer, Mike 178
Briggs, Pat 36
British and Irish Lions 3, 14, 31, 37,
    47, 59, 69, 80, 103
  fly-on-the-wall documentary 106
  Martin's Test debut 14, 107–45
  Premiership squabbles 111
Brooke, Robin 131
Brooke, Zinzan 174, 208
Brouzet, Oliver 164
Brown, Gordon ('Broonie') 211–13,
    262
BT Sport 202, 237, 246, 254, 262
budget filmmaking 230–2, 233
bullying 29, 30–1
Bunce, Frank 132, 144
Burgess, Sam 253
Burnell, Paul 129
Burrell, Luther 253

Cadbury Bourneville 26
Cadbury, Christopher 26
Calcutta Cup 74, 75
Callard, John 159
Campese, David ('Campo') 49, 60,
    170–1
Canada 93–4, 162
Canbannes, Lauren 164
Cannon, Vince 64
Captain's Run 97, 115
Carisbrook Stadium ('House of
    Pain') 148
Carling, Will 2, 13, 50, 57–9, 61,

    78, 83, 87, 88, 90–1, 97–8,
    119–21, 124, 126, 136, 154,
    162–5, 167–8, 174, 178, 194–5
Carreras, Chris 223–4
Carry On films 11
Castaignède, Thomas 192
Catt, Mike 174
Ceefax 105, 107–8
celebrity 2
Celebrity MasterChef 240, 241
Cemetery Hill 12, 13
CGI 234
Challenge Cup 55
The Chamber of Secrets, see under
    Harry Potter franchise
Champions' Cup 55, 271
Channel 4 167
Charron, Al 94
Clapton, Eric 144
Clarke, Allen ('Clarkey') 151, 193
Clarke, Ben 139, 157, 163–4
Clash of the Titans 234
Clement, Tony 125
Clohessy, Peter 109
Cockerill, Richard 54
Cohen, Ben 202
Cole, Dan 196
Coltrane, Robbie 4, 212, 215–28
Columbus, Chris 217, 219
Concept rower 11–12
Confederation of International
    Logistics and Transport
    (CILT) 261
Cooke, Geoff ('Cookey') 14, 15,
    56–8, 61, 80, 112, 114, 124,
    128, 152, 155
Cooksley, Mark 138–9
Cooper, Terry 168
Corless, Barrie 65
county and divisional rugby 37
'Cowboys bar' anecdote 248–9

cricket 28, 36, 273
Crimewatch 234–6
Cronin, Damian 112–13, 115
cross-border club competitions 55
Crystal, Terry 206
Cusworth, Les 48, 165
Cutler, Steve 49
Czechoslovakia 22

Daily Mail 191
Daily Telegraph 54
Dallaglio, Lawrence 6, 98, 106, 168
Dando, Jill 235–6
'Darth Vader' anecdote 237–9
Davidson, Jeremy 194
Davies, Gareth 253
Davison, Peter 231
Dawson, Matt 65, 69, 150, 194, 201
Diana, Princess of Wales 204
Dickinson, Sandra 231–2
Divisional Championship 54, 69
Doctor Who 231
Dooley, Wade ('Blackpool Tower') 2, 13, 15, 31, 55, 56, 70, 72–3, 79–81, 93–4, 99, 102, 108, 115, 118, 147, 169, 204–5
  caps totals 80, 87
  father's death 80, 126–8
  ill health/injuries 97
  retirement 127–9
Doyle, Craig 20
Doyle, Owen 84
Dudman, Nick 216, 221
Dwyer, Bob 50, 60
Dyke, Greg 167
Dylan, Bob 154

Eales, John 34, 60, 64, 171–2, 246

Easby, Dennis 168
East Midlands 38, 215
East Prussia 21, 24
Eden Park ground 135, 143–5
Edwards, Neil 73
Eiffel Tower 85
Elizabeth II 102
Elkington, David 91
Ellis Park ground 184
Elwood, Eric 101
Emerging Wallabies 9–10, 54
England B 9–10, 13
England Schools 14–15, 39–44, 40–1, 100
England v. Ireland, 1 February 1992 75–8
England v. Wales, 7 March 1992 87–91
European Champions' Cup 76, 271
European Professional Club Rugby (EPCR) 55
Evans, Ieuan 100, 112, 124–6, 131–2, 137–9
Events International 210–11
'Everest' rallying call 105
Exeter Chiefs 246–7, 275

'family connection' anecdote 132–3
Farr-Jones, Nick 49–50, 246
'fetish bar' anecdote 203
'57 old farts' jibe 167–8, 178
fighting 19, 22, 31, 45–6, 54, 93, 153, 202, 234, 236, 258
Fiji 10, 13, 14, 16, 95, 152, 253
  Lions 1991 tour 168, 168–9
  Midlands tour 56–9, 63, 70, 71–2
'filming bonus' anecdote 226
First Division 52–3, 80
Fitzpatrick, Sean ('Fitzy') 107, 138–41, 173, 177, 243, 244

Five Nations 37, 70–6, 84, 89, 96–7, 101, 108, 113, 129, 148, 151, 156, 162–3, 186, 192–3, 196
Flatman, David ('Flats') 241, 247
Fletcher, Guy 38, 40
Foley, Bernard 254
food rationing 27
football 3, 11, 45, 51
Fox, Grant 132
France 69, 97–8, 245, 247, 251
  back-to-back Grand Slams (1997/1998) 89
  'bloody victory' against 79–87, 102
France v. England, 15 February 1992 82–7
Francis, Neil 163
Franklin's Gardens ground 64, 69, 199, 209, 276
Fulcher, Gabriel 163
Fylde 80, 269

Galwey, Mick 103, 109, 129
Gambon, Sir Michael 225–6
Game of Thrones 236–7
Gang of Seven 64
Gatherer, Don 148–9
Gatland, Warren 108, 142
Geogheghan, Simon 151
Germany 21–4
  reunification 25
Getting Physical (Gibbs) 123
Gibbs, Scott ('Gibbsy') 123–5, 136, 140, 143
Ginger Pig 68–9
Gladiator 1
Glanville, Phil de 185
Glasgow 208
Gloucester 53, 127
Goldberg, Simon 221, 222

golf 257–65
Grahame Park ground 54
Grand Slam 173, 175, 255, 270
  1980 2, 14
  1984 49
  1990 70, 72
  1991 56
  1992 2, 3, 87–91
  1993 96–7, 166–7
  1995 2, 3, 162
  1997 89
  1998 89
  2017 89
  England's third campaign 96–7, 100, 103, 167
Grandstand 44–5
Grayson, Paul 65, 150, 194, 201
Greed, Richard 12–13
Green Howards Infantry 71, 159
Grewcock, Danny 187, 202
Greyfriars Police Station 11, 150
Grosvenor House 221
Guscott, Jeremy ('Jerry') 2, 13, 58, 74, 76–7, 83, 101, 124, 129, 139, 155, 165, 172, 192–3

Haden, Andy 161
Hadley, Norm ('Stormin' Norman') ('Super Norm') 93–4
Hall, John 57
Halliday, Simon ('Hallers') 13, 55, 76
Halliwell, Geri ('Ginger Spice') 69
Hands, David 58
Hardy, Robert 225
Harlequins ('Quins') 51, 52, 59, 61, 98, 185, 208
Harris, Richard 2, 4–5, 218, 225, 226

Harrow School 14–15, 40, 41
Harry Potter franchise 48, 232, 233–4, 235, 238–9, 245, 260, 261
  Harry Potter and the Chamber of Secrets 5
  Harry Potter and the Philosopher's Stone 1, 4, 212, 218
  Harry Potter and the Prisoner of Azkaban 222
  Leicester Square premiere 226–8
Hartley, Dylan 252
Haskell, James 251
Hastings, Gavin ('Big Gav') 70, 115–17, 120, 123–4, 126, 129, 132, 137–8, 140
Hastings, Scott ('Klunk') 118–19, 126
Hattingh, Drikus 95
Hawke's Bay 136
Heineken Cup (2000) 4, 208
Hendon 44, 46
Hepher, Ali 203
Herridge, Colin 58, 77, 149–50, 221
Hilditch, Stephen 81, 84
Hill, Jonny 246
Hill, Ted 45
Hill, Vincent 45
Himalaya, HMS 133
Hitler, Adolf 21
Hodgkinson, Simon 56
Hollywood 2, 5, 9, 216, 218, 229, 231
Holmes, Terry 131
Hopley, Damian 13, 57
Horan, Tim 60
How Was It Then (Bayfield, U.) 24
Howe, Mark 51
humour 30, 99, 112, 158, 168, 174

Hunter, Ian ('Hunts') 13, 65, 97, 115–16, 150
Hynes, Martin 72

Imber Court 44
independent films 230–2, 233
International Rugby Board (IRB) 184
Invictus 158
'Invincibles' tour (1974) 14, 106
IRA 102
Ireland 47, 75–8, 89, 96, 101–3, 125
Ireland Rugby Union (IRU) 125
Ischia, Italy 24
Italy 11, 101, 169, 255
Itoje, Maro 110
ITV 20, 42, 130, 140, 243, 246, 247, 252, 262

Jack and the Beanstalk 230
Jackson, Peter ('Jacko') 191
James Bond franchise 216, 238
Jauzion, Yannick 244
Jenkins, Neil 100
John Player Cup 42, 47, 269
Johns, Paddy 102–3, 108–9
Johnson, Martin ('Johnno') 3, 31, 36, 73, 81, 97–8, 106, 127, 128, 132, 135, 143, 156–7, 168, 193–4, 201, 224, 246, 247–52
  cover star 147
Jones, Eddie 6, 61, 89, 142, 144, 176, 254–6
Jones, Ian 31, 139, 143
Jones, James Earl 238
Jones, Robert 125, 126
Joseph, Jonathan 253

Kay, Ben 202
Keating, Frank 196

Kings Park ground 159
Kingston, Terry 193
Kirwan, John ('JK') 140, 246
Kirwan, Tony 140
'Knight's card' anecdote 225–6
Know, David 10
Kronfeld, Josh 118
Kruis, George 6

Lancaster Park 130, 131–3, 252
Land Rover sponsorship 250–1
Lansdowne Road ground 102–3, 264
Lascubé, Grégoire 83
'Le Crunch' 82, 84
Leavesden Film Studios 1, 212, 220, 226
Leicester Tigers 33, 47, 51, 98, 254
Lensbury Club 40
Leonard, Jason ('Jase') 6, 90, 94, 137, 139, 155, 160, 165–6
Les Bleus 81, 83, 243
Liebesman, Jonathan 234
Little, Jason 60
Living with the Lions 106
Llewellyn, Gareth 108
Lomu, Jonah 4, 130, 173–4
London Division 56, 61
London Irish 113
long-distance running 67
The Lord of the Rings franchise 234
Loughborough 204
Loveridge, Dave 131
Lucas, George 237–8
Luyt, Louis 159–60, 178
Lynagh, Michael 49, 171

McBride, John 106
McCann, Madeleine 236

McCaw, Richie 254
McGeechan, Ian ('Geech') 73, 103, 105–6, 112, 114, 124, 130, 131, 138
McGuigan, Barry 42
Major, Sir John 93
Malan, Adolf 95
Manako, David 115
Mandela, Nelson 153, 157, 158, 245
Marlow, Alan 109
'Martin Bayfield: (Extra)' anecdote 220
'Martin Bayfield/Hagrid drinking game' anecdote 226–8
MasterChef 240, 241
memorabilia 199–200, 259
Mendez, Federico 10
mental health 183, 189, 209
Met Police 10, 34, 42–8, 45, 48, 50–1, 111, 186
Michalak, Frederick 244
mid-tour blues 117–18
Middlesex 47
Midlands Schools 47–60, 95, 131
Milne, Kenny 118, 129
Miss World anecdote 77–8
Montana, Joe 231
Moore, Brian ('Mooro') 2, 19, 21, 48, 50–1, 58, 63, 70–1, 74, 84, 88, 95, 120, 124, 126, 135–7, 140–1, 162–3
Morris, Dewi ('Monkey') 3, 74, 76, 88, 100, 103, 118, 126, 129, 136, 139–40, 163–4, 171, 220
Moscato, Vincent 84
'Mountain' anecdote 236–7
Munster 4
Murdoch, Rupert 184
Murphy, Kevin 114

Murrayfield ground 57, 70–5, 151, 192, 193

Namibia 10
Navy, Army, Air Force Institutes (NAAFI) 24
NEC (National Exhibition Centre) 201
Nelson, Horatio 133
New South Wales 55, 56
New Tricks 232–3, 234
New Zealand 2, 20, 53, 89, 93, 247, 247–50, 254
  early settlers 132–3
  England B 1992 tour 98
  Lions 1983 tour 37, 131
  Lions 1993 tour 3, 14, 31, 80, 97, 103, 107–45, 147, 152, 156, 176, 210
  Lions 1995 tour 59
  Lions 2017 tour 107
  Martin's reporting in 20–1
  'shopkeeper' anecdote 137
  sister living in 29, 107
  v. Wales, 1978 162
New Zealand Maori ('Haka') 117, 131, 138–9
New Zealand Rugby Union (NZRU) 128
New Zealand Schools 40–1, 131
New Zealand v. British Lions, 3 July 1993 143–5
New Zealand v. British Lions, 12 June 1993 131–3
New Zealand v. British Lions, 26 June 1993 138–43
Newcastle 185, 200, 204
Newman, Andy 208–9
Newman, Lennie 116
News Corp. 184
'Nkosi Sikelel' iAfrika' 157

North America League 185
North Auckland 114, 115
North Harbour 115, 129, 137
Northampton Saints 4, 10, 33, 34, 49, 50–1, 64–6, 71, 73, 91, 113, 116, 151, 185, 187–8, 193–6, 199, 206, 207–10, 215, 224
Nothman, Rob 262–3
Notting Hill Carnival 20
Nottingham Law Society 260

Ofahengaue, Willie 60
Old Trafford 204
O'Leary, Sean 9, 10
Olver, John 65, 99
Olympic Park 237
Osborne, Glen 174
Ospreys 208
Otago Five 118
Otago 117–19, 126, 148
Oundle School 40

Pacino, Al 225–6
Packman, Frank 64
Paltrow, Gwyneth 9
pantomime 230
Parc des Princes 81, 82–7, 102, 152, 192
Pascall, Richard 53
Pask, Phil 66–7, 201
Pearce, Gary 64, 196
Pears, David 83
Peck, Ian ('Pecky') 37
Penaud, Alan 83
Perkins, John 39
Philadelphia Museum of Art 12
Phillips, Graham ('Granddad') 38
*The Philosopher's Stone, see under
  Harry Potter* franchise
Pienaar, François 158, 246

Pilgrims School 35
Pilkington Cup 167
Pinewood Studios 234, 238
plyometrics 67
Poidevin, Simon 49
'police officer + TV presenter'
    anecdote 234–5
Pontypool 39
Popplewell, Nick 109, 129
post-match events 42, 85, 102,
    141, 154–5, 269
Powell, Greg ('Dinny') 216
Premiership 111, 184, 269, 272,
    275–6
Preston Grasshoppers 6, 80
The Prisoner of Azkaban, see under
    Harry Potter franchise
Probyn, Jeff ('Probs') 70, 84, 109,
    129
professional status assigned to
    rugby (1995) 109, 184–9,
    205–6, 208
Prowse, David 237–8
Pugh, Vernon 184
punch-ups, see fighting

Queensland 55, 57
Quilley, Helen 10
Quins, see Harlequins
Quittenton, Roger 161

Radcliffe, Daniel 219–20, 221
Radcliffe, Paula 67
Radio 5 Live 234–5
Randt, Os du 124
Ranfurly Shield 136
Ready Steady Cook 234
Reason, John 54–5
red-letter moments 6, 139
Redmond, Nigel ('Ollie') 55, 57,
    64, 72, 149, 152, 157, 204

Reed, Andy ('Reedy') 114, 128,
    132
Rees, Gareth 94
Regan, Mark 192
Richards, Dean ('Deano') 3, 48,
    58, 70, 86, 93, 97, 102, 129,
    132, 139, 145, 153–4, 163,
    174–5
Richardson, Colin and John 68
Roberts, Jamie 253
Robshaw, Chris 42
Rocky 12
Rocky Steps 12
Rodber, Tim ('Rodders') 33, 65,
    71, 78, 102, 150, 157–9, 186,
    194, 200–1
Rogue One 238, 240
Romania 162
Rose Room 63, 81, 189
Rosslyn Park 41, 51
Roumat, Olivier 81, 86
Roux, Johan le 157
Rowell, Jack 155–6, 159, 163,
    165, 170, 172, 192–3, 200,
    203
Rowntree, Graham 54, 166
Royal and Derngate Theatre 230
Royal Marines 43
Royal Marsden 241
rugby academy 33–4, 208, 229,
    270
Rugby Football Union (RFU)
    11, 40, 43, 47, 63, 77, 86, 88,
    148–51, 167–8, 184–5, 221,
    249–54, 274–5
'Rugby Player 2' anecdote 232–3
Rugby Players' Association (RPA)
    205–6
Rugby School 36, 40
Rugby World 91, 147, 148
Rugby World Cup, see World Cup

Russia 22–3
Rutherford, Don 11
Ryan, Dean 158
Ryder, Steve 20

Samoa 95
Sandhurst 71
Sandy Park 246–7
Saracens 33–4, 194, 268
Scotland 73–5, 101, 112, 125, 128,
    151, 166, 173, 187, 192–3,
    211, 223, 225
Scotland v. England, 18 January
    1992 73–5
Scott-Young, Sam 56
Second Division 52–3, 64, 76,
    187, 194
Second World War 21–4, 22, 26–7
'serial killer' anecdote 98–9
Serkis, Andy 234
Sexton, Johnny 255
Sharman, Mark 245
Sharnbrook Upper School/
    Academy 67
Shaun of the Dead 231
Shaw, Simon 187, 202
Shelford, Wayne ('Buck') 10, 65
Shell sports ground 40
shorts pockets 115
Six Nations 89
skills link 6–7
Skinner, Mickey 59, 75, 85, 87–8
Sliding Doors 9
Smith, Damian 171
Snook, Ian 53
Sole, David 70
'Sony Walkman' anecdote 111,
    119–20, 121
South Africa 89, 95–6, 192
  Lions 1980 tour 37
  Lions 1993 tour 165

Lions 1994 tour 153–60, 189, 245
Lions 1995 tour 141, 160, 162–
    79, 194
Lions 1997 tour 105, 106, 124, 140
Lions 2021 tour 108, 118
Lions 'Invincibles' 1974 tour 14,
    106
South Africa 2
South African Union 159
South West 54
Southland 120, 129
'special leave' anecdote 109
speeches and Q&As (see also
    after-dinner speaking)
Spice Girls 69
Spielberg, Steven, acting career
    230
Springboks 95, 124, 157–60,
    176–8, 271
Stade de France 245–6
StagKnight 230–2, 233
Stallone, Sylvester 12
Star Trek 108
Star Wars 1–2, 223, 236, 237–40
Steele, John 65, 250
Stensness, Lee 143–4
Sting 144
Stoop 75, 86, 97
Stransky, Joel 184
Strydom, Hannes 157
Sumo wrestling 145, 219
Sun 147
Sun City 172–3, 177
Sunbury ground 113
Swain, Austin ('Neidermeyer')
    169–70, 172
Swansea University 43

Take That 191
Tavistock Sound & Vision 108
Taylor, Brett 207

Taylor, John 140
Teague, Mike ('Teaguey') ('Iron')
    2, 117–18, 126
Telfer, Jim 105
Terry, Paul 210–11
Thompson, Steve 202, 208
Thorp, Alan 36
The Times 58
Tindall, Mike 248
Tonga 95
Tordo, Jean-François 84–5
Transvaal 95, 157
Tremain, Kel 159
Tremain, Simon 159
Tuigamala, Inga 130, 131–2, 138
Tuilagi, Manu 251, 257–8
TV rights 184–5
Twickenham 4, 39–43, 46–7,
    50, 59–60, 63, 70, 75–8,
    81–2, 86–91, 94–8, 101, 120,
    148–51, 161, 164–8, 184, 189,
    192–3, 210–11, 221, 244,
    252–5, 263, 269–72, 275
Twigden, Dave 194

Ubogu, Victor 162, 165–6
Ulster 101
Underwood, Rory 2, 74, 76,
    83, 100, 101, 102, 129, 137,
    139–40, 164–6, 171, 174,
    187–8
Underwood, Tony 101
United States 94
Uttley, Roger 14, 59

Varsity match 26
Viar, Sébastien 83

Wacky Races 119
Waikato 142
Wales 39, 59, 86, 87–91, 96,
    98–101, 108, 123, 124–5, 142,
    162, 165, 192, 209, 253
Wallabies 34, 50, 59–60, 169–71
Wanderers 199, 263–4
Warburton, Sam 253
Warner Bros. 212, 222, 229
Wasps 9, 10, 57, 94, 98, 167
Waterloo 44
The Weakest Link 234
Webb Ellis Cup 167
Webb, Jonathan ('Webby') 56, 74,
    76–7, 83, 97
Webster, Richard 113, 129, 145
Weighill, Bob 128
weight training 39
Weir, Dodie 187, 203
Welford Road ground 47–8, 49–51,
    95, 254
Wells, John 54
'Welsh police "10–9"' anecdote 99,
    100–1
Wembley Stadium 93–4
Western Samoa 192
Wheeler, Peter 51
Wilding, Rav 235
Wilkinson, Johnny 175
'William' anecdote 230–2, 233
Williams, Roly 111–12
Winterbottom, Peter ('Wints') 3,
    78, 99, 120, 129, 136
Wood, Keith 162–3
Woodward, Sir Clive 6, 116, 156,
    202, 204
Worcester Warriors 254
World Cup 43, 81, 141, 170, 201, 274
    1969 95–6
    1984 250
    1987 178
    1988 59, 61
    1989 59
    1990 10

World Cup – *continued*
1991 10, 50, 61, 63–70, 82, 93,
    156, 177–8, 196
1992 82–6, 93–4, 250–1
1993 141, 156, 176
1994 153
1995 2, 4, 59–60, 118, 156–60,
    164–7, 167, 172–8, 181, 184,
    189, 191–2, 245
1996 157, 177
1998 10
1999 10, 244
2003 6, 54, 175, 185, 202–3, 222,
    224, 254, 273

2007 176, 243–6
2011 130, 247
2015 252–3
2017 255
2019 144, 176, 271–2
World League 184
Wrath of the Titans 234
Wright, Peter ('Teapot') 129, 142–3

York House 18
Young, Kirsty 235

zombies 231